# BRITISH LITERATURE UNLOCKED
## VOL II: ELIZABETHAN TO JACOBEAN

### A Complete Guide for UGC NET

## ANKIT SHARMA

## TO THE POINT NOTES BASED ON PREVIOUS YEARS QUESTION PAPERS

## Table of Contents

# **<u>Foreword</u>**

*The journey through British Literature is one marked by profound ideas, artistic transformations, and socio-political upheavals, all of which have shaped the literary canon as we know it. In "British Literature Unlocked: A Complete Guide for UGC NET," this literary heritage is meticulously unpacked, volume by volume, to serve as an essential resource for UGC NET English aspirants. Spanning six volumes, this series guides readers from the ancient foundations of the Greco-Roman period all the way to the nuanced expressions of the Modern and Postmodern ages. With each era, readers will find to-the-point notes, questions from the last decade of UGC NET exams, mnemonic codes, and strategic insights designed to simplify and streamline the study process, making preparation not only thorough but also deeply engaging.*

## **Volume by Volume Breakdown**

### **Volume I: Greco-Roman to Chaucer**

*Dive into the roots of Western literary thought, tracing the influences of classical antiquity up through the Middle Ages and Chaucer's groundbreaking contributions. This volume introduces foundational concepts and sets the stage for the evolution of British literature.*

### **Volume II: Elizabethan to Jacobean**

*Enter the vibrant Renaissance period, where the works of Shakespeare, Marlowe, and their contemporaries reflect the artistic flourishing and complex socio-political shifts of the time. Each page delves into the drama, poetry, and prose that defined these eras.*

### **Volume III: The Age of Milton, Restoration, and The Augustan Age.**

*Explore an age marked by poetic grandeur, the restoration of the monarchy, and the Augustan pursuit of clarity and wit. This volume captures the transformations in language, form, and ideology as literature moved into a reflective phase of transition.*

### **Volume IV: The Age of Transition and The Age of Romanticism**

*Witness the emotional and imaginative power of the Romantic movement, a response to the rigid rationality of the previous era. This volume celebrates the Romantic poets and novelists who embraced nature, individualism, and emotion in revolutionary ways.*

## Volume V: The Victorian Age

*This volume covers the prolific Victorian era, an age of dramatic change and conflict that grappled with industrialization, social reform, and expanding empire. Here, readers can explore the complex morality, realism, and unique characters of Victorian prose and poetry.*

## Volume VI: Modern and Postmodern Literature

*The journey concludes with an in-depth look at Modern and Postmodern literature, where literary form, narrative structure, and thematic depth are pushed to their limits. From the experimental techniques of Modernism to the playful and questioning nature of Postmodernism, this volume brings British literature into the contemporary era.*

# Why This Book is Essential?

*Designed for aspiring NET scholars, "British Literature Unlocked" offers a unique blend of academic precision and strategic insight. With mnemonics that transform complex historical timelines and literary movements into memorable codes, this guide ensures that vital information is readily accessible. Each volume is filled with analysed questions from the last ten years of UGC NET exams, helping you understand not only what to study but also how to approach the exam strategically. This guide offers a structured pathway through the vast landscape of British literature, reducing overwhelm and empowering students to confidently tackle their preparation.*

*An effective study companion, "British Literature Unlocked" is the result of years of dedicated analysis, scholarly research, and an in-depth understanding of the UGC NET requirements. The goal is to provide readers with more than just a study guide—it is to offer them a roadmap that navigates through the richness of British literary history with ease and engagement. As you turn these pages, may you not only prepare but also find joy in the timeless world of British literature, its stories, and its legacy.*

*This series invites you on an enlightening journey, guiding you through the ages and unlocking the potential for both academic success and a deeper appreciation of the literary arts. Welcome to "British Literature Unlocked: A Complete Guide for UGC NET."*

# CHAPTER 1

## THE AGE OF ELIZABETH (1560-1640)

### POETRY

**Blank Verse**

Blank verse is a type of poetry that doesn't rhyme, but it has a regular rhythm. The most common rhythm used in blank verse is called iambic pentameter, which means each line has ten syllables with a pattern of unstressed and stressed syllables, like a heartbeat: da-DUM, da-DUM, da-DUM, da-DUM, da-DUM.

**Parts in Blank Verse**

- **Blank Verse** is a type of poetry that has a regular meter but does not rhyme.
- **Iambic Pentameter** is the most common meter used in blank verse. Unstressed followed by Stressed.
- **Iambic Pentameter** means each line has ten syllables, divided into five pairs (or "feet") (da-DUM, da-DUM, da-DUM, da-DUM, da-DUM)

Now, let's break down the key points from the text:

- **What is Blank Verse?**
  Blank verse is poetry that has a regular beat (meter) but doesn't rhyme. It's like a song that keeps a steady beat, but the words don't necessarily sound the same at the end.
- **First Use in English:**
  The first time blank verse was used in English was by **Henry Howard, Earl of Surrey**, when he translated a famous story called the Aeneid around 1540.
- **Famous Early Examples:**
  **The play "Arden of Faversham" (around 1590) is one of the first known uses of blank verse** where the lines stop at the end of each

thought, making it easier to understand. **Another play called "Gorboduc" (1561) was the first English play to use blank verse**.

> **Christopher Marlowe's Contribution:**
> Christopher Marlowe was the first English writer to become famous for using blank verse. His work made it popular and important.

> **Shakespeare and Milton:**
> William Shakespeare used blank verse a lot in his plays, which made it even more popular. John Milton wrote an entire epic poem called **"Paradise Lost" in blank verse**, which became a masterpiece of English literature.

> **18th Century and Beyond:**
> In the 18th century, poets like James Thomson and William Cowper continued to use blank verse in their works. Later, Romantic poets like William Wordsworth, Percy Bysshe Shelley, and John Keats also used blank verse in their poetry.

> **19th Century:**
> Alfred, Lord Tennyson, another famous poet, loved blank verse and used it in many of his poems, including "The Princess" and "Ulysses."

> **American Poets:**
> In America, poets like Hart Crane and Wallace Stevens used blank verse in their long poems, even when many other poets were starting to write in free verse, which doesn't have a regular rhythm or rhyme.

## Thomas Wyatt and Henry Howard, Earl of Surrey Sonnet Form

### Thomas Wyatt:

> Introduced the **Petrarchan sonnet** to English poetry.
> Adapted the **octave and sestet structure** to suit the English language.
> Themes often include **love, beauty, and human emotion**.
> Famous sonnet: **"Whoso List to Hunt,"** an adaptation of Petrarch.
> Brought **Italian Renaissance influences** to English literature.

### Henry Howard, Earl of Surrey:

> Created the **English (Shakespearean) sonnet** form.
> Structure: **Three quatrains (ABABCDCDEFEF) and a rhymed couplet (GG)**.
> Wrote about **love, honor, and the human condition**.

- ➤ Introduced **blank verse** (unrhymed iambic pentameter) to English poetry.
- ➤ Famous sonnet: **"The soote season,"** exemplifying the English sonnet form.

## Shakespearean sonnet form:

A **Shakespearean sonnet** is a special type of poem that William Shakespeare made famous. It's like a little story or thought wrapped up in a neat, 14-line package. Here's how it works:

### Structure

- ➤ **14 Lines:** A Shakespearean sonnet always has 14 lines.
- ➤ **Iambic Pentameter:** Each line has 10 syllables, with a pattern that sounds like "da-DUM, da-DUM, da-DUM, da-DUM, da-DUM."
- ➤ **Rhyme Scheme:** The lines rhyme in a specific pattern: **ABAB CDCD EFEF GG**.

### Three Quatrains and a Couplet

- ➤ **Quatrains:** The first 12 lines are divided into three groups of four lines each. These are called **quatrains**. Each quatrain explores a part of the poem's main idea.
- ➤ **Couplet:** The last two lines are called a **couplet**. These lines usually wrap up the poem with a punchy conclusion or twist.

### Themes

- ➤ Shakespearean sonnets often talk about big ideas like love, beauty, time, and mortality (the idea that life doesn't last forever).

### Example: Sonnet 18

**Title:** "Shall I compare thee to a summer's day?"
**Quatrain 1 (ABAB):**
- ➤ *Shall I compare thee to a summer's day?*
- ➤ *Thou art more lovely and more temperate:*
- ➤ *Rough winds do shake the darling buds of May,*
- ➤ *And summer's lease hath all too short a date:*

**Quatrain 2 (CDCD):**
- ➢ *Sometime too hot the eye of heaven shines,*
- ➢ *And often is his gold complexion dimm'd;*
- ➢ *And every fair from fair sometime declines,*
- ➢ *By chance or nature's changing course untrimm'd;*

**Quatrain 3 (EFEF):**
- ➢ *But thy eternal summer shall not fade*
- ➢ *Nor lose possession of that fair thou owest;*
- ➢ *Nor shall Death brag thou wanderest in his shade,*
- ➢ *When in eternal lines to time thou growest:*

**Couplet (GG):**
- ➢ *So long as men can breathe or eyes can see,*
- ➢ *So long lives this, and this gives life to thee.*

**Breaking Down Sonnet 18**

- ➢ **Quatrain 1:** The poet wonders if he should compare someone to a summer day.
- ➢ **Quatrain 2:** He explains how summer can have flaws, like being too hot or too short.
- ➢ **Quatrain 3:** But he says that the person he's describing will never lose their beauty.
- ➢ **Couplet:** The poem will keep this person's memory alive forever.

## Petrarchan sonnet

A Petrarchan sonnet is another special type of poem, named after the Italian poet Francesco Petrarch, who popularized this form of poetry. It's different from the Shakespearean sonnet in its structure and rhyme scheme, but it also tells a story or explores an idea in a very compact, **14-line form**.

## 1. Structure

- ➢ **14 Lines:** Like the Shakespearean sonnet, a Petrarchan sonnet has 14 lines.
- ➢ **Iambic Pentameter:** The poem is usually written in iambic pentameter, which means each line has 10 syllables with a rhythm that sounds like "da-DUM, da-DUM, da-DUM, da-DUM, da-DUM."
- ➢ **Two Parts:** The sonnet is divided into two sections:

- o **Octave (8 lines)**
- o **Sestet (6 lines)**

## 2. Rhyme Scheme

- ➤ **Octave:** The first 8 lines follow a specific rhyme scheme of **ABBAABBA**.
- ➤ **Sestet:** The last 6 lines can have different rhyme schemes, like **CDECDE** or **CDCDCD**. The rhyme scheme of the sestet can vary, but it never rhymes the same way as the octave.

## 3. Themes

- ➤ Petrarchan sonnets often explore themes of love, beauty, unrequited love, and the pain and joy that come with them. The octave usually presents a problem or situation, and the sestet offers a resolution or reflection.

## 4. The "Volta" or Turn

- ➤ **Volta:** The ninth line, which is the first line of the sestet, often marks a "volta," or a turn in the poem. This is where the mood, tone, or focus of the poem shifts. For example, the octave might describe a problem, and the sestet might offer a solution or a new perspective.

## 5. Example:

- ➤ **Petrarch's Sonnet 90** (translated to English)
- ➤ **Octave (ABBAABBA):**
  - o *Upon the breeze she spread her golden hair*
  - o *That in a thousand gentle knots was turned,*
  - o *And the sweet light beyond all radiance burned*
  - o *In eyes where now that radiance is rare;*
  - o *And in her face there seemed to come an air*
  - o *As of a spirit, kindled and adorned*
  - o *With love, that over me his full power turned.*
  - o *Good God, the lovely look she had, to spare!*
- ➤ **Sestet (CDECDE):**
  - o *It was a sound that wept with me, that sighed;*
  - o *And its own harmony led out a song*
  - o *To comfort me in times of misery.*

- o   *And such a sweetness flowed from it, my guide,*
- o   *That in me still will linger, in me long,*
- o   *The greater good that what I see must be.*

## 6. Breaking Down the Example

➢ **Octave:** The speaker describes the beauty and grace of a woman, emphasizing how her hair, eyes, and presence enchanted him.
➢ **Volta:** The ninth line begins to shift the tone, focusing more on the emotional impact that her presence had on him.
➢ **Sestet:** The poem reflects on the memory of her beauty and the lasting emotional effect it has on him

### Spenserian sonnet

A **Spenserian sonnet** is a variation of the sonnet form that was developed by the English poet Edmund Spenser. It has some similarities to the more famous Shakespearean sonnet but also has unique features that set it apart. Here's an explanation of the Spenserian sonnet, broken down in a way that's easy to understand:

## 1. Structure

➢ **14 Lines:** Like other sonnets, a Spenserian sonnet consists of 14 lines.
➢ **Iambic Pentameter:** The poem is written in iambic pentameter, meaning each line typically has 10 syllables with a rhythm that goes "da-DUM, da-DUM, da-DUM, da-DUM, da-DUM."

## 2. Rhyme Scheme

➢ **Interlocking Rhyme:** The rhyme scheme of a Spenserian sonnet is unique because it links the quatrains together. The rhyme scheme is **ABAB BCBC CDCD EE.**
➢ This interlocking pattern creates a smooth flow from one quatrain to the next, leading up to a final rhymed couplet.

## 3. Quatrains and Couplet

- ➢ **Three Quatrains (12 lines):** The poem is divided into three 4-line sections (quatrains). Each quatrain develops a part of the theme or argument of the poem.
- ➢ **Final Couplet (2 lines):** The last two lines are a rhymed couplet, which typically presents a conclusion or a twist to the poem.

## 4. Themes

- ➢ Spenserian sonnets often explore themes of love, beauty, time, and nature. They might present an idea or problem in the first part of the poem and then resolve or reflect on it in the final couplet.

## 5. Example:

- ➢ **Sonnet 75** by Edmund Spenser
- ➢ **First Quatrain (ABAB):**
  - o *One day I wrote her name upon the strand,*
  - o *But came the waves and washed it away:*
  - o *Again I wrote it with a second hand,*
  - o *But came the tide, and made my pains his prey.*
- ➢ **Second Quatrain (BCBC):**
  - o *"Vain man," said she, "that dost in vain assay*
  - o *A mortal thing so to immortalize,*
  - o *For I myself shall like to this decay,*
  - o *And eek my name be wiped out likewise."*
- ➢ **Third Quatrain (CDCD):**
  - o *"Not so," quoth I, "let baser things devise*
  - o *To die in dust, but you shall live by fame:*
  - o *My verse your virtues rare shall eternize,*
  - o *And in the heavens write your glorious name."*
- ➢ **Final Couplet (EE):**
  - o *Where whenas death shall all the world subdue,*
  - o *Our love shall live, and later life renew.*

## 6. Breaking Down the Example

- ➢ **First Quatrain:** The speaker describes writing his beloved's name in the sand, only to have it washed away by the waves.

- ➤ **Second Quatrain:** The beloved questions the point of trying to immortalize something mortal, like a name in the sand.
- ➤ **Third Quatrain:** The speaker argues that his poetry will make her name eternal, even if her physical form fades away.
- ➤ **Final Couplet:** The poem concludes with the idea that their love will live on forever, even after death.

## Spenserian Stanza

## Structure:

- ➤ **9 lines** per stanza.
- ➤ **First 8 lines:** Iambic pentameter (10 syllables each).
- ➤ **9th line:** Iambic hexameter (12 syllables), called an "alexandrine."

## Rhyme Scheme:

- ➤ **ABABBCBCC** pattern.

## Example:

- ➤ From *The Faerie Queene*:
  *A gentle Knight was pricking on the plaine, (A)*
  *Yclad in mightie armes and silver shielde, (B)*
  *Wherein old dints of deepe woundes did remaine, (A)*
  *The cruell markes of many a bloody fielde; (B)*
  *Yet armes till that time did he never wield: (B)*
  *His angry steede did chide his foming bitt, (C)*
  *As much disdayning to the curbe to yield: (B)*
  *Full jolly knight he seemd, and faire did sitt, (C)*
  *As one for knightly giusts and fierce encounters fitt. (C)*

## Key Features:

- ➤ **Complexity:** Interlocking rhyme and varied meter.
- ➤ **Elegance:** Final line provides closure.

## Themes:

- ➤ Used in *The Faerie Queene* for both action and reflection.

**Table comparing the Petrarchan, Shakespearean, & Spenserian Sonnet:**

| Feature | Petrarchan Sonnet | Shakespearean Sonnet | Spenserian Sonnet |
|---|---|---|---|
| Origin | Italian (Petrarch) | English (Shakespeare) | English (Edmund Spenser) |
| Structure | 14 lines | 14 lines | 14 lines |
| Division | Divided into an octave (8 lines) and a sestet (6 lines) | Composed of three quatrains (4 lines each) and a couplet (2 lines) | Composed of three quatrains and a couplet |
| Rhyme Scheme | ABBAABBA (octave) + CDECDE or CDCDCD (sestet) | ABABCDCDEFEFGG | ABABBCBCCDCDEE |
| Volta (Turn) | Typically occurs between the octave and sestet (line 9) | Usually occurs at the beginning of the third quatrain (line 9) | Typically occurs at the beginning of the final couplet (line 13) |
| Themes | Love, unattainable beauty, philosophical musings | Love, time, beauty, mortality | Love, time, beauty, morality |
| Tone | Often introspective and reflective | Varied: reflective, dramatic, sometimes playful | Varied, but often more fluid and interwoven in theme |
| Example | Petrarch's Sonnet 90: "Upon the breeze she spread her golden hair..." | Shakespeare's Sonnet 18: "Shall I compare thee to a summer's day?" | Spenser's Sonnet 75: "One day I wrote her name upon the strand..." |

| Langua ge | Often ornate, with an emphasis on contrast between ideas | Often direct, with clear argument progression | Rich and elaborate, with a focus on interlocking themes |
| --- | --- | --- | --- |
| Purpos e of Form | To present a problem in the octave and a resolution in the sestet | To present a theme in the quatrains and a resolution or twist in the couplet | To create a more interwoven and flowing structure through linked quatrains |

## Literary Devices Used in Elizabethan Literature

### Blank Verse

- ➤ **Definition:** Unrhymed iambic pentameter, often used in drama and poetry.
- ➤ **Example:** William Shakespeare frequently used blank verse in his plays, such as in *Hamlet*:
  *"To be, or not to be: that is the question."*

### Metaphor

- ➤ **Definition:** A figure of speech in which a word or phrase is applied to an object or action to which it is not literally applicable.
- ➤ **Example:** In Shakespeare's *As You Like It*:
  *"All the world's a stage, And all the men and women merely players."*

### Simile

- ➤ **Definition:** A figure of speech involving the comparison of one thing with another thing of a different kind, using "like" or "as."
- ➤ **Example:** From Edmund Spenser's *The Faerie Queene*:
  *"Her angel's face, As the great eye of heaven shined bright."*

### Alliteration

- ➤ **Definition:** The occurrence of the same letter or sound at the beginning of adjacent or closely connected words.

> **Example:** In Christopher Marlowe's *The Passionate Shepherd to His Love*: *"And we will all the pleasures prove."*

## Personification

> **Definition:** The attribution of a personal nature or human characteristics to something nonhuman.
> **Example:** In Shakespeare's *Sonnet 18*: *"Rough winds do shake the darling buds of May."* (Here, winds are given the human ability to shake.)

## Hyperbole

> **Definition:** Exaggerated statements or claims not meant to be taken literally.
> **Example:** From Marlowe's *Doctor Faustus*: *"Was this the face that launched a thousand ships?"* (Referring to Helen of Troy.)

## Irony

> **Definition:** The expression of one's meaning by using language that normally signifies the opposite, typically for humorous or emphatic effect.
> **Example:** In Shakespeare's *Julius Caesar*, Marc Antony says: *"Brutus is an honourable man,"* while actually suggesting the opposite.

## Pun

> **Definition:** A play on words, often exploiting multiple meanings or similar sounds.
> **Example:** In Shakespeare's *Romeo and Juliet*, Mercutio says: *"Ask for me tomorrow, and you shall find me a grave man."* (Grave meaning serious and also a burial place.)

## Oxymoron

> **Definition:** A figure of speech in which apparently contradictory terms appear in conjunction.
> **Example:** From Shakespeare's *Romeo and Juliet*: *"O brawling love, O loving hate."*

## Soliloquy

➢ **Definition:** A speech given by a character alone on stage, expressing their thoughts aloud.
➢ **Example:** The famous "To be, or not to be" soliloquy in *Hamlet*.

## Antithesis

➢ **Definition:** A contrast or opposition between two things, often in parallel structure.
➢ **Example:** In Shakespeare's *A Midsummer Night's Dream*:
*"The more I hate, the more he follows me."*

## Foreshadowing

➢ **Definition:** A literary device in which a writer gives an advance hint of what is to come later in the story.
➢ **Example:** In *Macbeth*, the witches' prophecies foreshadow Macbeth's eventual downfall.

## Symbolism

➢ **Definition:** The use of symbols to represent ideas or qualities.
➢ **Example:** The green girdle in *Sir Gawain and the Green Knight* symbolizes Gawain's human frailty.

## Allusion

➢ **Definition:** An indirect reference to another literary work or to a famous person, place, or event.
➢ **Example:** In Shakespeare's *Hamlet*:
*"Hyperion to a satyr"* is an allusion to classical mythology, comparing King Hamlet to a god and Claudius to a goat.

## Rhetorical Question

➢ **Definition:** A question asked in order to create a dramatic effect or to make a point rather than to get an answer.
➢ **Example:** In Shakespeare's *Julius Caesar*:
*"Did this in Caesar seem ambitious?"*

## Allegory

- ➢ **Definition:** A narrative in which characters, events, or settings symbolize abstract ideas or moral qualities.
- ➢ **Example:** In Spenser's *The Faerie Queene*, the Redcrosse Knight represents the virtue of Holiness and the battle between good and evil, serving as an allegory for the Christian's journey toward spiritual perfection.

## Assonance

- ➢ **Definition:** The repetition of vowel sounds within close proximity in a sentence or line of poetry.
- ➢ **Example:** In Alfred, Lord Tennyson's *The Lady of Shalott*:
  *"The willow waves, the willow shivers."* (The repetition of the "i" sound in "willow" and "shivers" creates assonance.)

## Introduction of the Elizabethan Age

### Historical Background (1550–1630):

- ➢ **Reign of Elizabeth** saw **political** and **religious stability**.
- ➢ **Union of Crowns** settled **England-Scotland conflict**.
- ➢ **Religious quiescence** with **minor disturbances** occurred.
- ➢ **Expansion** in **mental** and **geographical horizons** noted.
- ➢ **New knowledge** from **East** and **West** influenced **literature**.
- ➢ **Voyages** chronicled by **Richard Hakluyt** impacted **literature**.
- ➢ **Hakluyt's work** highlighted **explorers' material** and **intellectual treasures**.
- ➢ **Elizabethan settlement** positively influenced **literary growth**.
- ➢ **English nation** attained **stability** in **politics** and **religion**.
- ➢ **Intellectual treasures** shaped the period's **literary output**.
- ➢ **Exploration** and **discovery** enriched **Elizabethan literature**.
- ➢ **Elizabethan Age** marked by a **sense of adventure**.
- ➢ **Stability** and **expansion** fueled **literary achievements**.
- ➢ **Union of Crowns** strengthened the **English nation**.
- ➢ **Elizabethan era** laid foundation for **English literature**.
- ➢ **Religious conflicts** resolved, fostering **literary creativity**.
- ➢ **Voyages to new worlds** inspired **literary imagination**.

- ➢ **Elizabethan stability** supported **literary experimentation**.
- ➢ **Intellectual curiosity** drove **literary innovation**.
- ➢ **Political stability** allowed **literature** to flourish.

## Literary Features of the Age:

- ➢ **New Classicism** revived **Greek** and **Latin studies**.
- ➢ **English language** tempered by **classical influences**.
- ➢ **Abundant literary output** characterized **Elizabethan era**.
- ➢ **Pamphlets** and **treatises** written in large numbers.
- ➢ **New Romanticism** emphasized the **wonderful** and **remote**.
- ➢ **Daring spirit of adventure** marked **literature**.
- ➢ **Elizabethan drama** matured **quickly** and **dramatically**.
- ➢ **Theaters** faced challenges from **actors** and **Puritans**.
- ➢ **Drama** reached zenith with **Shakespeare's works**.
- ➢ **Sidney's Apologie** defended **poetry** against **attacks**.
- ➢ **Poetry** of great **beauty** and **originality** produced.
- ➢ **Prose** rose to a position of **major importance**.
- ➢ **Latin influence** on **prose** began to wane.
- ➢ **Scottish literature** disappeared during this period.
- ➢ **Drama** dealt with contemporary **quarrels** and **controversies**.
- ➢ **Prose** developed a **tradition** and **universal application**.
- ➢ **Puritan opposition** to **drama** began to emerge.
- ➢ **Prose** became increasingly **important** in **literature**.
- ➢ **Poetry** reflected the **passion** and **disputes** of the time.
- ➢ **Shakespeare's art** marked the **height of the drama**.

## EDMUND SPENSER (1552–99)

### Life

- ➢ **Edmund Spenser** born in **London, 1552 or 1553**.
- ➢ **Little known** about his **family** or **childhood**.
- ➢ Attended **Merchant Taylor School** on **scholarship**.
- ➢ Studied **Latin** and **Greek** at the school.
- ➢ Graduated with a **B.A. in 1573** from **Cambridge**.
- ➢ Received an **MA** from **Cambridge in 1576**.
- ➢ First published work: **The Shepheardes Calender (1579)**.
- ➢ Dedicated **Shepheardes Calender** to **Sir Philip Sidney**.

- ➤ Edmund Spenser's first major work was **"The Shepheardes Calender,"** published in **1579**. His last work was **"A View of the Present State of Ireland,"** which was written in **1596** but published posthumously in **1633**.
- ➤ Best known for epic poem **The Faerie Queene**.
- ➤ Also wrote **Amoretti** and **Epithalamion (1595)**.
- ➤ Served as **secretary** for **Bishop of Rochester**.
- ➤ Later became **secretary** to the **Earl of Leicester**.
- ➤ Appointed **secretary** to **Lord Deputy of Ireland (1580)**.
- ➤ Lived in **Ireland** for **eighteen years**.
- ➤ Granted **Kilcolman Castle** and **3,000 acres**.
- ➤ Published first three books of **The Faerie Queene (1589)**.
- ➤ Returned to **London** with **second installment (1596)**.
- ➤ **Kilcolman Castle burned** during a **rebellion (1598)**.
- ➤ Lost a child in the fire, fled to **London**.
- ➤ Died in **1599**, buried in **Poets' Corner, Westminster Abbey**.

**Rhyme and Reason:**

In Worthies of England, Thomas Fuller included a story where the Queen told her treasurer, William Cecil, to pay Spenser one hundred pounds for his poetry. The treasurer, however, objected that the sum was too much. She said, "Then give him what is reason." Without receiving his payment in due time, Spenser gave the Queen this quatrain on one of her signs of progress:

*"I was promis'd on a time,*
*To have a reason for my rhyme:*
*From that time unto this season,*
*I receiv'd nor rhyme nor reason."*

She immediately ordered the treasurer to pay Spenser the original £100.

**His Works:**

- ➤ *The Shepheardes Calender* (**1579**),
- ➤ *The Faerie Queene*, Books 1–3 (**1590),**
- ➤ *Complaints, Containing Sundrie Small Poemes of the Worlds Vanitie (1991),*
- ➤ *Axiochus (1592),*
- ➤ *Daphnaïda (1592),*

- ➢ "Amoretti" "Epithalamion" (**1595**),
- ➢ *Astrophel. A Pastorall Elegie vpon the Death of the Most Noble and Valorous Knight, Sir Philip Sidney* (**1595**),
- ➢ *Colin Clouts Come Home Againe* (**1595**),
- ➢ *Fowre Hymnes* (**1596**),
- ➢ *Prothalamion* (**1596**),
- ➢ *The Faerie Queene*, Books 4–6 - (**1596**),
- ➢ *Two Cantos of Mutabilitie (1609),*
- ➢ *A Vewe of the Present State of Irelande (1633)*

<table>
<tr><td>

*Code to Remember:*
*Shefaer Camp*
*Amor Epic Astro*
*Pro Queen's Mutiny in Ireland*

- ➢ ***His Works starts from 1579 to 1633***
- ➢ ***His First work The Shepheardes Calender in 1579***
- ➢ ***First Faerie Queene 1590***
- ➢ ***Amoretti and Epithalamion Together in 1595***
- ➢ ***Prothalamion and The Next Faerie Queene together in 1596***
- ➢ ***His last work  A Vewe of the Present State of Irelande in 1633 which is prose.***

</td></tr>
</table>

**Remember the chronology order through Story:**

Once upon a time, in 1579, a young Shepherd named Calender set off on a journey through the mystical land. In 1590, he reached the enchanted Fairy land where he discovered a grand Queen ruling over the magical beings. As he wandered, he heard the Complaints of the creatures who were troubled by the vanity of the world, in 1591. In 1592, the shepherd found an ancient Axe that held the power to translate languages, called Axiochus. Nearby, in the same year, he encountered the weeping spirit of Daphne who had been transformed into a tree. By 1595, the shepherd fell in love with a maiden named Amorette and wrote her many love poems. On their wedding day, he sang a joyful Epic song called the Epithalamion to celebrate their union. Later that year, he composed an Astounding elegy for a fallen knight named Astrophel. When he returned home, Colin the shepherd shared tales of his journey, marking his return in 1595. In 1596, the shepherd composed Hymns to honor the gods and goddesses of the land. He then proclaimed a great Proclamation of peace throughout the kingdom, in 1596. During his travels, he visited the Fairy land again, witnessing the great Queen's ongoing battles in 1596. Many years later, in 1609, the shepherd learned of the Mutability of all things and wrote about the changes in the world. Finally, in 1633, the shepherd's journey brought him to Ireland, where he offered a View of the Present State of Ireland before his story ended.

- ➢ *Jan van der Noodt's A Theatre for Worldlings* (includes poems translated into English by Spenser) - **1569**
- ➢ *The Shepheardes Calender* (published under the pseudonym "Immerito") - **1579**
- ➢ *Iambicum Trimetrum* - **1579**
- ➢ *The Faerie Queene*, Books 1–3 - **1590**
- ➢ *Complaints, Containing Sundrie Small Poemes of the Worlds Vanitie,* includes:

  - o "The Ruines of Time"
  - o "The Teares of the Muses"
  - o "Virgil's Gnat"
  - o "Prosopopoia, or Mother Hubberds Tale"
  - o "Ruines of Rome: by Bellay"
  - o "Muiopotmos, or the Fate of the Butterflie"
  - o "Visions of the Worlds Vanitie"
  - o "The Visions of Bellay"
  - o "The Visions of Petrarch" - **1591**

- ➢ *Axiochus* (a translation of a pseudo-Platonic dialogue) - **1592**
- ➢ *Daphnaïda* (An Elegy upon the Death of the Noble and Vertuous Douglas Howard) - **1592**
- ➢ *Amoretti and Epithalamion*, containing:

  - o "Amoretti"
  - o "Epithalamion" - **1595**

- ➢ *Astrophel. A Pastorall Elegie vpon the Death of the Most Noble and Valorous Knight, Sir Philip Sidney* - **1595**
- ➢ *Colin Clouts Come Home Againe* - **1595**
- ➢ *Fowre Hymnes* - **1596**
- ➢ *Prothalamion* - **1596**
- ➢ *The Faerie Queene*, Books 4–6 - **1596**
- ➢ *Babel, Empress of the East* (a dedicatory poem prefaced to Lewes Lewkenor's *The Commonwealth of Venice*) - **1599**

- ➤ *Two Cantos of Mutabilitie* (published with a reprint of *The Faerie Queene*) - **1609** (Posthumous)
- ➤ First folio edition of Spenser's collected works - **1611** (Posthumous)
- ➤ *A Vewe of the Present State of Irelande* (a prose treatise on the reformation of Ireland) - **1633** (Posthumous)

## Key Points:

- ➤ **"The Shepherd's Calendar" (1579)**: First of Spenser's surviving poems.
- ➤ **Title adopted** from a popular compilation of the day.
- ➤ **Series of twelve eclogues**, one for each month.
- ➤ **Dialogue form** with stock pastoral characters like **Cuddie, Colin Clout, and Perigot.**
- ➤ **No great poetical merit**, but excellent poetic exercises.
- ➤ **Wide range in meter, skillful alliteration**, and pastoral phrases.
- ➤ **1591**: Published **"The Ruins of Time," "The Tears of the Muses,"** and **"Mother Hubberd's Tale."**
- ➤ **"Amoretti" (1595)**: Eighty-eight sonnets celebrating Spenser's love.
- ➤ **"Epithalamion"**: Magnificent ode, written for Spenser's marriage.
- ➤ **"Colin Clouts Come Home Againe"**: Contains interesting personal details.
- ➤ **"Four Hymns" and "Prothalamion"** published in **1596**.
- ➤ **Spenser's shorter poems** showcase his **lyrical ability**.
- ➤ **Diffuse and ornate style**, not intensely passionate.
- ➤ **Odes**: Sonorous, commanding measures, delight mind and ear.
- ➤ **"Mother Hubberd's Tale"**: Satirical, sharp, and censorious in tone.

## The Shepheardes Calender (1579)

- ➤ **First major poetic work by Spenser** published in **1579**.
- ➤ **Modeled after Renaissance eclogues** of Mantuanus, not Virgil.
- ➤ **Written in deliberately archaic spellings** to connect with **medieval literature.**
- ➤ **Spenser's The Shepherd's Calender, published in 1579, was dedicated to Philip Sidney**
- ➤ Introduces **Colin Clout**, a **folk character** originally by John Skelton.
- ➤ Represents **life as a shepherd** through the **twelve months**.
- ➤ **Extensive commentary or gloss** ascribed to a mysterious **"E.K."**.
- ➤ **E.K. provides ironic and intelligent** commentary on the poems.

- ➤ The term **sarcasm (Sarcasmus)** is **first recorded** in the **October eclogue**.
- ➤ **Spenser's innovations** anticipated Sidney's **Arcadia (1580)**.
- ➤ Establishes **Spenser's reputation** as a poet with **classical influences**.

## Amoretti (1595)

- ➤ **Sonnet cycle describing Spenser's courtship** and **marriage** to **Elizabeth Boyle**.
- ➤ **Published in 1595** as part of **Amoretti and Epithalamion**.
- ➤ Includes **89 sonnets** and a **series of short poems**.
- ➤ **Immortalizes the name** of his bride through **wordplay**.
- ➤ Chronicles the **progress of love** and records **his marriage**.
- ➤ **Sonnet 34** discusses the **breakup with his wife**.
- ➤ **Critically overlooked**, seen as **inferior** to other sonnet sequences.
- ➤ Celebrates **Elizabeth Boyle** and **Spenser's union** in a **poetic cycle**.
- ➤ Published by **William Ponsonby** in **London**.
- ➤ **Represents Spenser's personal** and **literary achievements** in the sonnet form.

## Epithalamion (1595)

- ➤ **Ode to his bride Elizabeth Boyle** on their **wedding day**.
- ➤ **Published in 1595** alongside **Amoretti** by **William Ponsonby**.
- ➤ **24 stanzas** represent the **hours of Midsummer Day**.
- ➤ Begins with **invocation to the Muses**, seeking their **help**.
- ➤ Chronicles the **wedding day**, from **dawn to night**.
- ➤ **Expresses hopes for fertility** and **future generations**.
- ➤ **Detailed recording of hours** throughout the **wedding day**.
- ➤ **One of Spenser's finest lyrical** and **narrative achievements**.
- ➤ Combines **youthful enthusiasm** with **middle-age concerns**.
- ➤ Considered a **masterpiece of celebratory** and **narrative poetry**.

## Prothalamion (1596)

- ➤ **Nuptial song** for the **double marriage** of Elizabeth and Katherine Somerset.
- ➤ **Published in 1596**, written in the **form of a marriage song**.

- ➤ Describes the **Thames River**, where Spenser finds **two maidens**.
- ➤ **Nymphs collecting flowers** for the **bridal crowns** of the brides.
- ➤ References the **myth of Jove and Leda**, adding **mythological depth**.
- ➤ **Repeated refrain**: "Sweet Thames, run softly till I end my song."
- ➤ **Celebrates the twin marriage** with **elegance and grace**.
- ➤ **Connected with Spenser's marriage poem**, the Epithalamion.
- ➤ **Quoted by T.S. Eliot** in **The Waste Land**.
- ➤ **Set to music** by **George Dyson** in **1954**.

## A View of the Present State of Ireland (1633)

- ➤ **Written in 1596**, discussing the **control over Ireland**.
- ➤ Defends **Lord Arthur Grey de Wilton's policies** in Ireland.
- ➤ Highlights the **need for reform** in **Irish laws, customs, religion**.
- ➤ **Criticizes Brehon law**, favoring **capital punishment** over fines.
- ➤ Warns of the **dangers of Irish language education**.
- ➤ **Shows Spenser's political views** on **colonial governance**.
- ➤ Suggests **radical changes** to **integrate Ireland into English rule**.
- ➤ Represents **Spenser's involvement** in **English colonial policies**.
- ➤ The work reflects **Spenser's disdain** for **Irish customs**.
- ➤ **Published posthumously** in **1633** by **Sir James Ware**.

## The Faerie Queene (1590-1596)

### The Faerie Queene Overview

- ➤ **Epic poem by Edmund Spenser** published in **1590 and 1596**.
- ➤ **One of the longest poems** in the **English language**.
- ➤ **Over 36,000 lines** and **4,000 stanzas** in total length.
- ➤ **Introduced the Spenserian stanza** as a **new verse form**.
- ➤ Follows **several knights examining different virtues** allegorically.
- ➤ **Primarily allegorical work**, with multiple **interpretive levels**.
- ➤ **Praises and criticizes Queen Elizabeth I** through allegory.
- ➤ **"Letter of the Authors"** reveals the poem's **allegorical intentions**.
- ➤ **Aims to fashion a noble person** through **virtue and discipline**.
- ➤ **First three books** presented to **Elizabeth I in 1589**.
- ➤ **Sponsored by Sir Walter Raleigh**, gaining **court favor**.
- ➤ **Elizabeth granted Spenser a pension** of **£50 a year**.
- ➤ No evidence **Elizabeth I read** the **poem**.

- ➤ **Work published in instalments** during Spenser's **lifetime.**
- ➤ **First three books published** in **1589.**
- ➤ **Second three books published** in **1596.**
- ➤ **Posthumous publication** of **Book VII** with **two cantos.**
- ➤ **Allegory used** to **explore virtues** and **court politics.**

## The Faerie Queene Plot and Allegory

- ➤ **Plot is obscure, "clowdily enwrapped in Allegorical devises".**
- ➤ **Spenser wrote a preface letter** to **Sir Walter Raleigh.**
- ➤ **Twelve books planned,** each focused on a **particular knight.**
- ➤ **Each knight represents a specific virtue** in the story.
- ➤ **First book:** Knight of the Red Cross represents **Holiness.**
- ➤ **Second book:** Focuses on **Temperance** as a central virtue.
- ➤ **Third book:** Dedicated to the virtue of **Chastity.**
- ➤ **Fourth book:** Explores the virtue of **Friendship.**
- ➤ **Prince Arthur** is the chief character, appearing at **critical moments.**
- ➤ **Arthur is destined** to marry **Gloriana,** Queen of "Faerie-londe."
- ➤ **Plot is leisurely, elaborate,** filled with **incident and digression.**
- ➤ By the fifth book, the plot **weakens and loses momentum.**
- ➤ Only half of the story was **completed by Spenser.**
- ➤ **Complex allegory** with **twelve divisions,** each branching further.
- ➤ **Three strands of allegory** run through the story.
- ➤ **Characters from Arthurian** and **classical romance** are included.
- ➤ **Poorly developed characters** like Arthur, Merlin, Saracens.
- ➤ **Moral and religious virtues** allegorized: **Una (Truth), Guyon (Temperance).**
- ➤ **Vices also allegorized: Duessa (Deceit), Orgoglio (Pride).**
- ➤ **Twisting and untwisting strands** create a **baffling yet delightful narrative.**

## Summary of "The Faerie Queene" Books I-VI

- ➤ **Book I (Holiness):**
    - ○ **Redcrosse Knight** represents **Holiness.**
    - ○ Travels with **Una,** fights **Errour,** tricked by **Archimago.**
    - ○ **Redcrosse** captured by **Orgoglio,** saved by **Una** and **Arthur.**
    - ○ Recovers at the **House of Holiness,** sees future vision.
    - ○ Rescues Una's parents from a **dragon**; the two are betrothed.

- ➤ **Book II (Temperance)**:
  - o **Sir Guyon** embodies **Temperance**.
  - o Tempted by **Archimago**, resists various evil knights.
  - o Meets **Arthur**, together they resist **Acrasia's temptations**.
  - o Captures **Acrasia**, destroys the **Bower of Bliss**.
- ➤ **Book III (Chastity)**:
  - o **Britomart**, a lady knight, represents **Chastity**.
  - o Defeats **Guyon** in a joust, searches for **Artegall**.
  - o Learns her destiny to marry **Artegall**, fights **Sir Marinell**.
  - o Rescues **Amoret** from the wizard **Busirane**.
- ➤ **Book IV (Friendship)**:
  - o Focuses on events from Book III, not true **friendship**.
  - o **Scudamore** misled by **Ate**, becomes jealous of **Britomart**.
  - o **Satyrane** holds a tournament; **Britomart** defeats **Artegall**.
  - o **Artegall** falls in love with **Britomart**, they pledge love.
  - o **Amoret** escapes **savage man**, reunited with **Scudamore**.
- ➤ **Book V (Justice)**:
  - o **Sir Artegall** embodies **Justice**.
  - o The book focuses on Artegall's quest to bring justice.
- ➤ **Book VI (Courtesy)**:
  - o **Sir Calidore** represents **Courtesy**.
  - o The book follows Calidore's efforts to maintain social grace and chivalry.

## Question

**Question 1**

**Arrange chronologically the following texts in terms of their years of first publication:**

    A.   Edmund Spenser's The Faerie Queene
    B.   Coleridge and Wordsworth's Lyrical Ballads
    C.   Pablo Neruda's Canto General
    D.   Charles Baudelaire's The Flowers of Evil

**Choose the correct answer from the options given below**
1. A, B, C, D
2. **A, B, D, C**
3. B, C, A, D
4. D, A, B, C

**Correct Explanations:**

"The Faerie Queene" is an English epic poem by Edmund Spenser. Books I–III were first published in **1590,** then republished in 1596 together with books IV–VI.

"Lyrical Ballads", with a Few Other Poems is a collection of poems by William Wordsworth and Samuel Taylor Coleridge, first published in **1798.**

"Les Fleurs du mal" is a volume of French poetry by Charles Baudelaire. Les Fleurs du mal includes nearly all of Baudelaire's poetry, written in **1840** and ending with his death in August 1867.

"Canto General" is Pablo Neruda's tenth book of poems. It was first published in Mexico in **1950.**

## Question 2

**Which of the following is true in relation to Edmund Spenser's Faerie Queene?**

1. A letter addressed to Sir Walter Raleigh was prefixed to the 1590 edition of the poem
2. A letter addressed to Sir Walter Raleigh was appended to the 1590 edition of the poem
3. A letter addressed to Sir Walter Raleigh was prefixed to the 1596 edition of the poem
4. A letter addressed to Sir Walter Raleigh was appended to the 1596 edition of the poem

**Explanation:**

**Answer: 2.** A letter addressed to Sir Walter Raleigh was appended to the 1590 edition of the poem.

Explanation: The letter addressed to Sir Walter Raleigh was added to the 1590 edition of Edmund Spenser's epic poem "Faerie Queene." The letter serves as a dedication to Raleigh and provides insights into the poem's purpose and themes. It was appended to the edition, meaning it was added at the end of the book rather than being prefixed or placed at the beginning.

## Question 3

**By Who among the following is the author of The Steele Glass**

1. The Earl of Surrey

2. Thomas Sackville
3. **George Gascoigne**
4. Edmund Spenser

**Correct Explanations:**
**"Steele Glass" is actually "The Steele Glas" and it is a poem by George Gascoigne, a 16th-century English poet.** The poem is a satirical work that critiques the vanity and greed of the court and aristocracy in Elizabethan England. It uses the metaphor of a glass mirror to represent the way in which individuals become obsessed with their own reflection and neglect the needs of others. The poem is also notable for its use of a unique and complex rhyme scheme, which adds to its overall satirical tone.

## Question 4

**Arrange the following poets in accordance with their years of birth.**

A. George Herbert
B. Edmund Spenser
C. Philip Sidney
D. John Donne
E. Oliver Goldsmith

Choose the correct answer from the options given below:

1 ABDCE
2. **BCDAE**
3. EBADC
4. ADEBC

**Explanations:**
➢ Edmund Spenser (1552/1553 – 1599)
➢ Philip Sidney (1554 – 1586)
➢ George Herbert (1593 – 1633)
➢ John Donne (1572 – 1631)
➢ Oliver Goldsmith (c. 1730 – 1774)

## Question 5

**Spenser's The Shepherd's Calender, published in 1579, was dedicated to**

1. Wyatt
2. Surrey
3. Sidney
4. Bacon

**Explanations:**

The Shepheardes Calender, originally titled The Shepheardes Calendar, Containing twelve Aeglogues proportionable to the Twelve monthes. Entitled to the Noble and Vertuous Gentleman most worthy of all titles both of learning and chevalrie M. Philip Sidney, marks Edmund Spenser's first significant poetic work, published in 1579. Inspired by Virgil's Eclogues, Spenser crafted a series of pastoral poems at the start of his career, drawing more from the Renaissance eclogues of Mantuanus. The deliberate use of archaic spelling in the title and throughout the work creates an intentional connection to mediaeval literature, particularly Geoffrey Chaucer. **Dedicated to Philip Sidney, the poem introduces Colin Clout, a character derived from John Skelton, and portrays his life as a shepherd across the twelve months of the year. The Calendar showcases formal innovations that anticipate Spenser's even more elaborate Countess of Pembroke's Arcadia (The "Old" Arcadia, 1580), a renowned pastoral romance by Sir Philip Sidney,** who was acquainted with Spenser. Notably, the first publication of The Shepheardes Calender includes extensive commentary and gloss attributed to an individual identified as "E.K." Often assumed to be an alias of Spenser himself, E.K. is a clever, subtly ironic commentator, occasionally mistaken but highly insightful. The term "sarcasm" (Sarcasmus) is first recorded in English in Spenser's poem (October).

Spenser presented the first three books of **The Faerie Queene to Elizabeth I** in 1589, probably sponsored by **Sir Walter Raleigh**.

## Question 6

**Which among the following are not true about The Defense of Poesie by Philip Sidney?**

A. The text was published posthumously in 1595
B. It is also titled as An Apology for Poetry
C. Philip Sidney criticises Geoffrey Chaucer's Troilus and Criseyde and Spenser's The Shepheardes Calendar
D. The text is the first major piece of literary criticism in English

E. The text defends Plato for his decision to ban poets from the ideal state as described in Republic

**Choose the correct answer from the options given below:**

1. A and B only
2. B and C only
3. C and D only
4. C and E only

**Explanations:**
**Answer: 4.** C and E only

*An Apology for Poetry*

> **An Apology for Poetry (or The Defence of Poesy)**
> Written by Elizabethan poet Philip Sidney around 1580.
> **It is the first major piece of literary criticism in English**
> **Published posthumously in 1595,** following Sidney's death.
> Partially motivated by Stephen Gosson's critique of English stage.
> **Sidney rebuts general objections to poetry, including Plato's.**

An example of the latter is his approach to Plato. **He reconfigures Plato's argument against poets by saying poets are "the least liar".** Poets never claim to know the truth, nor "make circles around your imagination," nor rely on authority.

> Integrates classical and Italian precepts on fiction.
> Argues poetry combines history's liveliness with philosophy's ethics.
> Claims poetry more effective in promoting virtue.
> **Offers significant commentary on Chaucer and Edmund Spenser.**

*"**Chaucer, undoubtedly, did excellently in his Troilus and Cressida:** of whom, truly, I know not whether to marvel more, either that he in that misty time could see so clearly, or that we in this clear age walk so stumblingly after him. Yet had he great wants, fit to be forgiven in so revered antiquity. I account the Mirror of Magistrates meetly furnished of beautiful parts; and in the Earl of Surrey's lyrics many things tasting of a noble birth, and worthy of a noble mind.*

*__The Shepherd's Calendar has much poetry in his eclogues, indeed worthy the reading, if I be not deceived.__* "

- Discusses the role and impact of the Elizabethan stage.
- Defense against criticism, elevating poetry's educational and moral value.
- **Sidney states that there "have been three general kinds" of poetry:**
   (i) "the chief" being religious which "imitate[d] the inconceivable excellencies of God",
   (ii) philosophical and
   (iii) imaginative poetry written by "right poets" who "teach and delight"

## Sir Thomas Wyatt - Key Points

- **Born in 1503**, descended from an ancient **Yorkshire family.**
- Family supported the **Lancastrian side** in the **Wars of the Roses.**
- Educated at **Cambridge**, entering the **King's service.**
- Entrusted with many **important diplomatic missions.**
- Principal patron was **Thomas Cromwell.**
- **Imprisoned in 1541** after Cromwell's death.
- Known for his **love-poems, ninety-six** in total.
- Poems appeared in **Tottel's Miscellany** (1557).
- **First sonnets** in English, **thirty-one** in number.
- Ten sonnets are in the **Italian/Petrarchan form.**
- Wrote **epigrams, songs, and rondeaux**, lighter than sonnets.
- Poems show **care and elegance**, part of the **new romanticism.**
- His **Satires** are composed in **Italian terza rima.**
- Wyatt was a significant innovator in **English poetry.**
- His works demonstrate a strong influence from **Italian literature.**

## Henry Howard, Earl of Surrey - Key Points

- **Born in 1518**, son of **Thomas Howard**, Earl of Surrey.
- Adopted the title of **Earl of Surrey** when his father became **Duke of Norfolk** (1524).
- Played a **prominent role in Court life** due to his father's position.
- Served as a **soldier in France and Scotland.**
- Known for his **reckless temper**, leading to many quarrels.
- Incurred the wrath of **Henry VIII** and was **beheaded** on **Tower Hill.**

- Began **literary collaboration with Sir Thomas Wyatt** around 1542.
- His poems were **published posthumously in Tottel's Miscellany** (1557).
- Primarily composed **lyrical poems**, including a few **sonnets**.
- Created the **first sonnets in English** using the **Shakespearean form**.
- Wrote numerous **love-poems** addressed to a mysterious **"Geraldine."**
- His poems are **smoother and more poetical** than Wyatt's.
- Most important work: **Certain Bokes of Virgiles Æneis** (1557).
- Introduced **blank verse** to English literature, an important poetic form.
- His blank verse paved the way for the achievements of **Shakespeare and Milton**.

## Thomas Sackville, Earl of Dorset - Key Points

- **Born in 1536** at **Buckhurst, Sussex**; educated at **Oxford and Cambridge**.
- **Called to the Bar** and entered **Parliament**.
- Participated in many **diplomatic and public missions**.
- Created **Lord Buckhurst** in **1566**.
- Temporarily fell out of favor with **Queen Elizabeth** due to his **plain speaking**.
- Later restored to favor; became **Lord High Treasurer**.
- Elevated to **Earl of Dorset** in **1604**.
- His poetry, though not extensive, is **highly significant**.
- Known for **The Induction** and **The Complaint of Henry, Duke of Buckingham**.
- Both poems appeared in **The Mirror for Magistrates** (1555).
- Composed in **rhyme royal stanza**, with a **melancholy and elegiac tone**.
- Language is **archaic**, but the poems show **nobility and grandeur**.
- His work influenced **Spenser's** composition of **The Faerie Queene**.
- Sackville collaborated with **Thomas Norton** on the early tragedy **Gorboduc**.
- **Sackville's poetry** marked a return to the grandeur last seen in **Chaucer's** time.

## George Gascoigne - Key Points

> - **Born in 1535** in **Bedfordshire**; educated at **Cambridge**.
> - Became a **lawyer** and later entered **Parliament**.
> - Composed **elegant lyrics** and one of the first regular **satires**.
> - **The Steel Glass** (1576) is a notable satire in **blank verse**.
> - Wrote the tragedy **Jocasta** (1566), a **landmark in drama**.
> - **Supposes** (1566), an early comedy, influenced **Shakespeare's Taming of the Shrew.**
> - Authored **Certayne Notes of Instruction** (1575), an early **critical essay** on verse.
> - Known for his **ease and versatility** in writing.
> - Considered one of the **founders of the Elizabethan tradition**.
> - His works contributed to the **growth of English drama and literature.**

## Question 7

**By Who among the following is the author of The Steele Glass**

5. The Earl of Surrey
6. Thomas Sackville
7. **George Gascoigne**
8. Edmund Spenser

**Correct Explanations:**

**"Steele Glass" is actually "The Steele Glas" and it is a poem by George Gascoigne, a 16th-century English poet.** The poem is a satirical work that critiques the vanity and greed of the court and aristocracy in Elizabethan England. It uses the metaphor of a glass mirror to represent the way in which individuals become obsessed with their own reflection and neglect the needs of others. The poem is also notable for its use of a unique and complex rhyme scheme, which adds to its overall satirical tone.

**Sir Philip Sidney (1554–86)**

> - **Philip Sidney** was born in **Kent, England, in 1554.**
> - He was educated at **Shrewsbury and Oxford University.**
> - Traveled extensively across **Europe** after leaving **Oxford**.
> - **Appointed cupbearer** to **Queen Elizabeth** in **1575.**
> - Served as an **ambassador to Germany** in **1577.**

- ➢ **Opposed Queen Elizabeth's marriage** to the **French heir.**
- ➢ Encouraged **Edmund Spenser** and was a **patron of the arts.**
- ➢ Known for the sonnet collection **"Astrophel and Stella"** (published posthumously).
- ➢ **"Astrophel and Stella"** foreshadowed the **Shakespearian sonnet form.**
- ➢ Also wrote the heroic prose romance **"Arcadia".**
- ➢ Authored **"The Defense of Poesy,"** a significant **literary criticism.**
- ➢ Did not publish his works during his **lifetime.**
- ➢ Became **governor** of the **Dutch town of Flushing** in **1585.**
- ➢ **Fought in the Battle of Zutphen** against the **Spanish** in **1586.**
- ➢ **Shot in the thigh** during the battle and died of **gangrene.**
- ➢ **Died at the young age of 31**, in **1586.**
- ➢ Famous for **giving water** to a **wounded soldier** while dying. Saying, *"Thy necessity is yet greater than mine."*
- ➢ Sidney's death is often viewed as **avoidable but heroic.**
- ➢ Composed a **song on his deathbed**, illustrating his **noble character.**
- ➢ **Buried** at **St. Paul's Cathedral**, London, in **1587.**

## His Notable Works:

- ➢ "Arcadia"
- ➢ "Astrophel and Stella"
- ➢ "The Defence of Poesie"

## The Countess of Pembroke's Arcadia:

- ➢ **It** is a **pastoral romance** by **Sir Philip Sidney.**
- ➢ Written **towards the end of the 16th century.**
- ➢ **Philip Sidney's Arcadia was influenced by The Spanish Romance of Montemayor.**
- ➢ Sidney created two versions: **Old Arcadia** and **New Arcadia.**
- ➢ The setting is in **Arcadia**, a **fairyland** of **idealistic beauty.**
- ➢ **Arcadia** features **shepherd boys** grazing **herds of cattle.**
- ➢ The story revolves around **Duke Basilius**, his wife **Gynecia**, and their daughters **Pamela** and **Philoclea.**
- ➢ **Two princes, Musidorus** and **Pyrocles**, fall in love with the **princesses.**
- ➢ **Musidorus** disguises as a **lady; Pyrocles** as a **shepherd** to enter the household.

- **Complications arise** when the **King** and **Queen** fall for **Musidorus** in disguise.
- The **King** attempts to take **Musidorus** as a **woman**; the **Queen** seeks to **win his heart**.
- **Pyrocles' courage** leads to the **girls' freedom**.
- **Musidorus escapes** from the **entanglement** and runs away with **Pamela**.
- All **complications are resolved** by the **end of the story**.
- **William Hazlitt criticized** the prose style of Arcadia as *"one of the greatest monuments of the abuse of intellectual power upon record."*
- **T.S. Eliot called Arcadia** *"a monument of dullness."*
- William Shakespeare based **the subplot of Gloucester in "King Lear"** on Sir Philip Sidney's Arcadia.
- Samuel Richardson **took the name of Pamela for his novel "Pamela."**
- Sir Philip Sidney's **"Arcadia" was appreciated by Charles Lamb and Virginia Woolf**.

The style of Arcadia is as artificial as that of John Lyly's "Euphues." It is highly conceited. Here are some examples –

- Sidney's reference to cool wine seems to laugh for joy as it nears a lady's lips.
- The water drops that slip down the bodies of daintily ladies seem to weep for sorrow.
- The name that a beautiful lady utters is perfumed by the scent of her breath.
- When the princesses put on their clothes, the clothes are described as glad.

## Astrophel and Stella (1591)

- **Astrophel and Stella is an Elizabethan sonnet sequence.**
- Written by **Sir Philip Sidney** in 1582.
- Published **posthumously** in 1591.
- Consists of **108 sonnets** and **11 interspersed songs**.
- Considered among the **finest Elizabethan sonnet cycles**.
- **Astrophel** represents **Sidney**; **Stella** represents his **beloved**.
- The name **"Stella"** means **"star"**; **"Astrophel"** means **"star lover"**.

> Sidney expresses **passionate feelings** for **Stella.**
> Explores themes of **love, reason,** and **conflicting emotions.**
> **Astrophel** struggles with his **unrequited love** for **Stella.**
> He ultimately decides to **abandon his pursuit** of **Stella.**
> Sidney reflects on **reason vs. passion** in the sonnets.
> **Astrophel** chooses a **life of public service** over **love.**
> The work inspired a **vogue for sonnet sequences.**
> **Edmund Spenser** wrote the elegy **"Astrophel"** after Sidney's death.

## An Apology for Poetry

> **The Defence of Poesie** by **Sir Philip Sidney** written **c. 1582.**
> **Published posthumously in 1595**; another edition titled **An Apologie for Poetrie.**
> Considered the **finest piece of Elizabethan literary criticism.**
> Sidney argues **literature teaches better than history or philosophy.**
> **Refutes Plato's ban on poets** in his **Republic.**
> **Sidney was partly motivated by Stephen Gosson's** attack on the stage.
> **Gosson dedicated his work** "The School of Abuse" to **Sidney in 1579.**
> **Gosson's work was written in a style known as euphuism, which was popular in the late sixteenth century.**
> Sidney **primarily addresses broader objections to poetry**, like **Plato's.**

## Text:

> Sidney calls poetry his "unelected vocation" yet defends it passionately.
> **He defends "poor poetry,"** arguing its **value in purifying wit.**
> Early in his defense, Sidney candidly remarks, *"having slipped into the title of a poet, [I] am provoked to say something unto you in the defense of that my unelected vocation."*
> Poetry's "final end" is to lead us to **spiritual perfection.**
> Sidney argues poetry can elevate our **"degenerate souls".**
> He uses a classical **seven-part structure** for his argument.
> > o **Introduction,**
> > o **Proposition,**
> > o **Division,**

- o **Examination.**
  - o **Refutation,**
  - o **Peroration,**
  - o **Digressio**
- ➢ Sidney references **classical texts** to support his defense of poetry.
- ➢ **He examines different forms of poetry** to build his case.
- ➢ Sidney laments readers who "cannot hear the planet-like music of poetry."
- ➢ **He criticizes those with "earth-creeping" minds** unable to appreciate poetry.
- ➢ Sidney concludes with a harsh judgment for poetry's detractors.
- ➢ **He sends a message "in the behalf of all poets"** to such readers.
- ➢ Sidney wishes they "never get favor for lacking skill of a sonnet."
- ➢ **He also curses them to have their "memory die from the earth"** without an epitaph.
- ➢ Poetry according to Sir Philip Sidney, **is of three kinds.**
  - ▪ Religious,
  - ▪ Philosophical,
  - ▪ Imaginative
- ➢ Sidney states that there *"have been three general kinds" of poetry:* **(i) "the chief" being religious** *which "imitate[d] the inconceivable excellencies of God",* **(ii) philosophical and (iii) imaginative poetry** *written by "right poets" who "teach and delight".*
- ➢ **Sidney argued that poetry should prioritize the expression of moral and philosophical ideas over the use of formal devices like rhyme,**
- ➢ In "An Apology for Poetry" Sidney discusses the **didactic function of poetry by comparing it to philosophy and Religion.**
- ➢ **Sidney rebuts general objections to poetry, including Plato's.**
- ➢ An example of the latter is his approach to Plato. **He reconfigures Plato's argument against poets by saying poets are "the least liar".** Poets never claim to know the truth, nor "make circles around your imagination," nor rely on authority.

Plato expressed his views on poetry and poets in **Book X of "The Republic".** In this section, he famously critiques poetry by arguing that it is a form of **imitation** and, therefore, far removed from the truth. He states that **poetry is the "mother of lies"** because it portrays a distorted version of reality, appealing to emotions rather than reason. For this reason, **Plato argues that**

**poets should be banished from his ideal state**, as they can mislead people and corrupt the minds of the citizens, especially the youth.

- ➤ Integrates classical and Italian precepts on fiction.
- ➤ Argues poetry combines history's liveliness with philosophy's ethics.
- ➤ Claims poetry more effective in promoting virtue.
- ➤ **Offers significant commentary on Chaucer and Edmund Spenser.**

*__"Chaucer, undoubtedly, did excellently in his Troilus and Cressida;__ of whom, truly, I know not whether to marvel more, either that he in that misty time could see so clearly, or that we in this clear age walk so stumblingly after him. Yet had he great wants, fit to be forgiven in so revered antiquity. I account the Mirror of Magistrates meetly furnished of beautiful parts; and in the Earl of Surrey's lyrics many things tasting of a noble birth, and worthy of a noble mind. __The Shepherd's Calendar has much poetry in his eclogues, indeed worthy the reading, if I be not deceived.__ "*

Famous Arguments in *An Apologie for Poetrie*

- ➤ *"having slipped into the title of a poet, [I] am provoked to say something unto you in the defense of that my unelected vocation."*
- ➤ *"to lead and draw us to as high a perfection as our degenerate souls, made worse by their clayey lodgings, can be capable of."*
- ➤ *"neither philosopher nor historiographer, could at the first have entered into the gates of popular judgments, if they had not taken a great passport of poetry."*
- ➤ *"only the poet, disdaining to be tied to any such subjection, lifted up with the vigor of his own invention, doth grow in effect into another Nature, in making things either better than Nature bringeth forth, or, quite anew forms such as never were in Nature, as the Heros, Demigods, Cyclops."*
- ➤ *"Nature never set forth the earth in so rich tapestry, as divers poets have done ... Her world is brazen, the poets only deliver a golden."*
- ➤ *"who having made man to his own likeness, set him beyond and over all the works of that second nature, which in nothing he showeth so much as in poetry: when with the force of a divine breath, he bringeth things forth far surpassing her doings."*
- ➤ *"our erected wit, maketh us know what perfection is, and yet our infected will, keepeth us from reaching unto it."*

> *"is an art of imitation, for so Aristotle termeth it in his word mimesis, that is to say, a representing, counterfeiting, or figuring forth: to speak metaphorically, a speaking picture: with this end, to teach and delight."*
> *"right poets ... who having no law but wit, bestow that in colors upon you which is fittest for the eye to see."*
> *"the poet ... nothing affirms, and therefore never lieth."*
> *"poetry ... is the mother of lies."*
> *"the poet doth not endeavor to make men good, but that their evil hurt not others."*
> *"the one giveth the precept, and the other the example."*
> *"the peerless poet ... he coupleth the general notion with the particular example."*
> *"poetry is philosophoteron and spoudaioteron, that is to say, it is more philosophical, and more studiously serious, than history."*
> *"feigned example ... as much force to teach, as a true example."*
> *"the poet is the food for the tenderest stomachs, the poet is indeed the right popular philosopher."*
> *"poetry ... far exceedeth prose."*
> *"poetry abuseth man's wit, but that, man's wit abuseth poetry."*
> *"there are many mysteries contained in poetry, which of purpose were written darkly, lest by profane wits, it should be abused."*
> *"so earth-creeping a mind, that it cannot lift itself up, to look to the sky of poetry."*

## Question 8

**Who among the following observed that "Nothing can please many, and please long, but just representations of general nature"?**

(1) Philip Sidney
(2) Samuel Johnson
(3) S.T. Coleridge
(4) William Wordsworth

**Explanations:**
**Answer: 3.** Philip Sidney

Philip Sidney, in his work "The Defence of Poesy," indeed refutes Plato's charge that poets are liars. He argues that poets do not aim to present factual truths but rather to explore universal truths and convey moral lessons through their art. According to Sidney, poets use imagination and fiction to create a heightened reality that can reveal deeper insights into human nature and the world. He asserts that poets do not claim their creations to be literal truth but rather offer a different form of truth that can inspire and instruct. In this sense, poets, according to Sidney, do not affirm or assert facts in the same way as philosophers or historians but convey truths through the power of their imaginative art.

## Question 9

**Poetry according to Sir Philip Sidney, is of three kinds. They are:**

1. Classical, romantic, neo-classical
2. Religious, philosophical, imaginative
3. Philosophical, imaginative, narrative
4. Religious, dramatic, romantic

**Explanations:**

**Ans**: Religious, Philosophical, Imaginative

An Apology for Poetry (or The Defence of Poesy) is a work of literary criticism by Elizabethan poet Philip Sidney. It was written in approximately **1580 and first published in 1595, after his death**. It is generally believed that he was at least partly motivated by **Stephen Gosson, a former playwright who dedicated his attack on the English stage, The School of Abuse,** to Sidney in 1579, but Sidney primarily addresses more general objections to poetry, such as those of Plato. In his essay, Sidney integrates a number of classical and Italian precepts on fiction. The essence of his defense is that poetry, by combining the liveliness of history with the ethical focus of philosophy, is more effective than either history or philosophy in rousing its readers to virtue. The work also offers important comments on Edmund Spenser and the Elizabethan stage. Sidney states that there **"have been three general kinds" of poetry:** (i) **"the chief" being religious which "imitate[d] the inconceivable excellencies of God", (ii) philosophical and (iii) imaginative poetry written by "right poets" who "teach and delight".**

## Question 10

**Who among the following believed that rhyme is not an integral part of poetry?**

A. William Wordsworth
B. Horace
C. Samuel Daniel
D. Philip Sidney

**Choose the most appropriate answer from the options given below**

1. A and C only
2. B and D only
3. A and D only
4. D and C only

**Explanations:**
**Answer: 2.** B and D only

**Horace and Philip Sidney both expressed reservations about the use of rhyme in poetry, but it is important to note that they did not completely reject rhyme as a poetic device.**

Horace, a Roman poet and literary critic who lived in the first century BCE, wrote in his "Ars Poetica" that a poem should be **"mellifluous without artifice," suggesting that the language should flow naturally without the forced use of rhyme.** He also wrote that "the sense should be as much polished as the verse," emphasizing the importance of conveying a clear and meaningful message in poetry.

Philip Sidney, an English poet and courtier who lived in the sixteenth century, expressed similar views in his essay "The Defence of Poesy." **Sidney argued that poetry should prioritize the expression of moral and philosophical ideas over the use of formal devices like rhyme.** He believed that rhyme should be used sparingly and only when it enhances the meaning of the poem, rather than serving as a decorative element.

## Question 11

**Who among the following refutes Plato's charge that poets are liars, by arguing that the poet "nothing affirms, and therefore never lieth"?**

1. John Dryden
2. George Puttenham
3. Philip Sidney
4. Richard Hooker

**Explanations:**
**Answer: 3.** Philip Sidney

Philip Sidney, in his work "The Defence of Poesy," indeed refutes Plato's charge that poets are liars. He argues that poets do not aim to present factual truths but rather to explore universal truths and convey moral lessons through their art. According to Sidney, poets use imagination and fiction to create a heightened reality that can reveal deeper insights into human nature and the world. He asserts that poets do not claim their creations to be literal truth but rather offer a different form of truth that can inspire and instruct. In this sense, poets, according to Sidney, do not affirm or assert facts in the same way as philosophers or historians but convey truths through the power of their imaginative art.

## Question 12

**Which two of the following poets defended poetry against Plato's denigration of Poetry?**

A. John Dryden
B. P.B. Shelley
C. T.S. Eliot
D. Philip Sidney

**Choose the most appropriate answer from the options given below**

1. (B) and (D) Only
2. (B) and (C) Only
3. (A) and (B) Only
4. (C) and (A) Only

**Explanations:**
**Answer: 1.** (B) and (D) Only

The poets who defended poetry against Plato's denigration of poetry are P.B. Shelley and Philip Sidney. Both Shelley and Sidney wrote influential works that argued for the value and significance of poetry. Shelley, in his essay "A Defence of Poetry," emphasized the role of poetry in inspiring moral and social progress. Sidney, in his work "The Apology for Poetry," defended poetry as a powerful form of art that has the ability to teach, delight, and elevate the soul. They countered Plato's criticism and championed the importance of poetry in human culture and society.

## Question 13

In "An Apology for Poetry" Sidney discusses the didactic function of poetry by comparing it to philosophy and:

1. **Religion.**
2. Aesthetics.
3. History.
4. ethics.

**Correct Explanations:**

**In "An Apology for Poetry," Sidney discusses the didactic function of poetry by comparing it to philosophy and religion.** He argues that poetry has a unique ability to instruct and delight, to convey important ideas in a way that is more engaging and memorable than philosophy or theology. He suggests that poetry has a special relationship to emotions and imagination and that it can reach people in a way that dry intellectual arguments cannot. While he does not reject the importance of philosophy or religion, he argues that poetry has a unique role to play in educating and inspiring people.

## Question 14

**Philip Sidney's Arcadia was influenced by....**

1. The Metaphysical Poetry
2. The Arthurian Legends
3. The Italian Paintings of Veronese
4. **The Spanish Romance of Montemayor**

**Correct Explanations**

**The Countesse of Pembroke's Arcadia by Philip Sidney, 1590:** Sir Philip Sidney (1554–1586) was an English courtier and poet. Arcadia, dedicated to his sister, Mary Herbert, the Countess of Pembroke, was a work in the new genre of prose romance. It traces the adventures of the princes Pyrocles and Musidorus and the fortunes of the Duke of Arcadia.

**Montemayor's Diana was also a major inspiration for Philip Sidney in writing the New Arcadia.** Montemayor's influence was noticed early on by Sidney's contemporaries: as John Hoskins stated in 1599, "For the web, as it were, of [Sidney's] story, he followed three: Heliodorus in Greek, Sannazarius' Arcadia in Italian, and Diana by Montemayor in Spanish." Sidney, in particular, seems to have modelled his opening scene between the shepherds Strephon and Klaus on Montemayor's Sireno and Sylvano.

**Shakespeare used an episode from Arcadia as the source for the Gloucester subplot in King Lear.**

**The Seven Books of the Diana (Spanish: Los siete libros de la Diana) is a pastoral romance written in Spanish by the Portuguese author Jorge de Montemayor.**

One of its most famous readers was William Shakespeare, who seems to have borrowed the Proteus-Julia-Sylvia plot of The Two Gentlemen of Verona from Felismena's tale in the Diana.

Question 15

Match List I with List II

| LIST I | LIST II |
| --- | --- |
| A. Plato | I. Rhetoric |
| B. Aristotle | II. Symposium |
| C. P. B. Shelley | III. Apology of Poetry |
| D. Philip Sydney | IV. Defence of Poetry |

**Choose the correct answer from the options given below:**
1. A-I, B-II, C-III, DIV
2. A-III, B-II, C-IV, D-I
3. A-IV, B-III, C-II, D - I
4. A-II, B-I, C-IV, D-III

**Explanations:**
**Ans:** A-II, B-I, C-IV, D-III

**Plato's "Symposium" is a philosophical text that explores the nature of love and desire through a series of speeches delivered by guests at a symposium, or drinking party.** The speeches range from the comic to the tragic, and include discussions of beauty, the nature of reality, and the relationship between love and philosophy.

**Aristotle's "Rhetoric" is a treatise on the art of persuasion.** It covers a wide range of topics, including the nature of rhetoric, the types of arguments that are most effective, and the relationship between rhetoric and ethics. Aristotle argues that rhetoric can be used for both good and evil purposes, but that it is ultimately up to the individual to decide how to use this powerful tool.

**P.B. Shelley's "Defence of Poetry" is a critical essay in which he argues that poetry is a powerful force for social and political change.** He believes that poetry has the ability to inspire people to strive for a better world, and that it can help to create a more just and humane society.

**Philip Sidney's "Apology for Poetry" is a work of literary criticism in which he defends poetry against its critics.** He argues that poetry is a noble art that has the power to teach and inspire, and that it should be celebrated rather than condemned. Sidney also discusses the role of the poet in society, and the importance of imagination and creativity in the poetic process.

## Question 16

**Identify the correct ones among the following:**

A.   The Apologie for Poetrie was written by Sir Philip Sidney.
B.   Sir Philip Sidney wrote the Apologie for Poetrie as a counterblast to Stephen Gosson's The School of Abuse.
C.   Stephen Gosson wrote The School of Abuse in the euphuistic style.
D.   Sidney's style was characterised by neoclassical restraint.
E.   Sidney and Gosson wrote their critical treatise in the eighteenth century.

**Choose the correct answer from the options given below:**

1.   **A, B and C only.**
2.   A, C and D only.
3.   A D and E only.
4.   A, C and E only.

**Explanations:**
**Sir Philip Sidney wrote the Apologie for Poetrie,** a work of literary criticism, around 1580. In this work, Sidney defends poetry against its detractors, arguing that poetry has a moral purpose and can be used to teach and inspire readers. He also explores the nature of poetry and its place in society.

**Sidney wrote the Apologie for Poetrie as a response to Stephen Gosson's The School of Abuse,** which was published in 1579. Gosson's work attacked the stage and poetry, claiming that they were morally corrupt and had a negative influence on society.

**Gosson's work was written in a style known as euphuism, which was popular in the late sixteenth century.** This style was characterized by elaborate wordplay, alliteration, and other rhetorical devices.

Sidney's Apologie for Poetrie is considered an important work of literary criticism and a key text in the development of English literary theory. It helped establish the idea that poetry had a moral and educational value and helped to elevate the status of poetry in English literature.

## Question 17

**Arrange the following poets in accordance with their years of birth.**

    A.   George Herbert
    B.   Edmund Spenser
    C.   Philip Sidney
    D.   John Donne
    E.   Oliver Goldsmith

**Choose the correct answer from the options given below:**

    1.   ABDCE
    **2.   BCDAE**
    3.   EBADC
    4.   ADEBC

**Explanations:**
- Edmund Spenser (1552/1553 – 1599)
- Philip Sidney (1554 – 1586)
- George Herbert (1593 – 1633)
- John Donne (1572 – 1631)
- Oliver Goldsmith (c. 1730 – 1774)

## Question 18

**Match List I with List II**

| List I | List II |
|---|---|
| A. Response to Stephen Gosson | I. Aristotle |
| B. The Individual Talent | II. Matthew Arnold |
| C. Catharsis | III. T.S. Eliot |
| D. Sweetness and Light | IV. Philip Sidney |

**Choose the correct answer from the options given below:**

1. A- IV. B- II, C- III. D-I
2. A - IV, B - III. C - I. D -II
3. A - IV. B - III, C - II, D - I
4. A- IV. B - I, C - II, D - III

**Explanations**
**Answer:** 2. A - IV, B - III, C - I, D -II

**I. Aristotle - Catharsis: In his work "Poetics,"** Aristotle introduced the concept of catharsis, which refers to the **emotional release or purification experienced by the audience of a tragedy**. According to Aristotle, through witnessing the suffering and downfall of tragic characters, audiences experience a cathartic purging of their own emotions. Catharsis allows for a psychological and emotional transformation, providing a sense of relief and a heightened understanding of the human condition.

**II. Matthew Arnold - Sweetness and Light: Matthew Arnold, a prominent Victorian critic, advocated for the pursuit of "sweetness and light" in his essay "Culture and Anarchy."** He believed that true culture, achieved through education and intellectual development, could lead to the harmonious progress of society. **"Sweetness" represents the aesthetic** and **artistic aspects of culture, while "light"** refers to rational and intellectual enlightenment. Arnold emphasised the importance of cultivating both aspects to create a balanced and enlightened society.

**III. T.S. Eliot - The Individual Talent: T.S. Eliot, in his influential essay "Tradition and the Individual Talent,"** discusses the role of the individual poet in relation to literary tradition. Eliot argues that the poet's creative expression is shaped by the collective wisdom of the past, and true originality emerges from the assimilation and transformation of that tradition. He highlights the necessity of humility and the ability to detach oneself from personal emotions and biases, urging poets to embrace the wider cultural and historical context in their work.

**IV. Philip Sidney - Response to Stephen Gosson: Philip Sidney, in his critical work "An Apology for Poetry,"** responds to the attacks on poetry made by Stephen Gosson. Gosson criticised poetry for its alleged moral corruption and lack of educational value. In his response, Sidney defends poetry as a noble art form that holds the power to inspire and educate through imaginative storytelling. He argues that poetry has the ability to convey moral and philosophical truths while entertaining and engaging the audience, refuting Gosson's negative portrayal and advocating for the value and significance of poetry in society.

## Question 19

**What is the correct chronological sequence of the following texts?**

 A. "The Advancement of Learning"
 B. "An Apology for Poetry"
 C. "The Uses of the Spectator"
 D. "My Relations"
 E. "How it Strikes a Contemporary**

**Choose the correct answer from the options given below:**

 1. A, B, C, D, E
 2. B, A, C, D, E
 3. C, A, D, E, B
 4. D, C, B, A, E

**Explanations**
**Answer:** 2. B, A, C, D, E

**The Defence of Poesie, literary criticism by Sir Philip Sidney, written about 1582 and published posthumously in 1595.** Another edition of the work, published the same year, is titled An Apologie for Poetrie. Considered the finest work of Elizabethan literary criticism, Sidney's elegant essay suggests that literature is a better teacher than history or philosophy, and it masterfully refutes Plato's infamous decision to ban poets from the state in his Republic.

**The Advancement of Learning (full title: Of the Proficience and Advancement of Learning, Divine and Human) is a 1605 book by Francis Bacon.** It inspired the taxonomic structure of the highly influential Encyclopédie by Jean le Rond d'Alembert and Denis Diderot, and is credited by Bacon's biographer-essayist Catherine Drinker Bowen with being a pioneering essay in support of empirical philosophy.

**The Spectator was a daily publication founded by Joseph Addison and Richard Steele in England, lasting from 1711 to 1712.**

**Essays of Elia is a collection of essays written by Charles Lamb; it was first published in book form in 1823**, with a second volume, Last Essays of Elia, issued in 1833 by the publisher Edward Moxon. My Relations is an essay part of this collection.

**Men and Women is a collection of fifty-one poems in two volumes by Robert Browning, first published in 1855.** While now generally considered to contain some of the best of Browning's poetry, at the time, it was not received well and sold poorly. How it Strikes a Contemporary is a part of this collection.

## Question 20

**Identify the poet who has said that poetry has fallen from its pedestal as the highest estimation of learning... to be the laughingstock of children?**

1. Willam Wordsworth
2. Sir Philp Sidney
3. Willam Blake
4. George Gascoigne

**Explanations:**
**Answer: 2.** Sir Philp Sidney

**Sir Philip Sidney began his journey as a poet in 1578,** with a relatively brief but impactful literary career spanning 7 to 8 years. His seminal work, **"The Defence of Poesy," also known under the titles "The Defence of**

**Poesie" and "An Apologie for Poetrie,"** stands as a powerful testament to the value of poetry, penned by someone deeply versed in both the practice and the classical understanding of the art.

Early in his defense, Sidney candidly remarks, ***"having slipped into the title of a poet, [I] am provoked to say something unto you in the defense of that my unelected vocation."*** He champions the often undervalued art of poetry, asserting its unparalleled ability to elevate human nature beyond its flawed state, stating poetry's ultimate goal *"to lead and draw us to as high a perfection as our degenerate souls, made worse by their clayey lodgings, can be capable of."* Sidney structures his argument meticulously, adhering to a seven-part classical format that includes an introduction, proposition, division, examination, refutation, and concludes with a peroration, incorporating a digressio to address a tangential topic. Throughout "The Defence of Poesy," Sidney draws upon classical works and scrutinizes various poetic forms.

He poignantly addresses the skeptics of poetry's enchanting power, stating, *"you cannot hear the planet-like music of poetry."* For those unable to appreciate the transcendent qualities of poetry, he laments, *"if you have so earth-creeping a mind that it cannot lift itself up to look to the sky of poetry"* then humorously cautions, *"I must send you in the behalf of all poets:—that while you live in love, and never get favor for lacking skill of a sonnet; and when you die, your memory die from the earth for want of an epitaph."*

*"Wherein if Pugliano's strong affection and weak arguments will not satisfy you, I will give you a nearer example of myself, who, I know not by what mischance, in these my not old years and idlest times, having slipped into the title of a poet, am provoked to say something unto you in the defense of that my unelected vocation, which if I handle with more good will than good reasons, bear with me, since the scholar is to be pardoned that follows the steps of his master. **And yet I must say that, as I have just cause to make a pitiful defense of poor poetry, which from almost the highest estimation of learning is fallen to be the laughing-stock of children, so have I need to bring some more available proofs, since the former is by no man barred of his deserved credit, the silly [weak—ed] latter has had even the names of philosophers used to the defacing of it, with great danger of civil war among the Muses.**"*

**Famous Arguments in *An Apologie for Poetrie***

- *"having slipped into the title of a poet, [I] am provoked to say something unto you in the defense of that my unelected vocation."*
- *"to lead and draw us to as high a perfection as our degenerate souls, made worse by their clayey lodgings, can be capable of."*
- *"neither philosopher nor historiographer, could at the first have entered into the gates of popular judgments, if they had not taken a great passport of poetry."*
- *"only the poet, disdaining to be tied to any such subjection, lifted up with the vigor of his own invention, doth grow in effect into another Nature, in making things either better than Nature bringeth forth, or, quite anew forms such as never were in Nature, as the Heros, Demigods, Cyclops."*
- *"Nature never set forth the earth in so rich tapestry, as divers poets have done ... Her world is brazen, the poets only deliver a golden."*
- *"who having made man to his own likeness, set him beyond and over all the works of that second nature, which in nothing he showeth so much as in poetry: when with the force of a divine breath, he bringeth things forth far surpassing her doings."*
- *"our erected wit, maketh us know what perfection is, and yet our infected will, keepeth us from reaching unto it."*
- *"is an art of imitation, for so Aristotle termeth it in his word mimesis, that is to say, a representing, counterfeiting, or figuring forth: to speak metaphorically, a speaking picture: with this end, to teach and delight."*
- *"right poets ... who having no law but wit, bestow that in colors upon you which is fittest for the eye to see."*
- *"the poet ... nothing affirms, and therefore never lieth."*
- *"poetry ... is the mother of lies."*
- *"the poet doth not endeavor to make men good, but that their evil hurt not others."*
- *"the one giveth the precept, and the other the example."*
- *"the peerless poet ... he coupleth the general notion with the particular example."*
- *"poetry is philosophoteron and spoudaioteron, that is to say, it is more philosophical, and more studiously serious, than history."*
- *"feigned example ... as much force to teach, as a true example."*
- *"the poet is the food for the tenderest stomachs, the poet is indeed the right popular philosopher."*
- *"poetry ... far exceedeth prose."*
- *"poetry abuseth man's wit, but that, man's wit abuseth poetry."*

> *"there are many mysteries contained in poetry, which of purpose were written darkly, lest by profane wits, it should be abused."*
> *"so earth-creeping a mind, that it cannot lift itself up, to look to the sky of poetry."*



**Which among the following are not true about The Defense of Poesie by Philip Sidney?**

A. The text was published posthumously in 1595
B. It is also titled as An Apology for Poetry
C. Philip Sidney criticises Geoffrey Chaucer's Troilus and Criseyde and Spenser's The Shepheardes Calendar
D. The text is the first major piece of literary criticism in English
E. The text defends Plato for his decision to ban poets from the ideal state as described in Republic

**Choose the correct answer from the options given below:**

1. A and B only
2. B and C only
3. C and D only
4. C and E only

**Explanations**:
**Answer: 4.** C and E only

*An Apology for Poetry*

> **An Apology for Poetry (or The Defence of Poesy)**
> Written by Elizabethan poet Philip Sidney around 1580.
> **It is the first major piece of literary criticism in English**
> **Published posthumously in 1595,** following Sidney's death.
> Partially motivated by Stephen Gosson's critique of English stage.
> **Sidney rebuts general objections to poetry, including Plato's.**

An example of the latter is his approach to Plato. **He reconfigures Plato's argument against poets by saying poets are "the least liar".** Poets never claim to know the truth, nor "make circles around your imagination," nor rely on authority.

> ➢ Integrates classical and Italian precepts on fiction.
> ➢ Argues poetry combines history's liveliness with philosophy's ethics.
> ➢ Claims poetry more effective in promoting virtue.
> ➢ **<u>Offers significant commentary on Chaucer and Edmund Spenser.</u>**

*<u>**"Chaucer, undoubtedly, did excellently in his Troilus and Cressida;**</u> of whom, truly, I know not whether to marvel more, either that he in that misty time could see so clearly, or that we in this clear age walk so stumblingly after him. Yet had he great wants, fit to be forgiven in so revered antiquity. I account the Mirror of Magistrates meetly furnished of beautiful parts; and in the Earl of Surrey's lyrics many things tasting of a noble birth, and worthy of a noble mind. <u>**The Shepherd's Calendar has much poetry in his eclogues, indeed worthy the reading, if I be not deceived.**</u> "*

> ➢ Discusses the role and impact of the Elizabethan stage.
> ➢ Defense against criticism, elevating poetry's educational and moral value.
> ➢ **Sidney states that there "have been three general kinds" of poetry:**
>> (i) "the chief" being religious which "imitate[d] the inconceivable excellencies of God",
>> (ii) philosophical and
>> (iii) imaginative poetry written by "right poets" who "teach and delight".

## Michael Drayton (1563–1631)

> ➢ **He** epresents the later epoch of **Elizabethan literature**.
> ➢ Born in **Warwickshire, studied at Oxford**, and became a tutor.
> ➢ Drayton moved to **London around 1590** and produced many poems.
> ➢ His first book was **The Harmony of the Church (1591)**.
> ➢ He wrote several **long historical poems**, including **England's Heroical Epistles**.
> ➢ **The Barons' Wars (1603)** is another of his long historical poems.
> ➢ His most important longer poem is **Polyolbion**, a tedious geographical description of England.
> ➢ **Polyolbion** is written in **alexandrines** and includes interspersed tales.

- Drayton's **shorter poems** include his well-known poem on **Agincourt**.
- He also wrote verse tales and pastorals like **The Man in the Moon**.
- **Nymphidia** is one of his most skillful and attractive shorter poems.
- Drayton is rarely an inspired poet, but **"Since there's no help"** is an exception.
- The sonnet **"Since there's no help"** is considered his most inspired work.
- Drayton was **painstaking, versatile,** and sometimes **delightful** in his poetry.
- **Nymphidia** showcases his skill in creating **charming and whimsical** verse.

## Thomas Campion (1567–1620)

- He was born in **London** and educated at **Cambridge**.
- He studied law at **Gray's Inn** but became a **physician** in 1606.
- Campion wrote popular **masques** during his career.
- His main fame comes from his **attractive lyrics** set to music.
- **Campion** composed some of the music for his own lyrics.
- His best-known collections include **A Booke of Ayres (1601)**.
- **Songs of Mourning (1613)** and **Two Bookes of Ayres (1613)** are also well-known collections.
- Campion was known for his **skillful adaptation** of words to tunes.
- He mastered **complicated meters** and had a knack for **sweet phrasing**.
- Campion excelled in the **technical aspects** of poetry, despite lacking the highest lyrical genius.
- **Thomas Campion wrote** *Observations in the Art of English Poesie* **(1602)**.

## Phineas Fletcher (1582–1650) and Giles Fletcher (1588–1623)

- They were **brothers and poets**.
- Both were **educated at Cambridge** and later took **holy orders**.
- **Phineas Fletcher's** chief poem is **"The Purple Island"** (1633).
- **The Purple Island** allegorically describes the **human body** in **twelve cantos**.
- The poem contains **much digression**, allowing for **real poetical passages**.

- The poem's structure is **cumbrous and artificial** but shows **Spenserian influence.**
- **Phineas's stanza** resembles the **Spenserian** but omits the **fifth and seventh lines.**
- **Giles Fletcher's** best-known work is **"Christ's Victorie and Triumph"** (1610).
- The poem is **epical**, with **four cantos** describing **Christ's triumph.**
- **Giles's style** is **descriptive, imaginative**, and **ornate in diction.**
- The poem's **melodious diction** partly inspired **Milton's Paradise Regained.**
- **Giles's stanza** is similar to **Spenserian**, lacking the **seventh line.**
- The **Fletchers** were known for their **Spenserian imitation.**
- They lacked **Spenser's genius** but excelled in **intensity, color, and melody.**
- Their works show **great metrical artistry** and **high-quality imitation.**

## Samuel Daniel (1562–1619)

- He was born near **Taunton in Somerset.**
- He was **educated at Oxford** and became a **tutor** to the son of the **Countess of Pembroke.**
- In **1599**, he was briefly **Poet Laureate.**
- In **1603**, he was made **Master of the Queen's Revels** by **James I.**
- His works include the **sonnet-series "Delia"** (1592).
- He wrote the romance **"The Complaint of Rosamund"** (1592).
- His historical poem **"The Civil Wars"** was published in **1595.**
- He also wrote **masques**, including **"The Queenes Wake"** (1610) and **"Hymen's Triumph"** (1615).
- His **sonnets** continue the tradition of **Sidney, Spenser, and Shakespeare.**
- His **longer poems** are considered **prosy and dull**, though the **masques** show **imaginative touches.**
- **A Defense of Rhyme:** Prose treatise defending the English verse's lack of adherence to classical standards, a response to **Thomas Campion's Observations in the Art of English Poesie (1602).**

## Question 22

**Match List I and List II List I**

| List I **Critics** | List II **Text** |
|---|---|
| A. Horace | I. A Defence of Rhyme |
| B. John Dryden | II. Timber: or, Discoveries |
| C. Samuel Daniel | III. Ars Poetica |
| D. Ben Jonson | IV. Of Dramatic Poesy |

**Choose the correct answer from the options given below:**

1. A – II, B – I, C – IV, D – III
2. A – III, B – IV, C – II, D – I
3. A – III, B – IV, C – I, D – II
4. A – II, B – IV, C – I, D – III

**Explanations:**
**Answer 3:** A – III, B – IV, C – I, D – II

**A. Horace's "Ars Poetica" is a treatise on the art of poetry.** It was written in ancient Rome around 18 BCE and provides guidelines for writing poetry, including the importance of unity, clarity, and avoiding clichés.

**B. John Dryden's "Of Dramatic Poesy" is a critical essay written in 1668.** It is a conversation between four characters discussing the relative merits of ancient versus modern drama. The essay also explores the idea of the "rules" of drama and whether they should be followed or broken.

**C. Samuel Daniel's "A Defence of Rhyme" is a 16th-century treatise defending the use of rhyme in poetry.** At the time, there was a debate about whether rhyme was an appropriate technique for serious poetry. Daniel argues that rhyme can be used effectively to enhance the beauty and musicality of poetry.

**D. Ben Jonson's "Timber: or, Discoveries" is a collection of notes and observations on literature and language.** It was written in the early 17th century and covers a wide range of topics, including poetry, drama, and the use of language. The work is notable for its insights into Jonson's own creative process and his thoughts on other writers of his time.

**Chronological order of the works with their respective dates:**

1. **Plato's Republic** – c. **375 BCE**
2. **Aristotle's Poetics** – c. **335 BCE**
3. **Horace's Ars Poetica** – c. **19 BCE**

4.  **Longinus's On the Sublime** – c. 1st century CE
5.  **Stephen Gosson's School of Abuses** – 1579
6.  **Philip Sidney's An Apology for Poetry** – 1595 (published posthumously)
7.  **Thomas Campion's Observations in the Art of English Poesie** – 1602
8.  **Samuel Daniel's A Defense of Rhyme** – 1603
9.  **John Dryden's "Of Dramatic Poesy"** – 1668

## John Donne (1573–1631)

- **He** was born in London in **1572** into a wealthy Catholic family.
- Donne's parents were **John Donne Sr.** and **Elizabeth Heywood**, daughter of playwright **John Heywood**.
- Donne was raised as a **Catholic** during a time of Protestant rule, which isolated him.
- He studied at **Hart Hall, Oxford** from **1584–1589**, but left without a degree due to his religion.
- In **1592**, he studied law at **Lincoln's Inn**, participating in the vibrant literary culture.
- Donne never practiced law, though his legal knowledge influenced his poetry.
- He worked as secretary to **Sir Thomas Egerton** by the end of **1597**.
- Donne secretly married **Ann More** in **1601**, causing a scandal that led to his imprisonment.
- The marriage cost Donne his position, and the couple faced financial struggles.
- Donne spent the next **14 years** writing and seeking office, without success.
- He wrote notable works like **Pseudo-Martyr** and **Biathanatos**, displaying his shift from Catholicism to Protestantism.
- Donne was ordained in the **Church of England** in **1615** and became **Royal Chaplain** to **James I**.
- His wife Ann died in **1617** after a stillbirth, deeply affecting Donne.
- Donne vowed never to remarry and gained fame as a powerful preacher.
- He was appointed **Dean of St. Paul's** in **1621**, a position he held until his death.
- **Donne's poetry** includes **Satires** (1593), **The Progress of the Soul** (1600), and **An Anatomy of the World** (1611).
- He wrote numerous **songs, sonnets, elegies**, and letters in verse.

- Donne's poetry is known for its **metaphysical style**, blending religious zeal with mystical, imaginative imagery.
- His prose works include **sermons**, theological treatises, such as **The Pseudo-Martyr** (1609).
- Donne's prose is marked by **vivid imagery, pessimism, and roughness**, mirroring his poetic style.
- Despite his **crabbed language and obscure expressions**, Donne's poetry shows flashes of **genius**.
- He was a key figure in **Elizabethan literature**, with a poetic voice that bridged the gap to the **Metaphysical poets**.
- Donne's poetry often blends **gloom and brilliance**, offering a unique mix of **melancholy and intensity**.
- His works, particularly his **sermons**, show his distinctive style with **soaring, exaggerated imagery** and **emotional frenzy**.
- **John Donne died** on **March 31, 1631**, after a final sermon, leaving behind a profound literary and theological legacy.

*Death, be not proud, though some have called thee*
*Mighty and dreadful, for thou art not so;*
*For those, whom thou think'st thou dost overthrow,*
*Die not, poor Death; nor yet canst thou kill me.*
*From rest and sleep, which but thy picture be,*
*Much pleasure; then from thee much more must flow:*
*And soonest our best men with thee do go,*
*Rest of their bones, and soul's delivery.*
*Thou'rt slave to fate, chance, kings, and desperate men,*
*And dost with poison, war, and sickness dwell,*
*And poppy or charms can make us sleep as well,*
*And better than thy stroke. Why swell'st thou then?*
*One short sleep past, we wake eternally;*
***And death shall be no more: Death, thou shalt die.***
**Holy Sonnetts X**


**List of Poems:**

- **"The Flea"**
- **"A Valediction: Forbidding Mourning"**
- **"Death Be Not Proud" (Holy Sonnet 10)**

- o This piece referenced Donne's portrayal of death in his "Holy Sonnet 10," famously beginning with "Death be not proud."
  - o During Bulstrode's illness and subsequent death, Donne, under the patronage of the Countess of Bedford, honored her memory with two elegies.
- ➤ **"The Sun Rising"**
- ➤ **"The Canonization"**
- ➤ **"The Good-Morrow"**
- ➤ "A Nocturnal upon St. Lucy's Day"
- ➤ "The Relic"
- ➤ **"The Anniversary"**
  - o **Written to commemorate the death of Elizabeth Drury, the 14-year-old daughter of his patron, Sir Robert Drury.**
- ➤ "The Ecstasy"
- ➤ "Love's Alchemy"
- ➤ "Batter My Heart" (Holy Sonnet 14)
- ➤ "The Apparition"
- ➤ **"A Hymn to God the Father"**
  - o The **poem "A Hymn to God the Father," also known under the title "To Christ."**
- ➤ "Air and Angels"
- ➤ "The Triple Fool"
- ➤ **"Elegy XIX: To His Mistress Going to Bed"**
- ➤ "Satire III"
- ➤ "A Lecture upon the Shadow"
- ➤ **"Valediction of Weeping"**
- ➤ **"Negative Love"** is a poem by John Donne in which the speaker expresses the idea that love cannot be controlled or constrained.
- ➤ **"Lovers Infitenesse"** is another poem by John Donne, which explores the idea of infinite love between two people.

## A Valediction Forbidding Mourning

- ➤ **It contains a conceit, a type of extended metaphor in which he compares the two lovers to the two legs of a compass.**
- ➤ **The poem is addressed to the speaker's wife, who he is about to leave for some time.**
- ➤ **'A Valediction Forbidding Mourning' by Adrienne Rich is a farewell of a poet focusing on her inability to express her thoughts in conventional terms.**

# Questions

**Question 23**
**What is the correct chronological sequence of British poets in order of their birth ?**

      A. Andrew Marvell
      B. John Milton
      C. John Donne
      D. Richard Lovelace
      E. Thomas Carew

**Choose the correct answer from the options given below :**

      (1) C, E, B, D, A
      (2) D, B, C, A, E
      (3) B, C, D, E, A
      (4) A, D, E, C, B

**Explanations:**
**Answer:** (1) C, E, B, D, A

**John Donne** (1572–1631) was one of the earliest poets in the Metaphysical tradition.
**Thomas Carew** (1595–1640) followed, known for his Cavalier poetry.
**John Milton** (1608–1674) was born next, famed for *Paradise Lost*.
**Richard Lovelace** (1617–1657) was a Cavalier poet.
**Andrew Marvell** (1621–1678) was known for his metaphysical and political poetry.

## Question 24
**Match List I with List II**

| List I (Poet) | List II (Poem) |
| --- | --- |
| A. John Donne | (i) "The Retreat" |
| B. Andrew Marvell | (ii) "A Valediction of Weeping" |
| C. George Herbert | (iii) "The Garden" |
| D. Henry Vaughan | (iv) "The Collar" |

**Choose the correct answer from the options given below:**

1. (a)-(iv), (b)-(iii), (c)-(ii), (d)-(i)
2. (a)-(ii), (b)-(iv), (c)- i), (d)-(iii)
3. (a)-(iv), (b)-(i), (c)-(ii),  d)-(iii)
4. (a)-(ii), (b)-(iii), (c)-(iv), (d)-(i)

**Explanations:**
**Answer: 4.** (a)-(ii), (b)-(iii), (c)-(iv), (d)-(i)

(a) - (ii) John Donne's poem "A Valediction of Weeping"
(b) - (iii) Andrew Marvell's poem "The Garden"
(c) - (iv) George Herbert's poem "The Collar"
(d) - (i) Henry Vaughan's poem "The Retreat"

**John Donne's poem "A Valediction of Weeping"** explores the theme of farewell and separation, expressing the speaker's emotions as they bid farewell to a loved one with tears.

**Andrew Marvell's poem "The Garden"** depicts a garden as a symbol of nature's beauty and purity, contrasting it with the corruption of the city and emphasizing the need for contemplation and connection with nature.

**George Herbert's poem "The Collar"** delves into themes of spiritual struggle and surrender, as the speaker wrestles with his desires and ultimately finds solace and freedom in submission to God.

**Henry Vaughan's poem "The Retreat"** reflects on the transitory nature of life and the search for inner peace, drawing on the imagery of nature and the contemplative retreat of the soul.

## Question 25

**Which two of the following writers do A. D. Hope address through his poetic responses in *A Book of Answers*?**
    A. Tolstoy
    B. Dostoevsky
    **C. Mallarme**
    D. Goethe

**Choose the correct answer from the options given below:**
1. A and D only
2. B and C only
3. B and D only
4. A and C only

**Correct Explanations:**
A. D. Hope's "A Book of Answers" is a collection of his poetic responses to other writers, including Shakespeare, Marvell, **Donne**, Milton, Tennyson, Heine, Yeats, **Mallarme**, and Auden. In these poems, Hope engages with the themes and ideas of these writers and provides his own commentary and insights through his unique poetic voice. By responding to the works of these esteemed writers, Hope contributes to the ongoing literary conversation and demonstrates how literature can inspire and influence future generations of writers.

## Question 26

**Which one of the following is a set of Metaphysical Poets?**

1. John Donne, Henry Vaughan, and Andrew Marvell.
2. John Dryden, George Herbert, and Alexander Pope.
3. Samuel Johnson, T. S. Eliot and Herbert Grierson.
4. Henry Vaughan, John Dryden, and John Donne.

**Explanations:**
**Ans**: John Donne, Henry Vaughan, and Andrew Marvell.

**Metaphysical poet**, is any of the poets in 17th-century England who were inclined to the personal and intellectual complexity and concentration that is displayed in the poetry of **John Donne, the chief of the Metaphysicals. Others include Henry Vaughan, Andrew Marvell, John Cleveland, and Abraham Cowley, as well as, to a lesser extent, George Herbert and Richard Crashaw**.

Their work is a blend of emotion and intellectual ingenuity, characterized by **conceit or "wit"**—that is, by the sometimes violent yoking together of apparently unconnected ideas and things so that the reader is startled out of his complacency and forced to think through the argument of the poem. Metaphysical poetry is less concerned with expressing feeling than with analyzing it, with the poet exploring the recesses of his consciousness. The boldness of the literary devices used—especially **obliquity, irony, and paradox** —are often reinforced by a dramatic directness of language and by rhythms derived from that of living speech.

Esteem for Metaphysical poetry never stood higher than in the 1930s and '40s, largely because of **T.S. Eliot's influential essay "The Metaphysical**

**Poets" (1921), a review of Herbert J.C. Grierson's anthology Metaphysical Lyrics & Poems of the Seventeenth Century.** In this essay, Eliot argued that the works of these men embody a fusion of thought and feeling that later poets were unable to achieve because of a **"dissociation of sensibility,"** which resulted in works that were either intellectual or emotional but not both at once. In their own time, however, the epithet **"metaphysical" was used pejoratively: in 1630 the Scottish poet William Drummond of Hawthornden** objected to those of his contemporaries who attempted to "abstract poetry to metaphysical ideas and scholastic quiddities." At the end of the century, **John Dryden censured Donne for affecting "the metaphysics" and for perplexing "the minds of the fair sex with nice speculations of philosophy when he should engage their hearts . . . with the softnesses of love." Samuel Johnson, in referring to the learning that their poetry displays, also dubbed them "the metaphysical poets," and the term has continued in use ever since.** Eliot's adoption of the label as a term of praise is arguably a better guide to his personal aspirations about his own poetry than to the Metaphysical poets themselves; his use of metaphysical underestimates these poets' debt to lyrical and socially engaged verse. Nonetheless, the term is useful for identifying the often intellectual character of their writing.

## Question 27

**Which of the following poems contains John Donne's famous conceit bringing a parallel between lovers and the hands of a compass?**

1. "Negative Love"
2. "Lovers Infinitenesse"
3. **"A Valediction: Forbidding Mourning"**
4. "A Valediction: Of Weeping"

**Correct Explanations:**
**John Donne's poem "A Valediction: Forbidding Mourning" contains a conceit, a type of extended metaphor in which he compares the two lovers to the two legs of a compass.** The conceit illustrates the idea that the two lovers are connected and yet separate, just like the two legs of the compass. The compass is an appropriate image because it is used for measuring and drawing circles, representing the completeness and perfection of love. Donne describes how the fixed leg of the compass (the lover who remains at home) supports and guides the moving leg (the lover who travels),

just as in a relationship, one partner must remain grounded while the other explores the world. The poem argues that true love is not diminished by distance or separation but rather strengthened by it. The two lovers are joined in a spiritual bond that transcends the physical realm, and the poet suggests that their separation will only make their reunion more joyous.

**Other Explanations:**
**"Negative Love" is a poem by John Donne in which the speaker expresses the idea that love cannot be controlled or constrained.** Instead, love is like a force of nature beyond human understanding or manipulation. The poem begins with the speaker describing how he tried to push away his love but found that it only grew stronger. Ultimately, he accepts that love is beyond his control and submits to its power.

**"Lovers Infinitenesse" is another poem by John Donne, which explores the idea of infinite love between two people.** The poem is structured around a paradox, in which the speaker argues that the more love is shared, the more there is to give. The poem also includes several striking images, including the idea of two lovers becoming like two spheres that are linked and rotate around each other.

**"A Valediction: Forbidding Mourning" is one of John Donne's most famous poems. The poem is addressed to the speaker's wife, who he is about to leave for some time.** In the poem, Donne uses a conceit to describe the nature of their love. He compares their love to the legs of a compass, with one leg fixed and the other leg moving around it. The fixed leg represents the wife who remains at home, while the moving leg represents the husband who travels. Despite the distance between them, their love remains constant and unchanging.

**"A Valediction: Of Weeping" is another poem by John Donne, in which he again uses a conceit to explore the nature of love.** In this poem, Donne compares tears to the "breath" of love. Just as a person's breath is essential to their life, tears are essential to expressing love. The poem is also notable for exploring the idea that separation can strengthen love and that distance can create a deeper bond between two people.

**Question 28**
**Match List I with List II**

| List I (Book) | List II (Poet) |
| --- | --- |
| A. Anniversaries | I. Abraham Cowley |
| B. The Temple | II. John Donne |
| C. The Rehearsal Transpros'd | III. George Herbert |
| D. Pindarique Odes | IV. Andrew Marvell |

**Choose the correct answer from the options given below:**
1.  A-I; B-IV; C-II; D-III
2.  **A-II; B-III; C-IV; D-I**
3.  A-III; B-I; C-IV; D-II
4.  A-IV; B-II; C-I; D-III

**Correct Explanations:**
**The correct match between List I (Book) and List II (Poet) is:**

*The Rehearsal Transpros'd* (1672–3), Marvell deploys Menippean satire to parry Samuel Parker's bullying intolerance and lobby Parliament to extend the royal indulgence for Dissenters.

Abraham Cowley, who published fifteen *Pindarique Odes* in 1656, was the poet most identified with the form though many others had composed irregular verses.

Donne's poems, the *Anniversaries*, were written to commemorate the death of Elizabeth Drury, the 14-year-old daughter of his patron, Sir Robert Drury.

The Temple is written by George Herbert.

## Question 29
**Arrange the following poets in accordance with their years of birth.**

A.  Rudyard Kipling
B.  Robert Browning
C.  John Masefield
D.  A.E. Housman
E.  John Donne

**Choose the correct answer from the options given below:**

1. E, A, B, D, C
2. E, B, A, C, D
3. E, B, A, D, C
4. A, D, B, C, E

**Explanations:**

**Ans:** E, B, A, D, C

**Here are the poets in order of their years of birth, along with their life spans:**

- John Donne (1572-1631)
- Robert Browning (1812-1889)
- Rudyard Kipling (1865-1936)
- A.E. Housman (1859-1936)
- John Masefield (1878-1967)

**John Donne was born in 1572 and lived until 1631.** He is considered a leading figure of the Metaphysical poets, known for their use of extended metaphors, paradoxes, and intellectual wit.

**Robert Browning was born in 1812 and lived until 1889.** He is known for his dramatic monologues, which give voice to a range of characters and perspectives.

**Rudyard Kipling was born in 1865 and lived until 1936.** He was a prolific writer of poetry and prose, and his work often celebrated British imperialism and the values of the British Empire.

**A.E. Housman was born in 1859 and lived until 1936.** He is known for his elegiac poems about unrequited love and the transience of life.

**John Masefield was born in 1878 and lived until 1967.** He was appointed Poet Laureate of the United Kingdom in 1930 and is known for his lyrical, narrative poetry.

## Question 30

"A Valediction Forbidding Mourning" is written by

A. John Donne
B. John Milton
C. Adrienne Rich
D. Sylvia Plath
E. Robert Frost

**Choose the correct answer from the options given below:**

1. **A and C only.**
2. A and B only.
3. D and E only.
4. B and C only.

**Explanations:**

**"A Valediction Forbidding Mourning" is a poem by John Donne, a 17th-century English poet, cleric, and lawyer.** It was first published in 1633 as part of a collection of Donne's poetry, entitled "Songs and Sonnets." The poem is known for its metaphysical conceit, or extended metaphor, which compares the love between the speaker and his wife to a compass, with the two legs representing the two lovers and the fixed center representing their unchanging love for each other. The poem is often interpreted as a farewell to Donne's wife before his departure on a long journey.

**'A Valediction Forbidding Mourning' by Adrienne Rich is a farewell of a poet focusing on her inability to express her thoughts in conventional terms.** In this poem, Rich talks about expressing herself through the frozen language of others.

## Question 31
**Arrange the following poets in accordance with their years of birth.**

A. George Herbert
B. Edmund Spenser
C. Philip Sidney
D. John Donne
E. Oliver Goldsmith

**Choose the correct answer from the options given below:**

1. ABDCE
2. **BCDAE**
3. EBADC
4. ADEBC

**Explanations:**
- ➢ Edmund Spenser (1552/1553 – 1599)
- ➢ Philip Sidney (1554 – 1586)
- ➢ George Herbert (1593 – 1633)
- ➢ John Donne (1572 – 1631)
- ➢ Oliver Goldsmith (c. 1730 – 1774)

## Question 32

**Name the poet who has composed the following poems:**

A. "A Hymn to God the Father"
B. "Elegy on Mistress Bulstrode"
C. "Hymn to God My God, in My Sickness"
D. "A Valediction of Weeping"

**Choose the correct option from the below:**

1. William Shakespeare
2. Christopher Marlowe
3. John Donne
4. Ben Jonson

**Explanations:**
**Answer: 3.** John Donne

**John Donne**, an esteemed English poet and clergyman, authored the **poem "A Hymn to God the Father," also known under the title "To Christ."** Classified among his Divine Poems, its composition date remains uncertain. The poem gained a musical adaptation by Pelham Humfrey in the 17th century and was posthumously featured in the 1688 publication of Harmonia Sacra, Book 1. Typically, a rendition of Humfrey's setting lasts around three minutes. Despite being incorporated into ten hymnals, often by its first line, "Wilt Thou Forgive That Sin, Where I Begun," credits to both Donne and Humfrey are occasionally omitted. The poem initiates with Donne inquiring of

God's willingness to pardon sins, including those rooted in original sin, committed even before his birth.

Cecily Bulstrode (1584–1609) served as a courtier and inspired poetry. Born to Edward Bulstrode and Cecily Croke, she was closely related to Lucy Russell, Countess of Bedford, and was part of her household in 1605. Following Bulstrode's demise, which John Donne witnessed during her illness at Twickenham Park, diagnosing her condition as hysteria, the Countess of Bedford composed "Elegy on Mistress Boulstred." **This piece referenced Donne's portrayal of death in his "Holy Sonnet 10," famously beginning with "Death be not proud." During Bulstrode's illness and subsequent death, Donne, under the patronage of the Countess of Bedford, honored her memory with two elegies**.

The exact timing of Donne's **"Hymn to God my God" is debated among scholars, with possibilities including his 1630 deathbed or during a severe fever in 1623**, each a period when Donne contemplated his mortality. This religious piece showcases a simpler form compared to his metaphysical secular poetry, structured into six stanzas of five lines each, adhering to an ABABB rhyme scheme and iambic pentameter.

**Donne's "Valediction of Weeping" stands out as one of his finest poems**, employing vivid imagery to explore the dynamics of a relationship facing separation. The speaker, addressing their lover, navigates through sorrow and mixed feelings about their impending parting, exemplifying Donne's mastery in crafting conceits.

**List of Poems:**

- "The Flea"
- "A Valediction: Forbidding Mourning"
- "Death Be Not Proud" (Holy Sonnet 10)
- "The Sun Rising"
- "The Canonization"
- "The Good-Morrow"
- "A Nocturnal upon St. Lucy's Day"
- "The Relic"
- "The Anniversary"
- "The Ecstasy"

- "Love's Alchemy"
- "Batter My Heart" (Holy Sonnet 14)
- "The Apparition"
- "A Hymn to God the Father"
- "Air and Angels"
- "The Triple Fool"
- "Elegy XIX: To His Mistress Going to Bed"
- "Satire III"
- "A Lecture upon the Shadow"
- "Valediction of Weeping"

**Dame Helen Gardner (1908-1986), served as a prominent English literary critic and academic.** She initiated her academic career at the University of Birmingham and, from 1966 to 1975, made history as the first woman to hold the position of Merton Professor of English Literature. Garner gained recognition for her scholarly contributions to the studies of poets John Donne and T.S. Eliot, alongside her works on John Milton and William Shakespeare.

**Bibliography**
- *The Art of T.S. Eliot (1949)*
- *The Divine Poems of John Donne (1952)*
- *The Metaphysical Poets (1957)*
- ***The Business of Criticism (1959)***
- *Edwin Muir: the W. D. Thomas Memorial Lecture (1961)*
- *The Elegies and the Songs and Sonnets of John Donne (1965)*
- *A Reading of Paradise Lost: the Alexander Lectures in the University of Toronto (1962)*
- *The Waste Land 1972: The Adamson lecture, 3rd May 1972*

<table>
<tr><td>

**Chronology to Remember**
**Code:**
- ➤ Oldest Spenser
- ➤ Older Sidney
- ➤ Twin Kyd and Lodge
- ➤ DanDruff
- ➤ Twin Marlow and Shakespeare
- ➤ Camp
- ➤ Another Twin Donne and Jonson
- ➤ Herbs Care
- ➤ Milton's Love
- ➤ Youngest Marvell

</td></tr>
</table>

> **Oldest Spenser** – Edmund Spenser (1552–99)
> Older-Philip Sidney (1554–86)
> **Kyd Twin** – , Thomas Kyd (1558–94)  and **Thomas Lodge (1558–1625)**
> **DanDruff** – Samuel Daniel (1562–1619), Michael Drayton (1563–1631)
> **Twin Marlow and Shakespeare** – Christopher Marlowe (1564–93), William Shakespeare (1564-1616)
> **Camp** – Thomas Campion (1567–1620)
> **Another Twin Donne and Jonson** – John Donne (1573–1631), Ben Jonson (1573–1637)
> **Herbs Care** – George Herbert (1593-1633), Thomas Carew (1595-1640)
> **Milton's Love** – John Milton (1608-1674), Richard Lovelace (1617-1657)
> **Youngest Marvell** – Andrew Marvell (1621-1678)

**Chronology Type Questions**

## Question 33

**Indicate the correct chronological order of birth for the following British poets:**

        (A) Edmund Spenser
        (B) William Shakespeare
        (C) John Milton
        (D) John Donne
        (E) Ben Jonson

**Choose the correct answer from the options given below:**

        (1) (A), (B), (C), (E), (D)
        (2) (A), (D), (E), (B), (C)
        (3) (C), (A), (B), (E), (D)
        (4) (A), (D), (E), (C), (B)

**Answer: (2) (A), (D), (E), (B), (C)**

**Explanation:**

    ➢   Edmund Spenser (1552–99)
    ➢   John Donne (1572–1631)

- ➢ Ben Jonson (1573–1637)
- ➢ William Shakespeare (1564–1616)
- ➢ John Milton (1608–1674)

---

## Question 34

**Indicate the correct chronological order of birth for the following British poets:**

    (A) Philip Sidney
    (B) Thomas Kyd
    (C) John Donne
    (D) Michael Drayton
    (E) Thomas Campion

**Choose the correct answer from the options given below:**

    (1) (A), (B), (D), (E), (C)
    (2) (A), (C), (B), (E), (D)
    (3) (A), (B), (C), (D), (E)
    (4) (A), (B), (D), (C), (E)

**Answer: (4) (A), (B), (D), (C), (E)**

**Explanation:**

- ➢ Philip Sidney (1554–1586)
- ➢ Thomas Kyd (1558–1594)
- ➢ Michael Drayton (1563–1631)
- ➢ John Donne (1572–1631)
- ➢ Thomas Campion (1567–1620)

---

## Question 35

**Indicate the correct chronological order of birth for the following British poets:**

(A) Richard Lovelace
(B) Andrew Marvell
(C) Thomas Carew
(D) George Herbert
(E) John Milton

**Choose the correct answer from the options given below:**

(1) (C), (D), (E), (A), (B)
(2) (A), (B), (C), (D), (E)
(3) (C), (E), (D), (A), (B)
(4) (C), (D), (A), (E), (B)

**Answer: (1) (C), (D), (E), (A), (B)**

**Explanation:**

- ➢ Thomas Carew (1595–1640)
- ➢ George Herbert (1593–1633)
- ➢ John Milton (1608–1674)
- ➢ Richard Lovelace (1617–1657)
- ➢ Andrew Marvell (1621–1678)

---

## Question 36

**Indicate the correct chronological order of birth for the following British poets:**

(A) Samuel Daniel
(B) Edmund Spenser
(C) Thomas Campion
(D) Ben Jonson
(E) Christopher Marlowe

**Choose the correct answer from the options given below:**

(1) (B), (A), (E), (C), (D)
(2) (A), (B), (D), (E), (C)

(3) (B), (A), (E), (D), (C)
(4) (B), (C), (A), (E), (D)

**Answer: (3) (B), (A), (E), (D), (C)**

**Explanation:**

- Edmund Spenser (1552–1599)
- Samuel Daniel (1562–1619)
- Christopher Marlowe (1564–1593)
- Ben Jonson (1573–1637)
- Thomas Campion (1567–1620)

---

## Question 37

**Indicate the correct chronological order of birth for the following British poets:**

(A) George Herbert
(B) Thomas Carew
(C) Richard Lovelace
(D) Andrew Marvell
(E) John Donne

**Choose the correct answer from the options given below:**

(1) (E), (A), (B), (C), (D)
(2) (B), (A), (D), (E), (C)
(3) (E), (B), (A), (C), (D)
(4) (A), (C), (B), (E), (D)

**Answer: (1) (E), (A), (B), (C), (D)**

**Explanation:**

- John Donne (1572–1631)
- George Herbert (1593–1633)
- Thomas Carew (1595–1640)
- Richard Lovelace (1617–1657)

> ➤ Andrew Marvell (1621–1678)

---

## DRAMA

## THE UNIVERSITY WITS

**Code to remember**: Lodge is peeling a Green marshmallow for breakfast (nashta) for his kids.
**Triplets:** Lodge, Peele and Kyd (1558)
**Twin**: Marlow and Shakespear (1564)
**Twin: Donne and Jonson** (1572)

- **Thomas Lodge (1558–1625)**
- **George Peele (1558–98)**
- **Robert Greene (1560–92)**
- **Christopher Marlowe (1564–93)**
- **Thomas Nash (1567–1601)**
- **John Lyly (1553/1554–1606)**
- **Thomas Kyd (1558–94)**

The University Wits is a phrase used to name a group of late 16th-century English playwrights and pamphleteers educated at the universities (Oxford or Cambridge) and became famous secular writers. Prominent members of this group were **Christopher Marlowe, Robert Greene, and Thomas Nashe from Cambridge,** and **John Lyly, Thomas Lodge, and George Peele from Oxford.** Thomas Kyd is also sometimes included in the group, though not from the universities mentioned above.

## Question 38

**Which of the following qualities of heroic treatment <u>was not needed</u> in the plays of the University Wits?**

1. Splendid descriptions
2. Long swelling speeches
3. The handling of violent incidents and emotions
4. Lives of common figures

**Explanations**
Answer: 4. Lives of common figures

The plays of the University Wits emphasized heroic themes, **focusing on the lives of significant figures, splendid descriptions, long speeches, and the intense portrayal of emotions and violent incidents**. These elements catered to the tastes of the Elizabethan audiences who favored grandiosity and drama over the mundane. **Consequently, the lives of common figures, which typically lack the grandeur and high stakes of heroic tales, were not a needed quality in the plays of the University Wits**. Their works aimed to awe and inspire through the depiction of larger-than-life characters and events, rather than reflecting the everyday lives of ordinary people. Thus, option 4, "Lives of common figures," is the correct answer as it was not a focus or requirement in the University Wits' approach to playwriting.

**The University Wits, a group of late 16th-century** dramatists and writers educated at Oxford or Cambridge, significantly influenced Elizabethan theatre with their innovative and secular writings. Members such as **Christopher Marlowe, Robert Greene, and Thomas Nash**e brought forth a new era of professional writing, setting the stage for **William Shakespeare**. Their entrance into the world of theatre stemmed from an overproduction of scholars by universities, with limited professional avenues available. These writers' preference for heroic narratives, characterized by vast themes, elaborate descriptions, extensive monologues, and intense portrayal of actions and feelings, defined their style. Although this approach often veered into excess, it found its best expression through blank verse's flexibility. Tragedy dominated their thematic choices, with comedy playing a minimal role, often marked by crude humor. **Lyly stands out as a notable exception for his comedic works**.

## Characteristics of the University Wits' Plays:
- ➤ **Heroic themes featuring significant historical figures.**
- ➤ Utilized grand and elaborate descriptions vividly.
- ➤ **Favored long, eloquent speeches in dialogue.**
- ➤ **Masterful handling of intense emotions and conflicts.**
- ➤ Predominantly employed blank verse for flexibility.
- ➤ Tragic narratives with earnest themes dominated.
- ➤ Minimal inclusion of comedy, often crude when present.
- ➤ Stylistic ambition led to bombast in weaker works.

> ➤ Marlowe exemplified the group's stylistic prowess impressively.
> ➤ Pioneered professional secular writing in Elizabethan England.

## Thomas Lodge (1558–1625)

> ➤ **English writer** and **medical practitioner**.
> ➤ **Abandoned legal studies** for a **literary career**, possibly **acting** too.
> ➤ Likely **collaborated with Shakespeare** in *Henry VI*.
> ➤ **Only surviving solo play** is *The Woundes of Civile War*.
> ➤ **Prolific pamphleteer** and **imitator** of **Lyly's euphuistic style**.
> ➤ Co-wrote **A Looking Glass for London and England** with Greene.
> ➤ The "Young Juvenal" theory from **Greene's Groatsworth** is now disputed.
> ➤ *Colin Clout's Come Home Again* may reference Lodge as **Alcon**.
> ➤ Published **Phillis** and *The Complaynte of Elsired* in **1593**.
> ➤ **A Fig for Momus** (1595) made him an **early English satirist**.

# Question 39

**Name the playwright who has written Gallathea? Name the playwright who has written Gallathea?**

1. Robert Greene
2. Thomas Lodge
3. Thomas Nashe
4. John Lyly

**Explanations:**
**Answer**: 4. John Lyly

**Gallathea, also known as Galatea, is a comedy written by John Lyly during the Elizabethan era.** The play was first performed on New Year's Day in 1588 at Greenwich Palace, before Queen Elizabeth I and her court, by the Children of St Paul's, a troupe of boy actors. By this time, Lyly had already achieved success with his prose romance Euphues and held a position as a writer in residence at Blackfriars theatre. The story unfolds in a village situated along the Lincolnshire shore of the river Humber and in the adjacent woods, featuring an array of characters such as Greek deities, nymphs, fairies, and shepherds.

## George Peele (1558–98)

> - Born in **London**, educated at **Christ's Hospital** and **Oxford**.
> - Became a **literary hack** and **free-lance** in **London**.
> - Known for his supposed but **disputed collaboration with Shakespeare** on *Titus Andronicus*.
> - Many **anonymous Elizabethan plays** have been attributed to him.
> - Associated with **Robert Greene** and the **university wits** in London.
> - Tried to make a living as a **professional author**.
> - **Experimented with poetry** in various forms and styles.
> - His earliest important work is *The Arraignment of Paris* (c. **1581–84**).
> - *The Arraignment of Paris* was performed before **Queen Elizabeth**.
> - Also wrote **commemorative poems** and **city pageants** for public events.

**Works**

> - *The Araygnement of Paris (1581)*, a kind of romantic comedy;
> - ***Edward I (1593)***
> - *The Famous Chronicle of King Edward the First (1593)*, a rambling chronicle-play;
> - *The Battle of Alcazar (1594)*
> - *The Old Wives' Tale (1595)*, a clever satire on the popular drama of the day;
> - *David and Bethsabe (1599)*
> - *The Love of King David and Fair Bethsabe* (published 1599).

## Question 40

**Which of the following are written by George Peele?**

A. *The Famous Chronicle of King Edward the First*
B. *A Moon for the Misbegotten*
C. *The Arraignment of Paris*
D. *The Scottish Historie of James the Fourth*
E. *The Old Wives' Tale*

**Choose the correct answer from the options given below:**

1. B, C and D only.
2. **A, C and E only.**
3. A, C and D only.

4.   C, D and E only.

**Explanations:**
George Peele was an English poet and playwright who lived in the 16th century. Some of his notable works include:

- ***The Arraignment of Paris (1581)***
- *David and Bethsabe (1599)*
- *The Battle of Alcazar (1594)*
- ***Edward I (1593)***
- ***The Old Wives' Tale (1595)***
- *Sir Clyomon and Sir Clamydes (1599)*
- *The Love of King David and Fair Bethsabe (published posthumously in 1599)*

**Note**: "The Scottish Historie of James the Fourth" is not a work by George Peele. It is a play by an anonymous author, first published in 1598.

**"A Moon for the Misbegotten" is a play by American playwright Eugene O'Neill.** The play was written in 1943 and is a sequel to O'Neill's play "Long Day's Journey into Night." It is a tragic story about the complex relationship between two siblings, James Tyrone Jr. and his older sister Josie, who live together on their family farm in Connecticut.

## Question 41

**Who among the following attached himself to the Earl of Nottingham's theatrical company?**

1.   William Shakespeare
2.   **Christopher Marlowe**
3.   Ben Johnson
4.   George Peele

**Correct Explanations:**

**Admiral's Men**
**The Admiral's Men (also called the Admiral's company, more strictly, the Earl of Nottingham's** Men; after 1603, Prince Henry's Men; after 1612, the Elector Palatine's Men or the Palsgrave's Men) was a playing company or

troupe of actors in the Elizabethan and Stuart eras. It is generally considered the second most important acting troupe of English Renaissance theatre (after the company of Shakespeare, the Lord Chamberlain's or King's Men)

If the Admiral's Men were having difficulties in the city in this period, they were still welcome at Court (28 December 1589; 30 March 1590), and still popular in the towns and shires, where they toured more in 1589–90. Indeed, this was perhaps the height of their achievement: in these years Alleyn was making a sensation acting the heroes of **Christopher Marlowe. Tamburlaine was printed in 1590 with their name on its title page. Some of the plays of Robert Greene, and Thomas Lodge's The Wounds of Civil War, were also in their repertory in the early 1590s.**

## Robert Greene (1560–92)

- ➢ Wrote prolifically and recklessly throughout his life.
- ➢ Born in **Norwich** and educated at **Cambridge (1575)** and **Oxford (1588)**.
- ➢ Lived a **debauched life in London**, by his own account.
- ➢ Died after an **orgy in a London ale-house**, from **surfeit of pickle herringe**.
- ➢ Wrote **thirty-five prose tracts**, showing his intense but erratic energy.
- ➢ His prose works are known for their **malicious wit** and **powerful imagination**.
- ➢ Greene's plays include **four major works** written between **1586 and 1592**.
- ➢ *Alphonsus, King of Arragon* (1587) was an imitation of **Marlowe's Tamburlaine**.
- ➢ *Friar Bacon and Friar Bungay* (1589) is considered his **best play**, representing Elizabethan life.
- ➢ *Orlando Furioso* (1586) was adapted from an **English translation of Ariosto**.
- ➢ *The Scottish Historie of James the Fourth* (1592) was based on an **imaginary incident** in the King's life.
- ➢ Greene was **weak in creating characters**, and his style was not remarkable.
- ➢ His **humor is genial**, contrasting with the severity of other tragedians.
- ➢ Greene wrote more than **35 works between 1580 and 1592**.

- ➤ He initially followed **literary fashions slavishly** to attract public attention.
- ➤ Greene's first model was **John Lyly's Euphues**, mimicking its style.
- ➤ He wrote **prose pastorals** in the style of **Sidney's Arcadia**, interspersed with lyrics.
- ➤ His pastoral **Pandosto (1588)** was the direct source of Shakespeare's **The Winter's Tale**.
- ➤ In his last year, he wrote exposés of the **Elizabethan underworld**, like *A Notable Discovery of Coosnage* (1591).
- ➤ He also wrote the **amusing disputation** between a **hee conny-catcher and a shee conny-catcher** (1592).

**Notable Works:**
**Code: Mnemonic: "Green elf Panda Frights A Scottish Knight Shakespeare"**

- ➤ *Alphonsus, King of Arragon* (1587)
- ➤ **Pandosto (1588)**
- ➤ *Friar Bacon and Friar Bungay* (1589)
- ➤ *A Notable Discovery of Coosnage* (1591)
- ➤ *The Scottish Historie of James the Fourth* (1592)

**Controversy with William Shakespeare**

In *Groats-worth* appears the first printed reference to Shakespeare, assailed as

*"an upstart Crow, beautified with our feathers, that with his Tygers heart wrapt in a Players hide, supposes he is as well able to bumbast out a blanke verse as the best of you . . . in his owne conceit the onely Shake-scene in a countrie."*

(The words in italics are from Shakespeare's I Henry VI.) Greene is thought to be criticizing Shakespeare, the actor.

## Question 42

**Which of the following are the plays written by Robert Greene?**

- A.  The Famous Chronicle of King Edward the First
- B.  Alphonsus
- C.  A Moon for the Misbegotten

D.  The Old Wives' Tale
E.  King of Aragon

**Choose the correct answer from the options given below:**

1.  B and D only.
2.  A and E only.
3.  **B and E only.**
4.  C and E only.

**Explanations:**
**Robert Greene (1558-1592)** was an English poet and playwright who lived during the Elizabethan era. He was a contemporary and colleague of William Shakespeare, and is best known for his plays and prose works. Some of his notable works include "Friar Bacon and Friar Bungay," "The History of Orlando Furioso," "A Quip for an Upstart Courtier," and "The Honorable History of Friar Bacon and Friar Bungay." Greene was also known for his pamphlets and works of prose fiction, such as "Pandosto: The Triumph of Time," which served as the basis for Shakespeare's play **"The Winter's Tale."** Some of the major works by Robert Greene are:

> Mamillia: A Mirror of Looking-Glass for the Ladies of England (1583)
> Pandosto: The Triumph of Time (1588)
> Friar Bacon and Friar Bungay (1589)
> The Scottish History of James IV (1590)
> **Alphonsus, King of Aragon (1591)**
> A Looking Glass for London and England (1594)
> The Battle of Alcazar (1594)
> The Famous Chronicle of King Edward the First (1595)
> The Honourable History of Friar Bacon and Friar Bungay (1595)
> Orlando Furioso (1599)
> A Quip for an Upstart Courtier (1592)
> The Defence of Conny-Catching (1592)
> A Groatsworth of Wit (1592)
> A Maiden's Dream (1591)
> Greene's Farewell to Folly (1591)
> The Comical History of Alphonsus, King of Aragon (1599)
> **The Old Wives' Tale (1595)**
> The Tragical Reign of Selimus (1594)

**Other Explanations:**
*The Famous Chronicle of King Edward the First, sirnamed Edward Longshankes, with his returne from the holy land. ALSO THE LIFE OF LLEVELLEN rebell In Wales. Lastly, the sinking of Queen Elinor, who sunck at Charingcrosse, and rose againe at Pottershith, now named Queenehith.* **is a play by George Peele**, published 1593, chronicling the career of Edward I of England.

**Eugene O'Neill's play, A Moon for the Misbegotten, is a sequel to his earlier work, Long Day's Journey into Night, featuring an older version of the Jamie Tyrone character, known as Jim Tyrone.** O'Neill began writing the play in late 1941, but set it aside after a few months. He returned to it a year later, completing the text in 1943, which became his final work due to his declining health that made it physically challenging for him to write. The play made its Broadway debut in 1957 and has had four revivals on Broadway, as well as a run in London's West End.

## Thomas Nash (1567–1601)

- ➤ He was born in **Lowestoft** and educated at **Cambridge**.
- ➤ Moved to **London in 1586** to pursue a literary career.
- ➤ Nash was a **born journalist**, mainly engaging in **pamphleteering**.
- ➤ Took part in **political and personal debates**, often using **truculent methods**.
- ➤ His actions landed him in **jail in 1600** due to his writings.
- ➤ Nash completed **Marlowe's Dido**, but only his play *Summer's Last Will and Testament* (1592) survives.
- ➤ *Jack Wilton, or The Unfortunate Traveller* **(1594)** is a significant prose work.
- ➤ This prose tale is important in the **development of the English novel**.

## John Lyly (1553/1554-1606)

- ➤ Lyly was educated at Magdalen College, Oxford, and went to London about 1576.
- ➤ Lyly's distinctive and much-imitated literary style, named after the title character of his two books, is known as euphuism.
- ➤ There he gained fame with the publication of two prose romances,

- o **Euphues: The Anatomy of Wit (1578) and Euphues and His England (1580)**
- o **Euphues: The Anatomy of Wit (1578)**

**The plays appear in the text in the following order; the parenthetical date indicates the year they appeared separately in quarto form:**
- ➢ Endymion (1591)
- ➢ Campaspe (1584)
- ➢ Sapho and Phao (1584)
- ➢ Gallathea (1592)
- ➢ Midas (1592)
- ➢ Mother Bombie (1594)
- ➢ The Woman in the Moon (1595-1597)

**Euphues**
- ➢ **Euphues: The Anatomy of Wit** was written by **John Lyly** and published in **1578**.
- ➢ **Euphues and his England** was registered in **1579** and published in **1580**.
- ➢ The name **Euphues** is derived from the Greek word meaning **"graceful, witty"**.
- ➢ Lyly adopted the name from **Roger Ascham's The Scholemaster**, describing an ideal student.
- ➢ Lyly's writing style is known for its **parallel arrangements and periphrases**, creating a mannered effect.

**Code**: Lill Anne Indian Saga of Moon

## Question 43

**Name the playwright who has written Gallathea? Name the playwright who has written Gallathea?**

1. Robert Greene
2. Thomas Lodge
3. Thomas Nashe
4. John Lyly

**Explanations:**
**Answer**: 4. John Lyly

**Gallathea, also known as Galatea, is a comedy written by John Lyly during the Elizabethan era.** The play was first performed on New Year's Day in 1588 at Greenwich Palace, before Queen Elizabeth I and her court, by the Children of St Paul's, a troupe of boy actors. By this time, Lyly had already achieved success with his prose romance Euphues and held a position as a writer in residence at Blackfriars theatre. The story unfolds in a village situated along the Lincolnshire shore of the river Humber and in the adjacent woods, featuring an array of characters such as Greek deities, nymphs, fairies, and shepherds.

## Christopher Marlowe (1564–93)

- He symbolizes both the best and worst of his era.
- Born the **eldest son of a shoemaker** in **Canterbury**, educated locally and at **Cambridge**.
- Adopted **literature as a profession** and became attached to the **Lord Admiral's players**.
- Known for his **great mental powers**, though often leading to **questionable actions**.
- Faced accusations of **atheism** and **immorality** during his lifetime.
- Marlowe's sudden death in a **tavern brawl** saved him from prosecution.
- Allegedly **stabbed to death by a rival** in a dispute over **romantic interests**.
- **Puritanical opponents** of the stage fueled many charges against Marlowe.
- Marlowe's work paved the way for the **tragedies of Shakespeare**.
- A gap remains between **Marlowe's tragedies** and **Shakespeare's depth of humanity**.
- In Robert Greene's deathbed tract, ***Greenes groats-worth of witte***, Marlowe is referred to as a ***"famous gracer of Tragedians"*** and is reproved for having said, like Greene himself, **"There is no god" and for having studied "pestilent Machiuilian pollicie."**
- **Kyd** alleged that specific papers "denying the deity of Jesus Christ" found in his room belonged to Marlowe, who had **shared the room two years before**.
- Marlowe's characters are often **bleak in nature** and **massive in outline**.
- His characters possess **enormous, majestic qualities**, but lack warmth or humanity.
- **Marlowe's style** is marked by **volcanic energy** and a soaring, mighty line.

- Ben Jonson referred to it as **"Marlowe's mighty line"** for its grandeur.
- Marlowe's style tends to be **diffuse, exaggerated**, and **bombastic** at times.
- The style lacks **humor, flexibility**, and **sweetness**, focusing on intensity.
- His characters are often **inhuman**, focused on grand, epic ambitions and desires.
- **Marlowe's tragedies** reveal a dark, intense side of the human spirit.
- **Tamburlaine the Great** (1587) is among Marlowe's earliest and most powerful plays.
- His other major works include **Doctor Faustus** (1588), **The Jew of Malta** (1590), and **Edward II** (1592).
- His tragedies often explore themes of **overreaching ambition** and **tragic downfall**.
- Marlowe is considered a **pivotal figure in Elizabethan drama**, despite his short life.
- He also **collaborated with Nash in the tragedy of Dido (1593)**.
- His **uncompleted a poor fragment of a play called The Massacre at Paris**.
- **Six dramas** have been attributed to the authorship of Christopher Marlowe either alone or in collaboration with other writers.
- **Tamburlaine was the first English play written in blank verse.**
- His **last play may have been The Jew of Malta**, in which he signally broke new ground.

## List of Works:

**Dido, Queen of Carthage** (c. 1585–1587; possibly co-written with Thomas Nashe; printed 1594) **(First Play with collaboration)**

- **The playwrights relied on Books 1, 2, and 4 of Virgil's Aeneid as primary sources.**
- **Plot**: It tells an intense dramatic tale of Dido and her passionate love for Aeneas (induced by Cupid), Aeneas' betrayal of her, and her eventual suicide on his departure for Italy.

**Tamburlaine; Part I** (c. 1587), Part II (c. 1587–1588; printed 1590) **(First play by his own, no collaboration)**

- **The best of that group of writers known as the University Wits**
- **Marlowe's "mighty line," as Ben Jonson called it.**
- **Tamburlaine: in Part 1, a Scythian shepherd;**

- ➤ **In Part 2, Tamburlaine becomes the King of Persia.**
- ➤ **Techelles: in Part 1, a follower of Tamburlaine;**
- ➤ **In Part 2, Techelles becomes the King of Fez**
- ➤ **Usumcasane: in Part 1, a follower of Tamburlaine:**
- ➤ **In Part 2, Usumcasane becomes the King of Morocco**
- ➤ **Theridamas: in Part 1, a Persian lord, later a follower of Tamburlaine;**
- ➤ **In Part 2, Theridamas becomes the King of Algiers**
- ➤ **Zenocrate: daughter of the Soldan of Egypt;**
- ➤ **In Part 2, Zenocrate becomes the wife of Tamburlaine**
- ➤ **Plot:**
  - ○ **Tamburlaine, a Scythian shepherd**, rises as a powerful warlord.
  - ○ Mycetes sends troops to **dispose of Tamburlaine** but fails.
  - ○ **Cosroe plots against Mycetes** but is betrayed by Tamburlaine.
  - ○ Tamburlaine wins the heart of **Zenocrate, Egyptian king's daughter**.
  - ○ **Bajazeth, the Turkish emperor**, is captured and humiliated.
  - ○ Tamburlaine makes **Bajazeth his footstool**, and he later dies.
  - ○ **Tamburlaine spares Zenocrate's father**, crowning her Empress of Persia.
  - ○ His son Calyphas **refuses to fight**, earning his father's wrath.
  - ○ **Holla ye pampered jades of Asia!**, Tamburlaine taunts defeated kings.
  - ○ **Tamburlaine dies after burning the Qur'an**, leaving legacy to sons.

## The Jew of Malta (c. 1589–1590; printed 1633) (Last printed work)

- ➤ In full *The Famous Tragedy of the Rich Jew of Malta*
- ➤ Five-act tragedy in blank verse
- ➤ Was produced about 1590 and published in 1633.
- ➤ Plot:
  - ○ The play opens with **Machiavel**, who introduces **"the tragedy of a Jew."**
  - ○ Barabas, a wealthy Jew, loses everything to the **Governor of Malta.**
  - ○ He tricks the **Governor's son** and his friend, causing their deaths.
  - ○ Barabas' daughter **Abigall**, horrified, becomes a **Christian nun.**
  - ○ In revenge, Barabas **poisons Abigall** and the whole nunnery.

- o Barabas strangles **Friar Barnadine** and frames another friar, **Jacomo**.
- o Ithamore, his slave, **betrays Barabas** to a prostitute and her friend.
- o Barabas poisons them all and **fakes his death** using a potion.
- o Barabas switches sides and plots to **kill the Turks** with gunpowder.
- o **Double-crossed by the Governor**, Barabas dies, cursing as he burns.

## Doctor Faustus (c. 1588–1592; printed 1604 & 1616)

➢ In full *The Tragicall History of D. Faustus*, tragedy in five acts published in 1604.

➢ **Characters:**
- o **Faustus**: Scholar who trades his soul for power.
- o **Mephastophilis**: Devil summoned by Faustus's magic.
- o **Chorus**: Narrates and comments on the story.
- o **Old Man**: Urges Faustus to repent and seek mercy.
- o **Good Angel**: Encourages Faustus to return to God.
- o **Evil Angel**: Dissuades Faustus from repentance.
- o **Lucifer**: Prince of devils, ruler of hell.
- o **Wagner**: Faustus' servant, learns magic from him.
- o **Clown**: Wagner's servant, provides comic relief.
- o **Robin**: Innkeeper, uses magic for trickery.
- o **Rafe**: Robin's friend, also uses basic conjuring.

➢ Plots:
- o **Chorus: Faustus**, though low-born, quickly earned a doctorate at the **University of Wittenberg**.
- o His pride and thirst for knowledge led him to **necromancy**.
- o **Faustus**, a German scholar, seeks power through magic.
- o **Good and Evil Angels** offer paths to salvation or damnation.
- o **Valdes and Cornelius** teach him black magic fundamentals.
- o **Faustus** summons **Mephistopheles**, makes a pact for power.
- o As soon as he does so, the words **"Homo fuge," Latin for "O man, fly,"** appear branded on his arm.
- o He bargains 24 years of power for his soul.
- o **Faustus** hesitates, but signs his soul in blood.
- o **Mephistopheles** distracts him with a dance of devils.
- o **Faustus** begins to regret and curses **Mephistopheles**.

- o Good and Evil Angels return, urging repentance and sin.
- o Mephastophilis and Lucifer bring in personifications of **the Seven Deadly Sins**.
- o **Faustus** flies to **Rome**, plays tricks invisibly at feast.
- o He disrupts the **pope's banquet by stealing food and boxing the pope's ears**.
- o He gains fame with his powers, deceiving others.
- o **Faustus** performs illusions to please **Charles V**'s court.
- o Who asks Faustus to allow him to **see Alexander the Great**.
- o A knight scoffs at Faustus's powers, and Faustus chastises him by making **antlers sprout from his head.** Furious, the knight vows revenge.
- o He swindles, humiliates others with his newfound powers.
- o Faustus sells **him a horse that turns** into a heap of straw when ridden into a river.
- o The horse-courser shows up there, along with Robin, a man named Dick
- o **Robin the Clown** and others seek justice at the court.
- o **Faustus** entertains the **Duke and Duchess** with illusions.
- o **Wagner** reveals **Faustus** is preparing for death soon.
- o **Faustus** summons **Helen of Troy** for love and comfort.
  - ▪ *"Was this the face that launched a thousand ships,*
  - ▪ *And burnt the topless towers of Ilium?"*
- o He reveals to friends that he's a damned soul.
- o **Mephistopheles** taunts him as **Faustus** pleads for mercy.
- o At midnight, devils drag **Faustus** to hell forever.

## Edward II (c. 1592; printed 1594)

- ➤ *The Troublesome Reign and Lamentable Death of Edward the Second, King of England, with the Tragical Fall of Proud Mortimer*
- ➤ The relationship between King Edward II of England and Piers Gaveston and Edward's murder on the orders of Roger Mortimer.
- ➤ Marlowe found most of his material for this play in the third volume of **Raphael Holinshed's Chronicles (1587).**
- ➤ **Plot:**
  - o **Gaveston returns from exile, causing lordly plots.**
  - o **Rebels capture Gaveston, Isabella betrays Edward.**
  - o **Gaveston is killed, Edward retaliates and wins.**
  - o **Isabella allies with France, Edward flees Ireland.**

- o   **Edward is killed, Mortimer executed, Edward III ascends.**

## The Massacre at Paris (c. 1593; printed c. 1594) (Incomplete)
- ➢ **Complete by Nathaniel Lee (1689).**
- ➢ **The latter is chiefly remembered for a song by Henry Purcell.**

## Poetry and Translations:
The poetry and translations credited to Marlowe primarily occurred posthumously, including:

- ➢ *Amores*, the first book of Latin elegiac couplets by Ovid with translation by Marlowe (c. 1580s); copies **publicly burned as offensive in 1599.**
- ➢ **The Passionate Shepherd to His Love, by Marlowe.** (c. 1587–1588);
  - o   famous lyric of the time known for its first line, "*Come live with me and be my love,*"
- ➢ **Hero and Leander, by Marlowe** (c. 1593, *unfinished; completed by George Chapman*, 1598; printed 1598).
  - o   After Marlowe's untimely death, it was completed by George Chapman.
  - o   **Hero**, a priestess, lives in **chastity** in **Sestos.**
  - o   **Leander**, from **Abydos**, falls in love with **Hero.**
  - o   He convinces her to abandon her vow of **chastity.**
  - o   **Leander** swims the **Hellespont** nightly to meet **Hero.**
  - o   **Neptune** mistakes **Leander** for **Ganymede**, returns him safely.
- ➢ Pharsalia, Book One, by Lucan, with translation by Marlowe. (c. 1593; printed 1600)

A brief extract to show the "mighty line." In the passage Tamburlaine, "the Scourge of God," mentally reviews his past conquests.

> *And I have marched along the river Nile*
> *To Machda where the mighty Christian priest,*
> *Called John the Great, sits in a milk-white robe,*
> *Whose triple mitre I did take by force,*
> *And made him swear obedience to my crown,*
> *From thence unto Cazates did I march,*
> *Where Amazonians met me in the field,*
> *With whom, being women, I vouchsafed a league,*
> *And with my power did march to Zanzibar,*
> *The eastern part of Afric, where I viewed*

*The Ethiopian sea, rivers and lakes,*
*But neither man nor child in all the land;*
*Therefore I took my course to Manico,*
*Where unresisted, I removed my camp,*
*And by the coast of Byather, at last*
*I came to Cubar, where the negroes dwell,*
*And conquering that, made haste to Nubia.*
*There having sacked Borno, the kingly seat,*
*I took the king, and led him bound in chains*
*Unto Damasco, where I stayed before.*

## Question 44

**To which mythological character is Faustus compared in the Prologue of Dr. Faustus?**

1. Perseus
2. Theseus
3. Icarus
4. Achilles

**Explanations:**
**Answer: 3.** Icarus

**In the Prologue of Christopher Marlowe's play "Doctor Faustus",** the eponymous protagonist is compared to Icarus, the character from Greek mythology who flew too close to the sun with wings made of feathers and wax, causing him to fall to his death.

Dr. Faustus by Christopher Marlowe is a tragedy that follows the story of a German scholar named Faustus who sells his soul to the devil in exchange for knowledge and power. Some important events and actions in the play include:

➢ Faustus is a successful scholar who becomes bored with his life and decides to turn to magic to gain power and knowledge.
➢ He summons the demon Mephistopheles and makes a deal with the devil to sell his soul in exchange for 24 years of unlimited power and knowledge.
➢ Faustus uses his powers to perform various tricks and amuse himself, but ultimately feels unfulfilled.
➢ He meets with the Pope and plays tricks on him, leading to a confrontation with the Holy Roman Emperor and his armies.

> Faustus realizes that his time is running out and tries to repent, but it is too late. The devil claims his soul and drags him to hell.

## Question 45

**The lives of which of the following writers have been the subject matter of novels by Anthony Burgess?**

- A. Milton
- B. Marlowe
- C. Shelley
- D. Keats

**Choose the correct answer from the options given below:**

1. A and B only
2. A and D only
3. B and C only
4. B and D only

**Explanations:**
**Answer: 4.** B and D only
Anthony Burgess, in addition to being a novelist and critic, was also a scholar of English literature. He was particularly interested in the lives and works of Romantic poets, **including Christopher Marlowe, Percy Bysshe Shelley, and John Keats**. Burgess wrote several novels that revolve around these poets, often exploring their lives, works, and the historical contexts in which they lived.

For example, his novel **"A Dead Man in Deptford" explores the life and death of Marlowe,** while "Byrne" is a fictionalized account of Shelley's life. Burgess's novel **"Nothing Like the Sun" is a fictionalized biography of William Shakespeare** that also features Marlowe as a character. Finally, **his novel "Abba Abba" is a fictionalized account of the final days of Keats's life.** In each of these novels, Burgess uses his extensive knowledge of literature and history to create rich and complex portraits of these writers and the worlds in which they lived.

## Question 46

**Which of the following characters instruct Faustus in the dark arts?**

1. Robin and Rafe
2. Wagner and Bruno
3. Cornelius and Valdes

4. Old Man and Evil Angel

**Explanations**:
**Answer: 3.** Cornelius and Valdes

In Christopher Marlowe's play "Doctor Faustus," the main character, Faustus, seeks knowledge and power beyond the realm of conventional learning. He desires to practice dark arts and make a pact with the devil. In his pursuit of forbidden knowledge, **Faustus is instructed in the dark arts by two characters: Cornelius and Valdes.**

Cornelius and Valdes are learned scholars who are well-versed in occult practices and the supernatural. They are knowledgeable in the mystical arts and serve as Faustus's guides into the world of forbidden knowledge. They introduce Faustus to the study of necromancy, divination, and other occult practices, enabling him to tap into supernatural powers.

**Extra Perk:**

**Robin and Rafe:** Comical servants and foils to Faustus, providing comic relief in the play.

**Wagner and Bruno:** Wagner is Faustus's servant and later becomes a scholar himself, while Bruno is a friend of Faustus who ultimately suffers due to Faustus's actions.

**Cornelius and Valdes:** Learned scholars who introduce Faustus to the dark arts and serve as his guides in his pursuit of forbidden knowledge.

**Old Man and Evil Angel:** The Old Man represents Faustus's conscience and tries to guide him towards repentance, while the Evil Angel tempts Faustus and encourages him to continue his pact with the devil.

## Question 47

**Who among the following attached himself to the Earl of Nottingham's theatrical company?**

1. William Shakespeare
2. **Christopher Marlowe**
3. Ben Johnson
4. George Peele

**Correct Explanations:**

**Admiral's Men**
**The Admiral's Men (also called the Admiral's company, more strictly, the**
**Earl of Nottingham's** Men; after 1603, Prince Henry's Men; after 1612, the
Elector Palatine's Men or the Palsgrave's Men) was a playing company or
troupe of actors in the Elizabethan and Stuart eras. It is generally considered
the second most important acting troupe of English Renaissance theatre (after
the company of Shakespeare, the Lord Chamberlain's or King's Men)

If the Admiral's Men were having difficulties in the city in this period, they
were still welcome at Court (28 December 1589; 30 March 1590), and still
popular in the towns and shires, where they toured more in 1589–90. Indeed,
this was perhaps the height of their achievement: in these years Alleyn was
making a sensation acting the heroes of **Christopher Marlowe. Tamburlaine**
**was printed in 1590 with their name on its title page. Some of the plays**
**of Robert Greene, and Thomas Lodge's The Wounds of Civil War, were**
**also in their repertory in the early 1590s.**

## Question 48

**Choose the correct chronological sequence in which the following texts**
**were written.**

- A.   Lycidas
- B.   Hero and Leander
- C.   Masque of Comus
- D.   Paradise Lost
- E.   The Waste Land

**Choose the correct option from the following**
1.   A, B, D, E, C
2.   B, C, A, D, E
3.   B, A, E, C, D
4.   B, E, D, C, A

**Explanations:**
**Ans:** B, C, A, D, E

**Hero and Leander: It is a narrative poem written by Christopher**
**Marlowe in 1593.** The poem tells the story of the love affair between Hero, a

priestess of Aphrodite, and Leander, a young man from Abydos. It is considered one of Marlowe's greatest works.

**Masque of Comus: It is a masque (a form of festive courtly entertainment) written by John Milton in 1634.** It tells the story of a virtuous lady who becomes lost in the woods and is tempted by the evil sorcerer Comus. The masque is notable for its use of music, dance, and elaborate stage effects.

**Lycidas: It is a pastoral elegy written by John Milton in 1637.** The poem mourns the death of Edward King, a fellow Cambridge student of Milton's, who drowned in the Irish Sea. It is considered one of Milton's greatest works.

**Paradise Lost: It is an epic poem written by John Milton in 1667.** The poem tells the story of Adam and Eve's fall from grace and their expulsion from the Garden of Eden. It is considered one of the greatest works of English literature.

**The Waste Land: It is a modernist poem written by T.S. Eliot in 1922.** The poem is a fragmented and highly allusive work that reflects the disillusionment and fragmentation of post-World War I Europe. It is considered one of the most important works of modernist literature.

### Thomas Kyd (1558–94)

- **Thomas Kyd** initiated the **revenge tragedy** genre with *The Spanish Tragedy*.
- The play is also known as **Hieronimo** or **Jeronimo**, after its protagonist.
- Kyd anticipated the **structure** of later plays, including **middle** and **final climaxes**.
- He displayed a natural sense of **tragic situations** in his works.
- **Hieronimo's** character in *The Spanish Tragedy* paved the way for Shakespeare's **Hamlet**.
- Kyd's work significantly influenced **Elizabethan drama** with its psychological depth.
- **His Works:** The dates of composition are approximate.
  - Don Horatio (partially extant in The First Part of Hieronimo, c. 1586)
  - **The Spanish Tragedy (c. 1587)**
  - The Householder's Philosophy (translation, 1588)

- o  Fair Em (attributed, c. 1590)
- o  Arden of Faversham (attributed, 1592)
- o  Solyman and Perseda (attributed, c. 1593)
- o  Cornelia (translation of Robert Garnier, 1594)
- o  **King Leir** (attributed, 1594)

## The Spanish Tragedy (1587)

- ➢ Started a new genre in English theatre, **the revenge play or revenge tragedy**.
- ➢ Many elements of The Spanish Tragedy, such **as the play-within-a-play** used to trap a murderer. **Same like in Shakespeare's Hamlet.**
  - o **Mouse Trap**
  - o **Ghost of King**
- ➢ The play within a play in The Spanish Tragedy is called Soliman and Perseda.
- ➢ The Spanish Tragedy begins with **the ghost of Don Andrea**, a Spanish nobleman killed in a recent battle with Portugal.

## Characters:

- ➢ **Hieronimo**: Loyal King's Marshal, becomes vengeful after his son's murder.
- ➢ **Bel-Imperia**: Headstrong, seeks revenge for her lovers Andrea and Horatio.
- ➢ **Lorenzo**: Manipulative murderer, contrasts with the honorable Horatio.
- ➢ **Balthazar**: Hot-headed prince, kills Horatio out of pride and jealousy.
- ➢ **Horatio**: Loyal son of Hieronimo, murdered by Lorenzo and Balthazar.
- ➢ **Ghost of Andrea**: Seeks revenge for his death, observes events as a ghost.
- ➢ **Isabella**: Hieronimo's tormented wife, eventually takes her own life.
- ➢ **The King**: Ambivalent King of Spain, supports Hieronimo yet remains complacent.
- ➢ **The Viceroy**: Weak Portuguese king, deceived and overcome with grief for Balthazar.
- ➢ **Pedringano**: Betrays Bel-Imperia, morally corrupt, eventually betrayed by Lorenzo.
- ➢ **Serberine**: Balthazar's servant, murdered on Lorenzo's orders due to suspicion.
- ➢ **Basulto**: Old man seeking justice, reminds Hieronimo of his duty.

- ➤ **The Ambassador**: Facilitates communication between the Spanish and Portuguese courts.
- ➤ **Alexandro**: Nobleman falsely accused of killing Balthazar, represents honor.
- ➤ **Villuppo**: Deceitful nobleman, betrays Alexandro for personal gain.

**Plots:**

- ➤ **The Viceroy of Portugal** rebelled against Spanish rule before the play.
- ➤ **Andrea's ghost and Revenge** serve as the chorus throughout.
- ➤ Andrea was killed by **Balthazar** before Balthazar was captured.
- ➤ **Andrea's ghost** seeks revenge for the injustices against him.
- ➤ The play opens with **Andrea's ghost** and **Revenge** onstage.
- ➤ The **King's nephew Lorenzo** and **Horatio** dispute over capturing Balthazar.
- ➤ **Horatio defeated Balthazar**, but Lorenzo takes partial credit.
- ➤ **Bel-imperia**, formerly in love with Andrea, falls for Horatio.
- ➤ **Bel-imperia** seeks revenge for **Andrea's death** by loving Horatio.
- ➤ **Balthazar** falls in love with **Bel-imperia** during the events.
- ➤ The **Spanish King** arranges a marriage between **Bel-imperia** and Balthazar.
- ➤ **Lorenzo** suspects Bel-imperia's new lover and bribes **Pedringano**.
- ➤ **Lorenzo and Balthazar** murder **Horatio** during a secret meeting.
- ➤ **Hieronimo and Isabella** find their son's body, leading to grief.
- ➤ **Isabella** goes mad after discovering her son's death.
- ➤ **Bel-imperia** sends a letter, written in blood, to **Hieronimo**.
- ➤ **Hieronimo** suspects Lorenzo and **Balthazar** as **Horatio's murderers**.
- ➤ **Lorenzo** arranges for **Pedringano** to murder **Serberine**.
- ➤ **Pedringano** is sentenced to death by **Hieronimo**, the judge.
- ➤ **Pedringano** expects a pardon from **Lorenzo**, which never comes.
- ➤ **Lorenzo convinces the King** that **Horatio** is still alive.
- ➤ **Hieronimo** is prevented from seeing the **King** to seek justice.
- ➤ **Isabella's suicide** pushes **Hieronimo** into madness and despair.
- ➤ **Hieronimo** digs at the ground, consumed by grief and rage.
- ➤ **Lorenzo** spreads rumors that **Hieronimo** is mad with jealousy.
- ➤ **Hieronimo** reconciles with **Lorenzo** and suggests performing a play.
- ➤ **Soliman and Perseda** is performed, with real daggers used.
- ➤ **Lorenzo and Balthazar** are killed during the play by **Hieronimo**.
- ➤ **Bel-imperia** stabs herself during the play to avenge **Horatio**.

> ➤ **Hieronimo** reveals the truth, kills the **Duke**, and takes his own life.

## Question 49

**Arrange the following plays in their chronological order:**

- A. The Country Wife
- B. Cymbeline
- C. The Spanish Tragedy
- D. The Rivals

**Choose the correct answer from the options given below:**

1. B, A, C, D
2. B, C, D, A
3. C, B, A, D
4. C, A, B, D

**Explanations:**
**Answer: 3**. C, B, A, D

**The Spanish Tragedy, or Hieronimo is Mad Again is an Elizabethan tragedy written by Thomas Kyd between 1582 and 1592.** It initiated the revenge tragedy of his day.

**Cymbeline, comedy in five acts by William Shakespeare, one of his later plays, written in 1608–10 and published in the First Folio of 1623** from a careful transcript of an authorial manuscript incorporating a theatrical playbook that had included many authorial stage directions. Set in the pre-Christian Roman world, Cymbeline draws its main theme, that of a wager by a husband on his wife's fidelity, from a story in Giovanni Boccaccio's Decameron.

**"The Country Wife" is a Restoration comedy written by William Wycherley in 1675. It follows the story of a man named Horner** who pretends to be impotent in order to gain access to the wives of wealthy men.

**"The Rivals" is a play written by Richard Brinsley Sheridan in 1775.** It is a classic comedy of manners that satirizes the pretensions and foibles of the upper class society of the time. The play follows the story of a young heiress named Lydia Languish who is courted by two men, Jack Absolute and Bob Acres. The play is known for its witty dialogue, memorable characters, and intricate plot. It has been widely performed and adapted over the years and remains a popular work of English drama.

## William Shakespeare (1564-1616)

### Life:

- **William Shakespeare** was born in **Stratford-upon-Avon** in **1564**.
- He was **baptized on April 26, 1564**, in Stratford.
- Shakespeare's **birthday is celebrated on April 23**, St. George's Day.
- He **died on April 23, 1616**, at 52 years old.
- **John Shakespeare**, his father, was a **glove-maker** and civic figure.
- Shakespeare's mother was **Mary Arden**, daughter of a wealthy family.
- William was the **eldest surviving child** out of **eight siblings**.
- Shakespeare likely attended the **local grammar school** in Stratford.
- **Ben Jonson** said Shakespeare knew "small Latin and less Greek."
- Shakespeare married **Anne Hathaway** at **age eighteen** in **1582**.
- Anne Hathaway was **eight years older** than Shakespeare.
- The couple had **three children**, Susanna, and twins Hamnet and Judith.
- **Hamnet**, Shakespeare's only son, **died at age eleven**.
- The period from **1585 to 1592** is called Shakespeare's **'Lost Years'**.
- **Robert Greene** called Shakespeare an "upstart crow" in **1592**.
- His first printed works were **'Venus and Adonis'** (1593) and **'The Rape of Lucrece'** (1594).
- He became a founding member of **The Lord Chamberlain's Men**.
- The company later became **The King's Men** under **King James I**.
- Shakespeare produced **two plays a year** for nearly **twenty years**.
- He wrote famous tragedies like **King Lear** and **Macbeth**.
- His great romances include **The Winter's Tale** and **The Tempest**.
- Shakespeare retired to **Stratford** in **1610**, staying at **New Place**.
- His connection with the **Globe Theatre** ended after it burned in **1613**.
- Shakespeare's will was signed on **March 25, 1616**, shortly before his death.
- He is buried in the **Holy Trinity Church** in **Stratford-upon-Avon**.

### Poetry:

- **Shakespeare's two long narrative poems** were among his **earliest writings**.
- **Venus and Adonis** (1593)
  - Showed **signs of immaturity** but great beauty.
  - **Heavily ornamented and conventional**.
  - It tells of **Venus' unrequited love** for **Adonis**.

- o The poem is **pastoral**, at times **erotic**, **comic**, and **tragic**.
- o **Written in stanzas of six lines** with **ABABCC rhyme scheme**.
- o Poem consists of **199 stanzas or 1,194 lines** in total.
- o Published as a **quarto pamphlet** by **Richard Field** from Stratford.
- o Poem begins with a dedication to **Henry Wriothesley**: "the first heir of my invention."
- o **Based on Ovid's Metamorphoses**, though Shakespeare's Venus differs from **Ovid's version**.
- o **Venus offers her body** to Adonis in **graphically explicit terms**.
- o Published five years before Marlowe's **Hero and Leander**, another **Ovid-inspired poem**.
- o **Reprinted fifteen times** before 1640, despite few original quartos surviving.

➤ **The Rape of Lucrece** (1594)
- o Written in **rhyme royal stanzas**.
- o The action in **Lucrece** was retarded with **long speeches**.
- o It is a narrative poem.
- o Dedicated to **Earl of Southampton**, it is a "graver labour."
- o Poem opens with a prose dedication: "The love I dedicate...is without end."
- o **"The Argument"** summarizes the historical context, starting *in medias res*.
- o Contains **1,855 lines** in **265 stanzas**, all in **iambic pentameter**.
- o Follows **ABABBCC rhyme scheme**, known as **"rhyme royal."**
- o Poets like **Chaucer, Milton, and Masefield** used "rhyme royal."

➤ **The Passionate Pilgrim (1599)**
- o It was published under **Shakespeare's name**.
- o It was **published by William Jaggard** and attributed to "W. Shakespeare."
- o The anthology includes **20 poems**, only **five authentically Shakespearean**.
- o **Two sonnets** later appeared in *Shakespeare's Sonnets* (1609) collection.
- o **Three poems** were extracted from Shakespeare's play *Love's Labour's Lost*.
- o **Stylometric analysis** by Elliott and Valenza linked **some poems to Shakespeare's style**.

- o  Jaggard's **augmented edition** included poems by **Thomas Heywood**, known to him.
- o  **"The Passionate Shepherd to His Love" (1599), by Christopher Marlowe,** is a pastoral poem from the English Renaissance (1485–1603).
- ➤ **Shakespeare's works include 38 plays, 2 narrative poems**, and **154 sonnets**.
- ➤ No **original manuscripts** of Shakespeare's plays **exist today**.
- ➤ **36 plays** were collected and published in **The First Folio in 1623**.
- ➤ The **First Folio** did not include **Shakespeare's poetry**.
- ➤ **Shakespeare's later poetical work** includes numerous **lyrics scattered through his plays**.
- ➤ Some of the songs may have been **based on popular tunes**.
- ➤ The lyrics show a **great range of accomplishment** in **Shakespeare's plays**.
- ➤ Examples include **Ariel's "Full fathom five"** from **The Tempest**.
- ➤ The **willow-song in Othello** is another example of **Shakespeare's lyrical talent**.
- ➤ **"Take, O take those lips away"** appears in **Measure for Measure**.
- ➤ The noble dirge **"Fear no more the heat o' the sun"** is in **Cymbeline**.
- ➤ Shakespeare would have been a **great lyrical poet** if not **our greatest dramatist**.

## Shakespeare's sonnets

- ➤ Thye were printed by **Thomas Thorpe in 1609**.
- ➤ The dedication mentions **"Mr. W. H.,"** sparking speculation about his identity.
- ➤ The sonnets consist of **154 numbers** in the **English sonnet form**.
- ➤ The sonnets are divided into **two groups of unequal size**.
- ➤ The first group may reference **Shakespeare's friendship** with a high-ranking youth.
- ➤ The second group focuses on **reproaches to the "Dark Lady."**
- ➤ The **Dark Lady's identity** is one of **literature's great mysteries**.
- ➤ She may have been **Mary Fitton**, though this is debated.
- ➤ Shakespeare likely followed the **common practice of sonneteers**.
- ➤ The rhyme scheme is ABAB CDCD EFEF GG. Using this scheme, Sonnets are known as Shakespearean sonnets
- ➤ At the end of the third quatrain occurs the volta ("turn"), where the mood of the poem shifts, and the poet expresses a turn of thought.

- ➤ The sonnets are praised for their **splendor of style** and **sensuous phraseology**.
- ➤ Certain sonnets like 30, 33, 55, 71, 116 are praised as **"thick clusters of starlight."**
- ➤ ***The Dark Lady of the Sonnets* (1910) is a short comedy by George Bernard Shaw** where Shakespeare, seeking the "Dark Lady," accidentally meets Queen Elizabeth I and tries to convince her to establish a national theatre.
- ➤ Here are some of the famous sonnets from Shakespeare's list:
- ➤ **Sonnet 18**: *Shall I Compare Thee To A Summer's Day?*
- ➤ **Sonnet 29**: *When In Disgrace With Fortune and Men's Eyes*
- ➤ **Sonnet 30**: *When To The Sessions Of Sweet Silent Thought*
- ➤ **Sonnet 33**: *Full many a glorious morning have I seen*
- ➤ **Sonnet 55**: *O! Not Marble, Nor The Gilded Monuments*
- ➤ **Sonnet 60**: *Like As The Waves Make Towards The Pebbled Shore*
- ➤ **Sonnet 73**: *That Time Of Year Thou Mayst In Me Behold*
- ➤ **Sonnet 104:** *To me, fair friend, you never can be old*
- ➤ **Sonnet 116**: *Let Me Not To The Marriage Of True Minds*
- ➤ **Sonnet 129**: *The expense of spirit in a waste of shame*
- ➤ **Sonnet 130**: *My Mistress' Eyes Are Nothing Like The Sun*
- ➤ **Sonnet 138**: *When My Love Swears That She Is Made Of Truth*

**1-5: Read the following stanza and answer the questions that follow :**

*"Shall I compare thee to a Summer's day*
*Thou art more lovely and more temperate:*
*Rough winds do shake the darling buds of May*
*And summer's lease hath all too short a date.*
*Sometimes too hot the eye of heaven shines,*
*And often is his gold complexion dimm'd."*

## Question 50

**" The poem is an example of:**

1. Parampariterupaka (consequential metaphor) because here the superimposition, undermined by a resemblance, is the cause of another superimposition.

2. Nirangarupaka (entire metaphor) because here upameya is superimposed by upamana together with its subordinate parts.

3. Malarupaka (deficient metaphorserial) because here upameya is superimposed by serial of upamanas.

4. Mishritarupaka (mixed metaphor) because here the common attribute, the words implying comparison, upamana and upameya, all are expressed.

**Explanations:**
**Answer: 1. Paramapariterupaka (consequential metaphor) because here the superimposition, undermined by a resemblance, is the cause of another superimposition.**

The poem "Shall I compare thee to a summer's day?" by William Shakespeare is an example of Paramapariterupaka (consequential metaphor) because it utilizes a chain of superimpositions based on resemblance. The initial comparison of the beloved to a summer's day leads to further comparisons—more lovely and more temperate, not subject to the rough winds or the brevity that characterizes summer—highlighting the superior and enduring nature of the beloved's beauty. The resemblance between the beloved and a summer's day triggers a series of additional comparisons, each building upon the last.

**The correct answer is identified by analyzing the structure and content of the poem. The poet begins with a comparison and then elaborates on it by contrasting the beloved's enduring beauty with the transient nature of summer.** This elaboration or superimposition of one comparison upon another, where the initial resemblance leads to further detailed comparisons, aligns with the definition of Paramapariterupaka.

**Why Other Options are Incorrect:**

**Nirangarupaka (entire metaphor)** is incorrect because the poem does not superimpose the qualities of summer (upamana) onto the beloved (upameya) along with all its subordinate parts. Instead, it selectively uses aspects of summer to make a point about the beloved's qualities.

**Malarupaka (deficient metaphor)** is incorrect because the poem does not employ a series of inadequate or partial comparisons. The metaphor of comparing the beloved to a summer's day fully serves its purpose by highlighting the beloved's loveliness and temperance.

**Mishritarupaka (mixed metaphor)** is incorrect because the poem maintains a consistent comparison without mixing different attributes, words of comparison, or subjects and objects of comparison in a way that would confuse the imagery or the qualities being compared.

**Lines from the Text that Reflect the Answer:**

*"Shall I compare thee to a Summer's day"* introduces the initial comparison. *"Thou art more lovely and more temperate"* and *"Rough winds do shake the darling buds of May / And summer's lease hath all too short a date"* **further elaborate on the comparison by contrasting the beloved's qualities with those of summer**, illustrating the superimposition of one metaphor upon another based on resemblance. This process characterizes Parampariterupaka, where the initial resemblance triggers a consequential superimposition of qualities.

## Question 51

**What is the addressee in the poem?**

1. Feminine gender
2. Masculine gender
3. Common gender
4. Neutral Gender

**Explanations:**
Answer: 2. Masculine gender

The correct answer is masculine gender. In many of Shakespeare's sonnets, the addressee, **known as the Fair Youth, is believed to be a young man to whom Shakespeare addresses his deep affections and admiration.** This interpretation is supported by the context of Shakespeare's sonnets and the pronouns used in other sonnets directed towards the Fair Youth.

The answer is derived from an understanding of the broader collection of Shakespeare's sonnets, **many of which are addressed to a young man known as the Fair Youth.** This context, combined with literary analysis and historical understanding of Shakespeare's works, points towards the masculine gender of the addressee.

**Why Other Options are Incorrect:**

**Feminine gender** is incorrect because, within the context of Shakespeare's sonnets, particularly those directed to the Fair Youth, the subject is traditionally understood to be male.

**Common gender is incorrect** because the specific sonnets addressed to the Fair Youth use language and pronouns that traditionally correspond to the masculine gender, suggesting a specific gender rather than a non-specific or universal one.

**Neutral Gender is incorrect** as the poem employs personal admiration and affection that signifies a specific person rather than an object or concept, and the broader context of Shakespeare's sonnets indicates the Fair Youth is of masculine gender.

**Lines from the Text that Reflect the Answer:**

While the provided stanza itself does not directly reveal the gender of the addressee through specific pronouns or gendered language, the understanding that the addressee is of masculine gender comes from the broader context of Shakespeare's sonnets. Therefore, the poem's direct lines do not explicitly indicate the gender; however, historical and literary context regarding Shakespeare's sonnets supports the interpretation of the addressee being masculine.

## Question 52

**What is upmeya (object compared) in the poem?**

1. Addressee
2. Rough winds
3. Buds of May (4)
4. Summer's day

**Explanations:**
Answer: 1. Addressee

**The correct answer is the addressee of the poem. In classical and modern literary analysis, the term "upameya" refers to the object being compared to something else in a metaphorical or simile structure. In this poem, Shakespeare is comparing the person to whom the poem is addressed (the beloved or the addressee) to a summer's day, making the addressee the upameya.**

The answer is found by identifying the structure of comparison used in the poem. Shakespeare opens the sonnet with a question about comparing the **addressee to a summer's day, directly establishing the addressee as the subject of comparison.** By analyzing the role of each element in the stanza, it becomes clear that the entire comparison is structured around highlighting the qualities of the addressee in relation to the characteristics of a summer's day.

**Why Other Options are Incorrect:**

**Rough winds are not the object being compared; they are part of the descriptive imagery used to contrast the qualities of the addressee with the imperfections of a summer's day.**

**Buds of May are also part of the imagery used to illustrate the vulnerabilities of summer, not the object of comparison.**

**Summer's day is the upamana (the comparator), not the upameya.** It is what the addressee is being compared to, not the object of comparison itself.

**Lines from the Text that Reflect the Answer:**

**"Shall I compare thee to a Summer's day"** – This line directly establishes the addressee as the object of comparison (upameya), indicating that the entire poem is about comparing the person addressed to the qualities of a summer's day.

**"Thou art more lovely and more temperate:"** – This line further supports the addressee as the upameya by directly comparing their qualities to those of a summer's day, highlighting their superior loveliness and temperance.

## What is upmana (object compared to) in the poem?

1. Addressee
2. Rough winds
3. Buds of May
4. Summer's day

**Explanations:**
Answer: 4. Summer's day

**The correct answer is "4. Summer's day." In the context of the poem, the upamana (object compared to) is "Summer's day." This means that in the comparison being made, "Summer's day" serves as the standard or the entity to which the subject (upameya), presumably the poet's beloved, is being compared. The poet uses "Summer's day" as a metaphorical benchmark to highlight the qualities of the beloved.**

The answer was found by analyzing the opening line of the poem, "Shall I compare thee to a Summer's day?" This question clearly establishes "Summer's day" as the basis of comparison—the entity to which the beloved's qualities are being compared. The subsequent lines further describe characteristics of a summer's day, thereby reinforcing its role as the upamana in this metaphorical comparison.

**Why Other Options are Incorrect:**

**1. Addressee:** Incorrect because the addressee (the beloved) is the subject being compared, not the object of comparison.

**2. Rough winds:** Incorrect because rough winds are mentioned as part of the description of summer's attributes, not as a standard of comparison for the beloved.

**3. Buds of May:** Incorrect because the "buds of May" are used to illustrate the transient and sometimes harsh nature of summer, rather than serving as the benchmark for comparison.

**Lines from the Text that Reflect the Answer:**

The very first line of the poem, "Shall I compare thee to a Summer's day," explicitly mentions "Summer's day" as the entity to which the poet is comparing the beloved. This directly indicates that "Summer's day" is the upamana (object compared to) in this poetic comparison.

## Question 54

**Which of the following statements rightly shows the relationship of upameya with upamana in the poem:**

1. Upameya is superior to upamana
2. Upamana is superior to upameya
3. Both upamana and upameya are equal
4. Both are governed by position and superimposition

**Explanations:**
Answer: 1. Upameya is superior to upamana

**In the poem, the beloved (upameya) is compared to a summer's day (upamana).** However, the comparison ultimately concludes that the **beloved surpasses the summer's day in terms of loveliness and temperance**. The poem highlights the imperfections of summer—its rough winds, variable temperature, and fleeting nature—to argue that the beloved's beauty is more enduring and stable. Therefore, upameya (the beloved) is shown to be superior to upamana (a summer's day).

The correct answer was identified through a close reading of the poem, paying particular attention to the descriptions of the summer's day and how they are used to contrast with the qualities of the beloved. The poem explicitly states the beloved is "more lovely and more temperate," pointing to the superiority of the beloved over the summer's day.

**Why Other Options are Incorrect:**

**Upamana is superior to upameya:** Incorrect because the poem specifically points out the flaws in the summer's day and contrasts these with the superior qualities of the beloved.

**Both upamana and upameya are equal:** Incorrect because the poem does not establish an equality between the summer's day and the beloved; rather, it emphasizes the superiority of the beloved.

**Both are governed by position and superimposition:** Incorrect because the poem's focus is not on their relational positions but on comparing two entities to demonstrate the superiority of one (the beloved) over the other (a summer's day).

**Lines from the Text that Reflect the Answer:**

*"Thou art more lovely and more temperate":* Directly states the superiority of the beloved over the summer's day.

*"Rough winds do shake the darling buds of May / And summer's lease hath all too short a date":* Highlights the imperfections and transience of summer, reinforcing the superiority of the beloved's enduring beauty.

*"Sometimes too hot the eye of heaven shines, / And often is his gold complexion dimm'd":* Illustrates the variability and imperfection of summer, further establishing the beloved's superior qualities.

## Shakespearean Actors

The actors in Shakespeare's company included **Richard Burbage, Will Kempe, Henry Condell, and John Heminges.**

## Richard Burbage (1567–1619)

- Richard Burbage was one of the most famous actors of **The Globe Theatre.**
- He played **Hamlet, Othello, Richard III,** and **King Lear** in **Shakespeare's plays.**
- Burbage was a theatre owner and lifelong **friend of William Shakespeare.**

## Richard Cowley (Died 1619)

- Richard Cowley was a **shareholder** in the Lord Chamberlain's Men.

> He played **Verges** in **Much Ado About Nothing**, alongside **William Kempe**.
> Cowley toured with Edward Alleyn and was active **until 1619**.

## William Kempe (1560–1603)

> William Kempe was renowned as a clown and dancer of **jigs**.
> He originated the role of **Dogberry** in **Much Ado About Nothing**.
> Kempe is believed to have played **Falstaff**, **Bottom**, and **Lancelot Gobbo**.

## Robert Armin (1568–1615)

> Robert Armin replaced **William Kempe** as the lead comedy actor in **Chamberlain's Men**.
> Armin played witty fools like **Feste** in **Twelfth Night** and the **Fool** in **King Lear**.
> He also performed as **Abel Drugger** in **Ben Jonson's The Alchemist**.

## Nathan Field (1587–1619?)

> Nathan Field acted with **Children of the Queen's Revels** and later **King's Men**.
> Field played key roles and replaced **Shakespeare** in **King's Men** after 1616.
> He wrote **A Woman is a Weathercock** and **Amends for Ladies**.

### His Plays:

> **Shakespeare's works include 38 plays, 2 narrative poems**, and **154 sonnets**.
> No **original manuscripts** of Shakespeare's plays **exist today**.
> **36 plays** were collected and published in **The First Folio in 1623**.
> **None of Shakespeare's plays were printed by him**; all manuscripts perished.
> "First Folio edition" of 1623 included **thirty-six dramas**.
> **Eighteen plays appeared in quarto form**, unauthorized during his lifetime.
> **The First Folio** does not arrange the plays **chronologically**.
> Dates registered at **Stationers' Hall** are for printing, not composition.

- Assigning play order requires **"ingenious deductive work"** due to scant evidence.
- **Francis Meres** provides a list of Shakespeare's plays in **Palladis Tamia** (1598).
- Meres mentions **twelve of Shakespeare's plays**, written before 1598.
- He also notes **"his Venus and Adonis, his Lucrece, and sugred sonnets"**.
- **Classification of the Plays.** It is customary to group the plays into sets that to some extent traverse the order given above.

## History Plays:
- **Total Henry Plays are 8:** *3 Henry VI, 3 Henry IV, 1 Henry V, 1 Henry VII.*
- **Total Richard Plays are 2:** *Richard III, and Richar II*.
- **Total Edward Plays are 1:** *Edward III.*
- **Total King John plays are 1:** *King John*
- **Total Roman Plays are 4 and all are tragedies:** *Antony and Cleopatra, Coriolanus, Julius Caesar, Titus Andronicus.*

**Total Comedy Plays are 12:** *The Comedy of Errors, The Taming of the Shrew, The Two Gentlemen of Verona, Love's Labour's Lost, A Midsummer Night's Dream, The Merchant of Venice, Much Ado About Nothing, As You Like It, Twelfth Night, The Merry Wives of Windsor, All's Well That Ends Well, Measure for Measure*

**Todal Tragey Plays are 10 and four of them are Romans:** *Romeo and Juliet, Hamlet, Othello, King Lear, Macbeth.*

**Total Tragic Comedies are 5:** *Cymbeline, The Winter's Tale, The Tempest, Pericles, Prince of Tyre (in part), The Two Noble Kinsmen (in part)*

**Total Problem Plays are 3:** *Measure for Measure, All's Well That Ends Well, Troilus and Cressida.*

**Total Unfinished work 1:** Timon of Athens (unfinished)

Remember this Shakespeare born in 1564 and Started his writing career in 1590 when he was only 26. He started his career in 1590 with Henry VI and ended his career in 1613 with Henry VIII. First two years from 1590 to 1591 he wrote only Henry VI part 1,2,3 and Richard III and Edwar III in 1993. In the same year his first immature comedy appeared *The Comedy of Errors (1593)*. **Next year in 1594 he wrote 4 plays** *(Code: Tit for tat) Titus Andronicus (1594), The Taming of the Shrew (1594),* **Then  (Code: Love story** *of Romeo* **and Juliete** *Love's Labour's Lost (1594), Romeo and Juliet (1594).*

In 1595, he wrote two play **(Code: A Midsummer in Verona)** *A Midsummer Night's Dream (1595), The Two Gentlemen of Verona (1595), King John (1595).*

In 1596 he wrote **(Code: Richard the merchant)** Richard II *(1596)*, The Merchant of Venice, *(1596)*

In next two years he wrote Henry IV (1597), 2 Henry IV (1598) and Much Ado about Nothing (1598), Henry V (1599) Julius Cæsar, (1599)

- ➢ **1600: The Merry Wives of Windsor, As You Like It**
- ➢ **1601: Hamlet, Twelfth Night**
- ➢ 1602: Troilus and Cressida, All's Well that Ends Well
- ➢ **1603: (Theaters closed)**
- ➢ 1604: Measure for Measure, Othello
- ➢ **1605: Macbeth, King Lear**
- ➢ **1606:** Antony and Cleopatra, Coriolanus
- ➢ 1607: Timon of Athens (unfinished)
- ➢ 1608: Pericles (in part)
- ➢ 1609: Cymbeline
- ➢ 1610: The Winter's Tale
- ➢ **1611: The Tempest**
- ➢ **1613: The Two Noble Kinsmen (in part), Henry VIII (in part)**

## Important Plays:

**Henry VI** (1590)
**Henry VI** (1591–2)
**Henry VI** (1591–2)

- ➢ **Falstaff provides comic relief** in *Henry IV*, balancing the serious political themes.
- ➢ **His relationship with Prince Hal** highlights themes of leadership and responsibility.

**Richard III** (1593)

➤ The story of Richard II was taken mainly from **Raphael Holinshed's Holinshed's Chronicles.**

**Edward III** (in part) (1593)

**The Comedy of Errors** (1593)
➤ **Egeon** of Syracuse is detained in **Ephesus**, facing execution.
➤ **Egeon** explains the loss of his twin sons and their slaves.
➤ **Duke Solinus** grants Egeon until sunset to raise his ransom.
➤ **Antipholus** and **Dromio** of **Syracuse** arrive in **Ephesus**, unaware of danger.
➤ Confusions begin when **Dromio of Ephesus** mistakes **Antipholus of Syracuse.**
➤ **Antipholus of Syracuse** is surprised by **Adriana**, claiming to be his wife.
➤ **Luciana**, Adriana's sister, catches **Antipholus of Syracuse's** eye.
➤ **Antipholus of Ephesus** is enraged after being locked out of his home.
➤ **Goldsmith's chain** causes further confusion, leading to wrongful arrest.
➤ **Antipholus of Ephesus** and **Dromio** are accused of madness and restrained.
➤ **Syracusian twins** seek refuge in a **priory**, escalating panic in **Ephesus**.
➤ **Duke Solinus** prepares to execute **Egeon** when the twins appear.
➤ **Abbess Emilia** reveals herself as **Egeon's** long-lost wife.
➤ Families reunite, and **Antipholus of Syracuse** proposes to **Luciana**.
➤ **Two Dromios**, hand in hand, leave the stage joyfully.

**Titus Andronicus** (1594)
➤ Believed to have been written between 1588 and 1593, probably **collaborating with George Peele.**
➤ Titus, a general in the Roman army, presents Tamora, Queen of the Goths, as a slave to the new Roman emperor, Saturninus.
➤ **"But, soft! methinks I do digress too much,"** — TITUS ANDRONICUS, ACT 5 SCENE 3

**The Taming of the Shrew** (1594)
➤ was written around **1590–94.**
➤ The play was first printed in the **First Folio of 1623.**
➤ The main plot follows the **courtship of Petruchio and Katherina.**
➤ **Katherina** is portrayed as a **shrewish and headstrong** woman.
➤ **Petruchio "tames" Katherina** using **psychological tactics.**

- ➤ His methods include **denying her food and drink**.
- ➤ **Katherina eventually becomes compliant** and marries Petruchio.
- ➤ The subplot involves a **competition for Katherina's sister Bianca**.
- ➤ Bianca is seen as the **"ideal" obedient woman**.

**Love's Labour's Lost** (1594)
- ➤ **King Ferdinand** and his friends pledge to avoid women and focus on studies for three years.
- ➤ **Costard** is arrested for pursuing **Jacquenetta**, while **Don Armado** secretly falls in love with her.
- ➤ The **Princess of France** arrives with her ladies, and the men immediately fall in love with them.
- ➤ **Biron's love letter** to **Rosaline** mistakenly reaches **Jacquenetta**, who plans to inform the King.
- ➤ The men spy on each other declaring their love and decide love can be part of their studies.
- ➤ The men, disguised, attempt to woo the women but are tricked by the ladies into revealing their feelings.
- ➤ After news of the **French King's death**, the **Princess** declares a year-long separation before the couples can reunite.

**Romeo and Juliet** (1594)
- ➤ **Feuding Families in Verona**: The play begins with the **Montagues and Capulets** feuding in **Verona's streets**.
- ➤ **Romeo's Heartbreak**: In **Montague's home**, **Romeo** is heartbroken over **Rosaline**.
- ➤ **Capulet's Ball Setting**: At the **Capulet's grand mansion**, **Romeo sneaks in** and meets **Juliet**, instantly falling in love.
- ➤ **Balcony Scene**: In **Capulet's garden**, **Romeo and Juliet** confess their secret love during the iconic **balcony scene**.
- ➤ **Friar Lawrence's Cell**: In the **Friar's cell**, **Friar Lawrence** agrees to marry the lovers to **end the feud**.
- ➤ **Tybalt's Challenge in the Streets**: **Tybalt** confronts **Romeo** in the **streets of Verona**, challenging him to a duel.
- ➤ **Mercutio's Death**: **Tybalt kills Mercutio** during the duel in **Verona's square**, escalating tensions.
- ➤ **Romeo's Revenge**: **Romeo kills Tybalt** in a duel at the same location, and is **banished** from **Verona**.

- ➤ **"O, I am Fortune's fool!"**: In the **streets**, **Romeo laments** his fate after killing **Tybalt**.
- ➤ **Juliet's Room**: In her bedroom, **Juliet receives** the sleeping potion from **Friar Lawrence**, planning to **fake her death**.
- ➤ **Romeo's Return to Verona**: In the **Capulet tomb**, **Romeo**, unaware of the plan, finds **Juliet "dead"**.
- ➤ **Romeo's Death**: Inside the **tomb, Romeo drinks poison**, believing **Juliet is truly dead**, and dies beside her.
- ➤ **Juliet Awakens in the Tomb: Juliet awakens** in the **Capulet tomb**, finding **Romeo's lifeless body**, and stabs herself.
- ➤ **Families Reconcile at the Tomb**: At the **Capulet tomb**, the **Montagues and Capulets** finally end their feud after their children's deaths.
- ➤ **Prince's Final Words**: In the **town square**, the Prince concludes, "**Never was a story of more woe** than this of Juliet and her Romeo."

**A Midsummer Night's Dream** (1595)
- ➤ The play is set in **Athens**, focusing on **Theseus** and **Hippolyta's** wedding.
- ➤ One subplot features a conflict among **four Athenian lovers**.
- ➤ Another subplot follows six **amateur actors** preparing a play for the wedding.
- ➤ Both groups enter a forest inhabited by **fairies**.
- ➤ The **fairies** manipulate humans and engage in their own intrigues.
- ➤ Four **Athenians** flee to the forest, where **Puck** interferes.
- ➤ **Puck** causes both boys to fall in love with the same girl.
- ➤ The four lovers chase each other through the forest.
- ➤ **Puck** also helps his master play a trick on the **fairy queen**.
- ➤ In the end, **Puck** reverses the magic spell.
- ➤ The two couples reconcile and return to Athens.
- ➤ The lovers marry, resolving the conflicts.

**The Two Gentlemen of Verona** (1595)
- ➤ It is a **pastoral story** about two friends traveling to **Milan**.
- ➤ **Proteus and Valentine** are best friends who travel to **Milan**.
- ➤ **Valentine** falls in love with **Silvia**, daughter of the Duke.
- ➤ **Proteus** betrays Valentine by pursuing **Silvia** himself.
- ➤ **Proteus** already has a girlfriend, **Julia**, back in Verona.
- ➤ **Silvia** remains faithful to Valentine despite **Proteus' advances**.
- ➤ **Julia** disguises herself as a page to **follow Proteus**.
- ➤ **Proteus** repents his betrayal and reconciles with **Valentine**.

- **Julia** reveals herself, and **Proteus returns to her**.
- **Both couples**, Valentine and Silvia, Proteus and Julia, marry.
- The primary source was **Los Siete Libros de la Diana** by **Jorge de Montemayor**.
- Shakespeare adapted the play from **various sources** like **Damon and Pythias**.
- **Geoffrey Chaucer's** *The Knight's Tale* also inspired aspects of the plot.
- The story of **Titus and Gisippus** from *The Boke Named the Governour* influenced the ending.

**King John** (1595)

**Richard II** (1596)
- Joan of Gaunt is a character in **Richard II** by William Shakespeare.
- He is the Duke of Lancaster and the father of Henry Bolingbroke, who later becomes King Henry IV.
- Joan of Gaunt's famous "This England" speech occurs in Act 2, Scene 1 of the play.

**The Merchant of Venice** (1596)
- It is best known for Shylock and his famous "Hath not a Jew eyes?" speech on humanity.
- Also notable is Portia's speech about "the quality of mercy."
- **Antonio** borrows money from **Shylock** for **Bassanio's** courtship of **Portia**.
- **Shylock** demands a **pound of flesh** if loan defaults.
- **Portia's suitors** must choose between **gold**, **silver**, or **lead** caskets.
- **Jessica** elopes with **Lorenzo**, taking **Shylock's wealth**.
- **Bassanio** chooses the **lead casket**, winning **Portia's hand**.
- **Shylock insists** on the **pound of flesh** as **Antonio's ships sink**.
- **Portia** disguises as a lawyer, saving **Antonio** in court.
- **Shylock** is denied his bond and forced to **convert**.
- **Bassanio and Graziano** unknowingly give their **rings** to their disguised wives.
- **Antonio's ships return**, and the couples prepare to **celebrate**.

**Henry IV** (1597)
**Henry IV** (1598)

**Much Ado about Nothing** (1598)
- ➢ The play explores **false accusations of unfaithfulness** comically.
- ➢ **Claudio-Hero plot** derives from **Matteo Bandello's Novelle**.
- ➢ **Beatrice-Benedick plot** is Shakespeare's original creation.
- ➢ The play combines themes from **Orlando Furioso** and **The Faerie Queene**.
- ➢ **Claudio falls in love** with Hero, Leonato's daughter.
- ➢ **Beatrice and Benedick** are tricked into thinking they're in love.
- ➢ **Don John** plots to ruin Hero and Claudio's relationship.
- ➢ Claudio is **deceived into believing Hero** is unfaithful.
- ➢ Claudio **publicly denounces Hero** at their wedding ceremony.
- ➢ **Hero faints** and is thought dead after the accusation.
- ➢ A **chance discovery reveals Hero's innocence** of wrongdoing.
- ➢ **Benedick defends Hero**, winning Beatrice's love and admiration.
- ➢ **Claudio mourns Hero's death** before learning she's alive.
- ➢ **Hero and Claudio reunite**, and all ends in marriage.

**Henry V** (1599)

**Julius Cæsar** (1599)
- ➢ **Brutus joins a conspiracy led by Cassius to murder Julius Caesar** to prevent Caesar from becoming a tyrant.
- ➢ **"Et tu, Brute?"** — JULIUS CAESAR, ACT 3 SCENE 1

**The Merry Wives of Windsor** (1600)
- ➢ Falstaff decides to fix his financial woe by seducing the wives of two wealthy merchants.
- ➢ The wives find he sent them identical letters and take revenge by playing tricks on Falstaff when he comes calling.
- ➢ With the help of their husbands and friends, the wives play one last trick in the woods to put Falstaff's mischief to an end.

**As You Like It** (1600)
- ➢ **Shakespeare based the play on Rosalynde (1590), a prose romance by Thomas Lodge.**
- ➢ Jaques, who speaks many of Shakespeare's most famous speeches, such as
  - ○ "All the world's a stage."
  - ○ "too much of a good thing."
  - ○ "A fool! A fool! I met a fool in the forest."

- **Orlando**, mistreated by his brother **Oliver**, challenges **Charles** the wrestler.
- **Duke Frederick** has deposed **Duke Senior**, but allowed **Rosalind** to stay.
- Rosalind falls in love with **Orlando** during the wrestling match.
- **Rosalind** gives Orlando a chain, sparking mutual feelings of love.
- Orlando flees to the **Forest of Arden** to escape his brother's plot.
- **Rosalind**, disguised as **Ganymede**, and **Celia**, as **Aliena**, flee to Arden.
- In the forest, **Ganymede** meets the lovesick shepherd **Silvius**.
- **Orlando** writes love poems for **Rosalind**, hung on trees in Arden.
- Ganymede (Rosalind) pretends to "cure" **Orlando** by acting as Rosalind.
- **Phoebe**, a shepherdess, falls in love with **Ganymede** (Rosalind in disguise).
- **Touchstone** woos country girl **Audrey**, winning her from **William**.
- **Orlando** saves his brother **Oliver**, leading to Oliver's transformation.
- **Oliver** and **Celia** fall in love, while **Rosalind** plans everyone's marriages.
- **Rosalind**, with the help of **Hymen**, reveals her true identity.
- The play ends with a joyful **dance**, celebrating four marriages in Arden.

**Hamlet** (1601)

- **Setting: Elsinore Castle, Denmark**: The play is set in the **royal court of Elsinore**, haunted by the **ghost of the late King Hamlet**.
- **Ghost's Appearance: King Hamlet's ghost** appears to his son, **Prince Hamlet**, revealing that **Claudius**, his brother, murdered him.
- **"Revenge His Foul and Most Unnatural Murder!"**: In the castle battlements, the ghost instructs **Hamlet** to **avenge his death**, setting the play's central conflict.
- **Hamlet's First Soliloquy**: In **Elsinore**, Hamlet delivers his famous soliloquy: **"O that this too too sullied flesh would melt"**, expressing his despair.
- **Claudius' Guilt and Marriage to Gertrude**: **Claudius**, now the king, has **married Gertrude**, Hamlet's mother, quickly after the old king's death, adding to Hamlet's disgust.
- **Play within a Play**: **Hamlet stages** "The Murder of Gonzago" to confirm Claudius' guilt by **mirroring the king's murder** in the play.
- **"The Play's the Thing"**: Hamlet declares, **"The play's the thing wherein I'll catch the conscience of the king"**, after deciding to observe **Claudius' reaction**.

- **Hamlet's Soliloquy - "To Be or Not to Be"**: In his famous soliloquy, Hamlet contemplates **life and death**, asking, **"To be or not to be, that is the question."**
- **Ophelia's Madness**: **Ophelia** descends into **madness** after Hamlet's rejection and **her father Polonius' death**, eventually leading to her tragic end.
- **Polonius' Death**: In **Gertrude's chamber**, **Hamlet accidentally kills Polonius**, mistaking him for **Claudius** behind the arras.
- **Hamlet's Exile to England**: After Polonius' murder, **Claudius sends Hamlet** to **England** with secret orders for his **execution.**
- Claudius sends **Rosencrantz and Guildenstern**, Hamlet's former friends, to **accompany him to England** with secret orders for Hamlet's **execution.**
- **Ophelia's Death**: **Ophelia drowns** in the **river**, a tragic outcome of her **father's death and Hamlet's actions.**
- **Return and Duel**: **Hamlet returns** to Denmark, and **Laertes challenges him** to a duel, plotting with **Claudius** to kill Hamlet.
- **Poisoned Cup and Duel**: During the duel, **Gertrude drinks the poisoned cup** meant for Hamlet, and **Laertes wounds Hamlet** with a poisoned sword.
- **Hamlet's Death**: Hamlet kills **Claudius**, but not before being **mortally wounded** himself, ending with his final words, **"The rest is silence."**
- **Play within a Play**: "The Murder of Gonzago" is used by Hamlet to **reveal Claudius' guilt** for murdering King Hamlet.
- **Famous Soliloquy**: The **"To be or not to be"** soliloquy highlights Hamlet's **internal struggle** over life, death, and action.
- **Yorick** was a jester in *Hamlet*, his **skull** held by **Hamlet** in the graveyard scene.
- **Three Sisters** and *The Seagull* by Chekhov draw from **Shakespeare's Hamlet.**
- *The Seagull* explores **lost opportunities** and **generational conflicts**, referencing *Hamlet.*
- **Alfred Jarry's Ubu Roi** parodies **Macbeth**, incorporating elements of **Hamlet** and **King Lear.**
- **"When sorrows come, they come not single spies,"** a line from **Hamlet.**
- **Marcellus** says **"Something is rotten in the state of Denmark"** in *Hamlet.*
- **"Time out of joint"** is spoken by **Hamlet** after seeing his father's **ghost.**

**Twelfth Night** (1601)
- **Duke Orsino** loves **Countess Olivia**, but she continually **rejects him.**
- **Viola** is shipwrecked and believes her twin, **Sebastian**, is dead.
- Viola disguises as a boy, **Cesario**, and enters Orsino's service.
- **Orsino sends Cesario (Viola)** to court **Olivia** on his behalf.
- Olivia falls for **Cesario (Viola)** instead of **Orsino.**
- **Malvolio**, Olivia's steward, is tricked into thinking **Olivia loves him.**
- Malvolio follows **the letter's demands** and behaves bizarrely, **wearing yellow stockings.**
- **Sebastian** survives and arrives in Illyria with **Antonio,** a former pirate.
- **Sir Toby, Sir Andrew**, and others plot to **humiliate Malvolio.**
- Mistaken for **Cesario, Sebastian marries Olivia**, deepening the confusion.
- **Viola and Sebastian** are reunited when they realize they are **both alive.**
- **Malvolio** is imprisoned, but vows **revenge** after learning of the trick.
- **Orsino** discovers his attraction to **Viola**, promising to **marry her.**
- The play ends with **two marriages: Olivia and Sebastian, Viola and Orsino.**
- **"Journey's end in lovers meeting"** symbolizes **reconciliation** and **happy unions.**
- *"Some are born great, others achieve greatness." - William Shakespeare, Twelfth Night*

**Troilus and Cressida** (1602)
- Based on George Chapman's translation of the Iliad and 15th-century accounts of the Trojan War by John Lydgate and William Caxton

**All's Well that Ends Well** (1602)
- Bertram is compelled to marry Helena.
- Bertram refuses to consummate their marriage.
- He goes to Italy
- In Italy, Bertram courts Diana.
- Helena meets Diana.
- They perform the bed trick.
- **The play is considered one of Shakespeare's "problem plays,"** which poses complex ethical dilemmas that require more than typically simple solutions.

**Measure for Measure** (1604)

- Measure for Measure, a "dark" comedy in five acts
- The Duke leaves Angelo in charge of Vienna, where he quickly condemns Claudio to death for immoral behavior.
- Angelo offers to pardon Claudio if his sister, Isabella, sleeps with him.
- Isabella agrees but has Angelo's fiance switch places with her.
- The Duke returns to spare Claudio, punish Angelo, and propose to Isabella.

**Othello** (1604)
- **Othello**, a Moorish general in the Venetian army, marries **Desdemona** in secret.
- **Iago**, Othello's ensign, is resentful and jealous of **Cassio**, who was promoted over him.
- **Iago** manipulates **Roderigo**, who loves Desdemona, to help him seek revenge on **Othello**.
- **Cassio** is appointed as Othello's lieutenant, making Iago furious and fueling his schemes.
- **Iago** plots to make Othello believe **Desdemona** is unfaithful with **Cassio**.
- The **handkerchief**, a gift from Othello to Desdemona, becomes a key **symbol of fidelity**.
- **Iago** plants the handkerchief in Cassio's possession, making Othello suspicious of **Desdemona's loyalty**.
- Othello's jealousy deepens as **Iago** convinces him that **Desdemona** is unfaithful.
- **Othello** confronts **Desdemona**, who remains unaware of the **handkerchief's significance**.
- In a fit of jealousy and rage, **Othello smothers Desdemona**, believing she betrayed him.
- **Emilia**, Iago's wife, exposes Iago's deceit and explains the truth about the **handkerchief**.
- **Iago kills Emilia** when she reveals his plot to Othello and the others.
- Realizing his mistake, **Othello kills himself**, overwhelmed with guilt and sorrow.
- **Iago** is arrested, but his ultimate fate is left ambiguous by the end of the play.
- The play ends with **Cassio** being promoted to governor and tasked with punishing **Iago**.
- **Schlegel** viewed Othello's downfall as a return to his "wild nature."

- **Samuel Johnson** praised Othello for its compelling human behavior depiction.
- Johnson highlighted Othello's "fiery openness" and Desdemona's "soft simplicity."
- **Coleridge** saw Othello as driven by "wounded honor" and moral indignation.
- Coleridge described **Iago** as "motive-hunting of motiveless malignity."
- **A.C. Bradley** viewed Othello as noble, exploited by Iago's manipulation.
- Bradley emphasized the **tragic** and emotionally intense nature of Othello.
- **Wilson Knight** criticized Bradley's romanticism, focusing on Othello's "formal beauty."
- **F.R. Leavis** criticized Bradley for overly sentimentalizing Othello's character.
- **William Empson** focused on the repeated use of the word "honest."
- **John Campbell Shairp** questioned Shakespeare's hatred for Iago and Edmund.
- **Thomas Rymer** criticized Othello for deviating from neoclassical principles.
- **"I will wear my heart upon my sleeve"** is a famous quote by Iago.
- **Derek Walcott** critiqued racism using lines from Othello in his poem.
- In his poem, **"Goats and Monkeys,"** Walcott refers to Othello's dilemma.

## Macbeth (1605)

- **Macbeth**, a tragedy in five acts by William Shakespeare, is primarily based on historical accounts found in **Raphael Holinshed's *Chronicles of England, Scotland, and Ireland* (1577)**.
- Three witches tell the Scottish general Macbeth that he will be King of Scotland.
- Encouraged by his wife, Macbeth kills the King, becomes the new King, and kills more people out of paranoia.
- Civil war erupts to overthrow Macbeth, resulting in more death.
- **Macbeth's Ambition**: After hearing the witches' prophecy, Macbeth is consumed by ambition to become king, despite his initial hesitation.
- **Lady Macbeth's Influence**: Lady Macbeth persuades her husband to murder King Duncan, symbolizing her role in fueling his ambition.
- **Dagger Soliloquy**: Macbeth hallucinates a bloody dagger before killing Duncan, symbolizing his inner conflict: *"Is this a dagger which I see before me?"*.

- **Murder of King Duncan**: Macbeth kills Duncan while he sleeps, and Lady Macbeth frames the guards, starting Macbeth's spiral into guilt and paranoia.
- **Symbol of Blood**: After the murder, blood becomes a recurring symbol of guilt: *"Will all great Neptune's ocean wash this blood clean from my hand?"*.
- **Banquo's Murder**: Fearing Banquo's descendants will inherit the throne (as per the witches' prophecy), Macbeth has Banquo murdered, but Banquo's son, Fleance, escapes.
- **Banquo's Ghost**: At a banquet, Macbeth sees Banquo's ghost, symbolizing his overwhelming guilt and fear of losing power.
- **Witches' Riddles**: Macbeth seeks out the witches again, and they present him with riddles, such as "no man born of woman shall harm Macbeth," giving him false confidence.
- **Lady Macbeth's Guilt**: Lady Macbeth begins to unravel, sleepwalking and obsessively washing her hands, saying: *"Out, damned spot!"*, symbolizing her guilt.
- **Macduff's Exile**: Macduff, suspicious of Macbeth, flees to England to gather an army to overthrow him. Meanwhile, Macbeth has Macduff's family murdered.
- **Macduff's Revenge**: The English army, led by Malcolm and Macduff, advances on Macbeth. Macbeth learns that Macduff was "from his mother's womb untimely ripped" (born via C-section), fulfilling the witches' prophecy.
- **Death of Lady Macbeth**: Lady Macbeth dies off-stage, possibly by suicide, showing the ultimate price of her guilt and ambition.
- **Macbeth's Death**: In the final battle, Macduff kills Macbeth, bringing an end to his tyrannical rule: *"Turn, hellhound, turn!"*.
- **Crowning of Malcolm**: Malcolm is crowned king, restoring order to Scotland and ending the cycle of violence that Macbeth's ambition unleashed.
- ***"Come what come may, time and the hour runs..."* – Angus reflects** on time's endurance through hardships in *Macbeth*.
- ***"There is no art to find mind's construction..."* – King Duncan, in *Macbeth*,** laments trusting the man who murders him.
- ***"Maqbool" (2004) – A Hindi crime drama reimagining *Macbeth* directed by Vishal Bhardwaj.***
- *"Ubu Roi"* – A parody of *Macbeth*, blending elements from *Hamlet* and *King Lear*.
- ***Girish Chandra Ghosh* translated *Macbeth* into Bangla in 1893.**

**King Lear** (1605)

- **King Lear** begins by dividing his kingdom among his three daughters based on their flattery.
- **Lear disowns Cordelia**, the youngest, for refusing to flatter him, though she loves him most.
- Lear's elder daughters, **Goneril and Regan**, falsely profess love and receive the kingdom.
- **Lear** soon realizes Goneril and Regan's betrayal as they strip him of power and respect.
- **The storm** symbolizes Lear's internal chaos and descent into madness.
- **Edmund**, the illegitimate son of Gloucester, schemes to betray his father and brother.
- **Cordelia** returns from France to save Lear but is ultimately captured.
- Lear's madness deepens, and he wanders the heath in the raging storm, lamenting his fate.
- **Gloucester**, blinded by Regan's husband, seeks to join Lear in his suffering.
- **Edgar**, Gloucester's loyal son, disguises himself as "Poor Tom" to protect his father.
- **Cordelia** and Lear reunite in a touching scene, symbolizing forgiveness and lost love.
- **"We two alone will sing like birds in a cage"**, Lear tells Cordelia as they await their fate.
- **Edmund** orders Cordelia's death, and despite his last-minute remorse, she is hanged.
- Lear dies of a broken heart, holding Cordelia's body and lamenting, **"Howl, howl, howl!"**
- The play ends with **Edgar** and **Albany** taking control of the kingdom after the chaos.
- **Edward Bond's "Lear"** reimagines Shakespeare's Lear as a paranoid autocrat.
- **"I am a man more sinned against than sinning"** – Lear laments his unjust suffering.
- **George Orwell's essay "Lear, Tolstoy, and the Fool"** critiques Tolstoy's views on Shakespeare.
- **"Is man no more than this?"** – Lear reflects on man's vulnerable, unadorned state.
- **"A dog's obeyed in office"** – Lear condemns the unjust authority figures.

- **"Plate sin with gold"** – Lear criticizes hypocrisy and social inequality.
- **The Gloucester subplot** in *King Lear* was inspired by an episode from **Arcadia**.
- **"Thou rascal beadle, hold thy bloody hand!"** – Lear denounces societal hypocrisy.
- **"The usurer hangs the cozener"** – Lear reflects on corrupt justice systems.
- **Tolstoy's critique of Shakespeare** was the inspiration behind Orwell's essay.
- **Bond's Lear** builds a wall, symbolizing paranoia and self-isolation.
- **Lear's reflection** in Act 4 shows his growing awareness of human frailty.
- **"Through tatter'd clothes small vices do appear"** – Lear observes how wealth conceals sin.
- **Lear's breakdown** highlights his evolving empathy for the poor and powerless.
- **Shakespeare's use of Arcadia** enriches the tragic depth of the Gloucester subplot.

**Antony and Cleopatra** (1606)
- The principal source of the play was **Sir Thomas North's Parallel Lives (1579), an English version of Plutarch's Bioi parallēlo**i.
- **Mark Antony**, one of Rome's three rulers, falls in love with **Cleopatra**, Queen of Egypt.
- **Antony** neglects Roman duties, prioritizing his love for **Cleopatra** over his political responsibilities.
- **Octavius Caesar**, his rival, grows concerned about Antony's disregard for Rome's power.
- Antony is forced to return to Rome after the death of his wife, **Fulvia**.
- Antony marries **Octavia**, Caesar's sister, as a political alliance but quickly returns to Cleopatra.
- **War between Antony and Caesar** begins as their alliance breaks due to Antony's betrayal.
- **Cleopatra** offers her fleet in support of Antony, but they are defeated in the Battle of Actium.
- Antony accuses Cleopatra of betrayal after their defeat, but they reconcile shortly after.
- **Antony** is tricked into believing Cleopatra has died and attempts to kill himself.

- **Antony**, gravely wounded, is brought to Cleopatra, where he dies in her arms.
- Cleopatra prepares for her own death rather than being humiliated by Caesar's triumph.
- **Cleopatra** arranges her suicide, famously using an **asp (poisonous snake)** hidden in a basket of figs.
- **Cleopatra's final line**: "Give me my robe, put on my crown; I have / Immortal longings in me."
- **The wasp** symbolizes **Cleopatra's manipulative charm**, used to both allure and sting Antony.
- The play ends with **Caesar mourning** their deaths, realizing he's lost his greatest rival and ally.
- **All For Love - Written by John Dryden, it was first performed in 1677** and is a tragedy based on the story of Antony and Cleopatra.

**Coriolanus** (1606)

**Timon of Athens** (unfinished) (1607)
- Timon of Athens (The Life of Tymon of Athens) is a play written by William Shakespeare and probably also Thomas Middleton in about 1606.
- The earliest-known production of the Play was in 1674 when Thomas Shadwell wrote an adaptation under the title The History of Timon of Athens, The Man-hater.

**Pericles** (in part) (1608)
- **Pericles**, written **1606-08**, was published in **1609**.
- The play is based on **Apollonius of Tyre** story.
- **Pericles** leaves Tyre to escape death, winning a **jousting contest**.
- A storm separates **Pericles** from his family during the journey.
- Years later, **Pericles** reunites with his **lost wife** and daughter.

**Cymbeline** (1609)
- **Cymbeline**, set in **Ancient Britain**, written around **1611**.
- The play is based on the legend of **King Cunobeline**.
- King **Cymbeline** banishes his daughter **Innogen's** husband over a **bet**.
- **Innogen** is wrongly accused of infidelity and runs away.
- **Innogen** disguises herself as a **page** in the Roman army.
- In the end, **Innogen** clears her name of **false accusations**.
- She discovers her **long-lost brothers** during her journey.

- ➤ **Innogen** reunites with her **husband** after resolving the misunderstanding.
- ➤ King **Cymbeline** makes **peace with Rome**, ending the conflict.

## The Winter's Tale (1610)

- ➤ Relabelled the play as one of Shakespeare's late romances.
- ➤ Some critics consider it one of Shakespeare's "problem plays" because the first three acts are filled with intense psychological drama, while the last two acts are comic and supply a happy ending.
- ➤ The jealous King Leontes falsely accuses his wife, Hermione, of infidelity with his best friend, and she dies.
- ➤ Leontes exiles his newborn daughter Perdita, who is raised by shepherds for sixteen years and falls in love with the son of Leontes' friend.
- ➤ When Perdita returns home, a statue of Hermione "comes to life," and everyone is reconciled.

## The Tempest (1611)

- ➤ **The Tempest** was written and performed around **1611**.
- ➤ The play is set on a **remote island** after a **tempest**.
- ➤ **Prospero**, the usurped Duke of Milan, is a **sorcerer**.
- ➤ **Miranda** is Prospero's **daughter**, raised on the island.
- ➤ **Caliban**, Prospero's **savage servant**, plots against his master.
- ➤ **Ariel**, a spirit, serves Prospero but desires **freedom**.
- ➤ **Prospero** conjures the storm to shipwreck his enemies.
- ➤ **King Alonso**, his son **Ferdinand**, and **Antonio** are shipwrecked.
- ➤ **Miranda** meets and falls in love with **Ferdinand**.
- ➤ **Ferdinand** is thought dead but survives on another shore.
- ➤ **Prospero** tests **Ferdinand** by forcing him into **labor**.
- ➤ **Antonio** and **Sebastian** plot to kill **King Alonso**.
- ➤ **Ariel** foils **Sebastian** and **Antonio's** assassination attempt.
- ➤ **Caliban**, **Stephano**, and **Trinculo** plan to kill **Prospero**.
- ➤ **Ariel** informs Prospero of the **murderous plot**.
- ➤ **Prospero** sets a **trap** with magical clothes for the trio.
- ➤ **The masque** of goddesses celebrates **Ferdinand and Miranda's marriage**.
- ➤ **Ariel** leads the courtiers to **Prospero's cell**.
- ➤ **Prospero renounces magic** and forgives **his enemies**.
- ➤ **Ferdinand** and **Miranda** are **betrothed**.
- ➤ **The sailors** announce the **ship is safe**.

- ➤ **Prospero** fulfills his promise to **free Ariel.**
- ➤ **Caliban** is rebuked but **learns from his mistakes.**
- ➤ The play ends with **celebration** and **reconciliation.**
- ➤ **Prospero asks the audience** to release him from the play.
- ➤ **"The Sea and the Mirror: A Commentary on Shakespeare's The Tempest" is a long poem by W.H. Auden,** written 1942–44, and first published in 1944. Auden regarded the work as "my Ars Poetica, in the same way I believe The Tempest to have been Shakespeare's."

**The Two Noble Kinsmen** (in part) (1613)
- ➤ A tragicomedy in five acts by **William Shakespeare and John Fletcher.**
- ➤ The primary source for the story was The Knight's Tale from Geoffrey Chaucer's Canterbury Tales,
- ➤ But earlier plays concerning the friendship of Palamon and Arcite are known to have been performed.
- ➤ Three queens come to plead with Theseus and Hippolyta, rulers of Athens, to avenge their husbands' deaths at the hand of the tyrant Creon of Thebes.

**Henry VIII** (in part) (1613)
- ➤ "My drops of tears I'll turn to sparks of fire." — HENRY VIII, ACT 2 SCENE 4

**Other Important Facts Asked in Exam**

Almost three centuries after Shakespeare's death, **the scholar F. S. Boas also coined a fifth category, the "problem play," Although Shakespeare experts don't always agree, the plays generally called problem plays are:**

- ➤ All's Well that Ends Well
- ➤ Measure for Measure
- ➤ The Merchant of Venice
- ➤ Timon of Athens
- ➤ Troilus and Cressida
- ➤ The Winter's Tale

**Wolfgang Iser** was a German literary scholar. **Iser is known for his reader-response criticism in literary theory. This theory began to evolve in 1967 while he was working at the University of Konstanz, which he**

**helped to find in the 1960s. In his study of Shakespeare's histories, particularly Richard II, Iser interprets Richard's continually changing legal policy as an expression of the desire for self-assertion.**

In 1668, Dryden published *Of Dramatick Poesie, an Essay,* he remarked that **Whether French drama, as Lisideius maintains, is better than English drama (supported by Neander, who famously calls Shakespeare "the greatest soul, ancient or modern");**

**Julius Caesar: Shakespeare's tragedy based on Plutarch's "Parallel Lives,"** where conspirators plot against Caesar, leading to his assassination and the subsequent power struggles in Rome.

**"On Heroes and Hero Worship" is a series of lectures by Thomas Carlyle, published in 1841.** In the lectures, Carlyle discusses the concept of heroism and examines the lives of several notable figures from history, including Muhammad, Shakespeare, and Napoleon.

For example, his novel **"A Dead Man in Deptford" explores the life and death of Marlowe,** while "Byrne" is a fictionalized account of Shelley's life. Burgess's novel **"Nothing Like the Sun" is a fictionalized biography of William Shakespeare** that also features Marlowe as a character.

A. D. Hope's "A Book of Answers" is a collection of his poetic responses to other writers, including Shakespeare, Marvell, Donne, Milton, Tennyson, Heine, Yeats, **Mallarme**, and Auden.

**William Hazlitt, a British essayist, wrote the essay "My First Acquaintance with Poets" in 1823. The essay recounts Hazlitt's early encounters with poets and his appreciation for their work.**

In the essay, Hazlitt describes his love for poetry and how he was first introduced to it as a child by his father, who would read him poems by Shakespeare, Milton, and other great poets.

**James Burbage (1530–1597) was a prominent figure in the English Renaissance theatre.** He shared a close friendship and **business partnership with the renowned playwright William Shakespeare.**

The Plays of William Shakespeare, edited by Samuel Johnson and George Steevens, is an 18th-century edition of Shakespeare's dramatic works. Johnson's comprehensive edition, published in 1765.

**Shakespeare used an episode from Arcadia as the source for the Gloucester subplot in King Lear.**

**The Seven Books of the Diana (Spanish: Los siete libros de la Diana) is a pastoral romance written in Spanish by the Portuguese author Jorge de Montemayor.**

One of its most famous readers was William Shakespeare, who seems to have borrowed the Proteus-Julia-Sylvia plot of The Two Gentlemen of Verona from Felismena's tale in the Diana.

Mathew Arnold said in his study of poetry that **Chaucer does not have the high seriousness that Homer, Shakespeare, Milton, and many others had.**

**William Hazlitt,** a notable writer of the 19th century, produced several influential works. Among them are **"Characters of Shakespeare's Plays" (1817)**

**"Ariel"** is the title poem of Plath's posthumously published poetry collection. The poem is **named after the spirit Ariel from Shakespeare's "The Tempest"** and is a highly personal and confessional work that explores themes of mental illness, death, and identity.

**"The Sea and the Mirror: A Commentary on Shakespeare's The Tempest" is a long poem by W.H. Auden,** written 1942–44, and first published in 1944. Auden regarded the work as "my Ars Poetica, in the same way I believe The Tempest to have been Shakespeare's."

**Charles Dickens, in the 1850s, took on the role of editor for the English weekly magazine _Household Words_,** named after a phrase from Shakespeare's Henry V. Throughout its conception, Dickens considered various titles such as The Robin, The Household Voice, The Comrade, The Lever, and The Highway of Life before settling on Household Words.

**Holinshed** was a chronicler and translator who is best known for his "**Chronicles of England, Scotland, and Ireland,"** a history of the British Isles that was widely used by Shakespeare as a source for his plays.

**Alan Sinfield and Jonathan Dollimore were British literary critics and cultural theorists** who played an important role in the development of cultural materialism. **They jointly edited the influential collection of essays "Political Shakespeare: Essays in Cultural Materialism,"** which applied the principles of cultural materialism to the study of Shakespearean texts.

**Jonathan** Bate is a British literary critic and scholar who has written extensively on the work of **William Shakespeare, Romantic poetry, and ecocriticism**.

**"The Love Song of J. Alfred Prufrock," also known as "Prufrock," is the debut poem of T. S. Eliot (1888–1965),** an American-born British poet. Eliot's poem draws influence from Dante Alighieri and incorporates references to the Bible, as well as works —including William **Shakespeare's plays Henry IV Part II, Twelfth Night, and Hamlet, the poetry of seventeenth-century metaphysical poet Andrew Marvell, and the nineteenth-century French Symbolists. This repeated mention of Michelangelo by the women in "The Love Song of J. Alfred Prufrock" serves as more than just a representation of the idle chatter of the attendees of the tea party.**

**Peter Brook (1925 – July 2, 2022)** was an acclaimed English theatre and film director. He began his career in England, working at the Birmingham Repertory Theatre in 1945, then at the Royal Opera House in 1947, and later joined the Royal Shakespeare Company (RSC) in 1962.

**Alan Sinfield (17 December 1941 – 2 December 2017) was a prominent English theorist known for his groundbreaking contributions in the fields of Shakespeare and sexuality, modern theatre, gender studies, queer theory, queer studies, post-1945 politics, and cultural theory.**
  - Shakespeare, Authority, Sexuality: Unfinished Business in Cultural Materialism (2006)
  - Political Shakespeare: Essays in Cultural Materialism (1994) (With Jonathan Dollimore)

**Raja Rao wrote** *The Cat and Shakespeare: A Tale of India (1965)*

Questions:



**Match List | with List Il**

| List I | List II |
|---|---|
| A. Some are born great, others achieve greatness. | I. The Tempest |
| B. Love looks not with the eyes, but with the mind, And therefore is winged Cupid painted blind. | Il. The Comedy of Errors |
| C. lll deeds is doubled with an evil word. | lll. A Midsummer Night's Dream |
| D. We are such stuff as dreams are made on, and our little life is rounded with a sleep. | IV. Twelfth Night |

Choose the correct answer from the options given below:

1. **A-IV, B-IlI, C-II, D-I**
2. A-l, B-Il, C-IlI, D-IV
3. A-lII B- IV, C-I, D-III
4. A-ll, B-II, C-I, D-IV

**Explanations:**

A. *"Some are born great, others achieve greatness." - William Shakespeare, Twelfth Night*

B. *"Love looks not with the eyes, but with the mind, And therefore is winged Cupid painted blind." - William Shakespeare, A Midsummer Night's Dream*

C. *"Ill deeds are doubled with an evil word." - William Shakespeare, The Comedy of Errors*

D. *"We are such stuff as dreams are made on, and our little life is rounded with a sleep." - William Shakespeare, The Tempest*

## Question 56

**Name the play during the performance of which the Globe Theatre was burned down in 1613.**

1. *Henry VI*
2. *Henry VIII*
3. *Richard II*
4. *Richard III*

**Explanations**
**Answer:** 2. *Henry VIII*

"Henry VIII" is a history play created through the collaborative efforts of William Shakespeare and John Fletcher. It delves into the life of King Henry VIII. While contemporary documents refer to an alternative title, "All Is True," the play was ultimately published as "Henry VIII" in the First Folio of 1623. Stylistic analysis suggests that certain scenes were individually penned by either Shakespeare or his collaborator and successor, John Fletcher. In terms of structure, the play bears a resemblance to the late romances. Notably, it stands out among Shakespeare's works for its extensive stage directions, surpassing any of his other plays in this regard.

During a performance of **"Henry VIII" at the Globe Theatre in 1613, a cannon shot used for special effects ignited the thatched roof of the theatre, causing a fire that consumed the original Globe building.**

## Question 57

**Match List I with List IT:**

| List I | List II |
|---|---|
| (A) Hamlet | (I) 1606 |
| (B) Macbeth | (II) 1599 |
| (C) Julius Caesar | (III) 1604 |
| (D) Othello | (IV) 1600 |

**Choose the correct answer from the options given below: (DROP)**
1. (A)-(III), (B)- (IV). (C)-(II), (D)-(I)
2. (A)-(I), (B)-(II). (C)-(IV). (D)-(II)
3. (A)-(II). (B)-(I). (C)-(III), (D)-(IV)

4.  **(A)-(IV or II). (B)-(I). (C)-(II). (D)-(III)**
5.  (A)-(IV). (B)-(I). (C)-(II). (D)-(III)

**Correct Explanations:**

**Hamlet,** in full Hamlet, Prince of Denmark, is a tragedy in five acts by William Shakespeare, written about **1599–1601 and published in a quarto edition in 1603** from an unauthorized text concerning an earlier play. The First Folio version was taken from the **second quarto of 1604,** based on Shakespeare's own papers with some annotations by the bookkeeper.

**Macbeth**, a tragedy in five acts by William Shakespeare, was written sometime in **1606–07 and published in the First Folio of 1623 from a playbook or a transcript of one.** Some portions of the original text are corrupted or missing from the published edition. The play is the shortest of Shakespeare's tragedies, without diversions or subplots. It chronicles Macbeth's seizing of power and subsequent destruction, his rise and fall resulting from blind ambition.

**Julius Caesar**, a tragedy in five acts by William Shakespeare, **was produced in 1599–1600 and published in the First Folio of 1623** from a transcript of a promptbook.

**Othello**: The Moor of Venice, a tragedy in five acts by William Shakespeare, written in **1603–04 and published in 1622** in a quarto edition from a transcript of an authorial manuscript. The text published in the First Folio of 1623 seems to have been based on a version revised by Shakespeare himself that sticks close to the original almost line by line but introduces numerous substitutions of words and phrases, as though Shakespeare copied it over himself and rewrote as he copied. The play derives its plot from Giambattista Giraldi's De gli Hecatommithi (1565), which Shakespeare appears to have known in the Italian original; it was available to him in French but had not been translated into English.

## Question 58

**Who among the following, after watching the performance of William Shakespeare's play, A Midsummer Night's Dream, observed that "it is the most insipid, ridiculous play that I ever saw in my life"**

1.  John Evelyn

2.  Samuel Pepys
3.  John Dryden
4.  Robert Greene

**Explanations:**
**Ans:** Samuel Pepys.

The diarist **Samuel Pepys is the one who, after watching the performance of William Shakespeare's play, A Midsummer Night's Dream, observed that** "it is the most insipid, ridiculous play that I ever saw in my life." Pepys recorded his thoughts on the play in his diary on **September 29, 1662,** after seeing a performance at the theatre in **London's Lincoln's Inn Fields.**

## Question 59

**Who among the following has used lines from the Shakespearean play Othello to critique racism in one of his poems?**

1.  Edward Braithwaite
2.  Franz Fanon
3.  **Derek Alton Walcott**
4.  Ngigi wa Thiong'o

**Correct Explanations:**
Derek Walcott was a prolific Caribbean poet and playwright, and he often drew upon themes of race, identity, and colonialism in his work. He was also known for his deep knowledge of and engagement with classical literature, including the works of William Shakespeare.

**In his poem, "Goats and Monkeys", he has referred to Othello's dilemma in Shakespeare's play.** The poem reads like an extended example of Walcott's thesis on historicity and identity.

Othello represents all of Africa/ the other which is both enticing and repulsive, that must remain alien, for the social law "halves the world. **Walcott employs racial stereotypes in his poem in drawing analogy between whiteness of Desdemona & fight and on the other hand comparing Othello with the dark ominous night.**

**Arrange the following plays in their chronological order:**

    A.  The Country Wife
    B.  Cymbeline
    C.  The Spanish Tragedy
    D.  The Rivals

**Choose the correct answer from the options given below:**

    1.  B, A, C, D
    2.  B, C, D, A
    3.  C, B, A, D
    4.  C, A, B, D

Explanations:

**Answer: 3.** C, B, A, D

**The Spanish Tragedy, or Hieronimo is Mad Again is an Elizabethan tragedy written by Thomas Kyd between 1582 and 1592.** It initiated the revenge tragedy of his day.

**Cymbeline, comedy in five acts by William Shakespeare, one of his later plays, written in 1608–10 and published in the First Folio of 1623** from a careful transcript of an authorial manuscript incorporating a theatrical playbook that had included many authorial stage directions. Set in the pre-Christian Roman world, Cymbeline draws its main theme, that of a wager by a husband on his wife's fidelity, from a story in Giovanni Boccaccio's Decameron.

**"The Country Wife" is a Restoration comedy written by William Wycherley in 1675. It follows the story of a man named Horner** who pretends to be impotent in order to gain access to the wives of wealthy men.

**"The Rivals" is a play written by Richard Brinsley Sheridan in 1775.** It is a classic comedy of manners that satirizes the pretensions and foibles of the upper class society of the time. The play follows the story of a young heiress named Lydia Languish who is courted by two men, Jack Absolute and Bob Acres. The play is known for its witty dialogue, memorable characters, and intricate plot. It has been widely performed and adapted over the years and remains a popular work of English drama.



**Who is the author of the short play The Dark Lady of the Sonnets?'**

1. Ben Jonson
2. George Bernard Shaw
3. Oscar Wilde
4. Oliver Goldsmith

**Explanations:**
**Answer: 2.** George Bernard Shaw

The Dark Lady of the Sonnets is a 1910 short comedy by George Bernard Shaw in which William Shakespeare, intending to meet the "Dark Lady", accidentally encounters Queen Elizabeth I and attempts to persuade her to create a national theatre. The play was written as part of a campaign to create a "Shakespeare National Theatre" by 1916.

## Question 62

**Dev Virahsawmy's Toufann is an adaptation of Shakespeare's play**

1. Hamlet
2. Macbeth
3. The Twelfth Night
4. **The Tempest**

**Correct Explanations:**
**Dev Virahsawmy's novel Toufann is an adaptation of William Shakespeare's play The Tempest.** Like its source material, Toufann explores the themes of power, colonialism, and the struggle for freedom. However, Toufann also draws on Virahsawmy's personal experience as a writer and activist in Mauritius. The novel is set in a fictional island in the Indian Ocean, where the French colonizers and the local population are in conflict. The protagonist, Prosper, is a former slave who has gained power over the island through his mastery of sorcery. He finds himself caught between his desire for revenge against his former oppressors and his desire to use his power for the good of his people. Through Prosper's journey, Virahsawmy explores the complexities of power, justice, and the struggle for freedom in the postcolonial world.

## Question 63

**Match List I with List II**

| List I | List II |
| --- | --- |
| A. "There is no art to find mind's construction in the face". | I. Hamlet |
| B, "Time out of joint". | II. Richard III |
| C. "The better part of valour is discretion", | III. Macbeth |
| D. "My Kingdom for a horse". | IV. Twelfth Night |

**Choose the correct answer from the options given below:**

1. A - I, B - IV, C - III, D - II
2. **A - III, B - I, C - IV, D - II**
3. A - IV, B - III, C - II, D - I
4. A - II, B - III, C - IV, D - I

**Correct Explanations:**

**A. This is a quote from William Shakespeare's play "Macbeth." It is spoken by King Duncan in Act 1, Scene 4,** as he expresses his trust in the character of the man who will eventually murder him.

**B. This is a quote from William Shakespeare's play "Hamlet." It is spoken by Hamlet in Act 1, Scene 5,** after he has just seen the ghost of his father and is struggling to come to terms with the idea that his entire world is out of joint.

**C. This is a quote from William Shakespeare's play "Henry IV, Part One." It is spoken by Falstaff in Act 5, Scene 4,** as he justifies his decision to flee from battle rather than fight.

**D. This is a quote from William Shakespeare's play "Richard III." It is spoken by King Richard III in Act 5, Scene 4,** as he rides into battle and expresses his desperation for a horse.

## Question 64

**Which of the following statements is correct in relation to Shakespeare's works?**

1. The Folio edition appeared in the sixteenth century and the 'quartos' appeared in the seventeenth century
2. The 'quartos' appeared during his lifetime and the Folio edition appeared posthumously
3. The Folio edition appeared during his lifetime and the 'quartos' appeared

posthumously
4. The 'quartos' refer to works written between 1594 and 1599, and the Folio includes works written between 1608 and 1613.

**Explanations:**
**Answer: 2.** The 'quartos' appeared during his lifetime and the Folio edition appeared posthumously

**The statement suggests that the "quartos" of a particular work were published during the author's lifetime, while the "Folio" edition was published after the author's death.**

In the context of English Renaissance drama, especially the works of William Shakespeare, "quartos" refer to small-sized books that contained individual plays. These quartos were often published during Shakespeare's lifetime and were typically cheaper and less authoritative versions of his plays. They were printed and sold to meet the demand of the time.

On the other hand, the "Folio" edition refers to a larger-sized book known as the "First Folio." It is a collection of Shakespeare's plays compiled by his colleagues after his death. The First Folio, published in 1623, seven years after Shakespeare's death, was a more authoritative and comprehensive edition that included many of his works for the first time.

## Question 65

**Arrange the following plays in their chronological order:**

    (A) The Tempest
    (B) All For Love
    (C) Volpone
    (D) The School for Scandal

**Choose the correct answer from the options given below :**

1. (A), (C), (B), (D)
2. (C), (B), (A), (D)
3. (C), (A), (B), (D)
4. (A), (D), (B), (C)

**Explanations:**
**Answer: 3.** (C), (A), (B), (D

**(C) Volpone** - Written by Ben Jonson, it was first performed in **1605** and is a satirical comedy that explores themes of greed, deception, and corruption in

Venetian society.

**(A) The Tempest** - Written by William Shakespeare, it is believed to be one of his last plays and was likely composed around **1610-1611.** It is a complex play that combines elements of romance, comedy, and tragedy, centring around themes of power, magic, and forgiveness.

**(B) All For Love - Written by John Dryden, it was first performed in 1677** and is a tragedy based on the story of Antony and Cleopatra. It explores themes of love, loyalty, and the conflict between personal desires and duty.

**(D) The School for Scandal - Written by Richard Brinsley Sheridan, it premiered in 1777** and is a witty comedy of manners that satirizes gossip, hypocrisy, and social conventions of the time. It remains one of the most popular and enduring plays of the 18th century.

**96-97: Read the given passage and answer the questions that follow:**

> *And the creature run from the cur?*
> *There thou mightst behold the great image of authority: a dog's obeyed*
> *in offce,—*
> *Thou rascal beadle, hold thy bloody hand!*
> *Why dost thou lash that whore? Strip thine own back;*
> *Thou hotly lust'st to use her in that kind for which thou whipp'st her.*
> *The usurer hangs the cozener.*
> *Through tatter'd clothes small vices do appear;*
> *Robes and fiord gowns hide all. Plate sin with gold,*
> *And the strong lance of justice hurtless breaks;*
> *Arm it in rags, a pigmy's straw cloth pierce it.*

> **-King Lear**

Question 66

**In the passage, the church oficer is asked to whip his own back rather than the prostitute's because:**

1. as a religious man he should punish himself for others' sins.
2. he at one time had lusted after her.
3. men like him make them prostitutes.
4. he does not have the authority to whip a woman.

**Explanations:**

**Answer: 3.** men like him make them prostitutes.

In the given passage from Shakespeare's "King Lear," the speaker is questioning the authority of the church official who is punishing a prostitute. The speaker suggests that the official himself has desired the woman in the past and that he should therefore punish himself instead of her. The speaker then goes on to say that people like the church official are responsible for creating prostitutes, implying that it is not the fault of the women themselves. **This is the reason why the church official is asked to whip his own back rather than the prostitute's**. The passage highlights the hypocrisy and corruption of those in positions of authority who abuse their power.

## Question 67

**Who speaks these lines and to whom?**

1. Edgar to Lear
2. Goneril to Edgar
3. Lear to Gloucester
4. Gloucester to Lear

**Explanations:**
**Answer: 3.** Lear to Gloucester

**Lear speaks these lines to his loyal companion Gloucester in Act 4, Scene 6 of William Shakespeare's play King Lear.**

In these lines, Lear expresses his frustration with the corruption and injustice he sees in society. He starts by asking a rhetorical question about why a creature, such as a cur or dog, is able to run from those in authority while others are punished for their small vices. Lear then comments on the power of the dog as an image of authority, saying that even dogs are obeyed when they are in office.

Lear then turns his attention to the beadle, who is whipping a prostitute. He criticizes the beadle for lashing the woman and accuses him of having lustful intentions towards her. Lear asserts that those who punish others for small vices are often guilty of much larger sins themselves. He then makes a broader statement about how wealth and power can be used to cover up sins and injustices.

## Question 68

**The two sentences in the lines from -Through tatter'd clothes.: to -... straw doth pierce it deal with two foibles, (i) vice and (ii) sin. About these two, the speaker says that**

1. Vice aflicts all but sin aflicts only the weak.
2. Sin aflicts all but vice aflicts only the strong.
3. Sin and vice are seen in both the weak and the strong.
4. Sin and vice are palpable in the weak and impalpable in the strong.

**Explanations:**

**Answer: 4.** Sin and vice are palpable in the weak and impalpable in the strong.

The lines "Through tatter'd clothes small vices do appear; Robes and furr'd gowns hide all. Plate sin with gold, And the strong lance of justice hurtless breaks; Arm it in rags, a pigmy's straw doth pierce it" are suggesting that vices, which are small faults or flaws in character, are easily visible in people who are weak and powerless, symbolized here by the "tatter'd clothes." However, when people are powerful and wealthy, symbolized by "robes and furr'd gowns," their sins are often hidden and disguised. The speaker is saying that by using wealth and power to cover up one's sins, it becomes difficult for justice to hold them accountable, as the strong lance of justice can break when it strikes at those who are powerful and influential. However, if one's sins are displayed through weakness and poverty, like "a pigmy's straw," then it becomes easy to pierce them with the lance of justice. Therefore, the speaker is suggesting that vice and sin are more easily noticeable in the weak and vulnerable, and are often hidden and protected in the powerful and wealthy.

Read the following extract and answer the questions:

> *The solemn temples, the great globe itself,*
> *Yea, all which it inherit, shall dissolve.*
> *And, like this insubstantial pageant faded,*
> *Leave not a rack behind. We are such stuff*
> *As dreams are made, and our little life*
> *Is rounded with a sleep.*
>
> **Shakespeare, *The Tempest***

## Question 69

'[T]his insubstantial pageant' refers to:
1. the shutdown of Globe theatre.
2. **a non-real performance.**
3. the destroyed mother earth.

4.   enactment with the support structure.

**Correct Explanations:**
For Question 9, the phrase 'insubstantial pageant' is a metaphor for life being like a non-real performance, **compared to a theatrical production or shows that is temporary and fleeting, and will eventually disappear without leaving a trace behind.**

## Question 70

'We are such stuff as dreams are made on' means:

1.   Human life is full of imaginary colours.
2.   Our life is a text of what happened.
3.   We are a bundle of past reality.
4.   **There is no substance to human life.**

**Correct Explanations:**
For Question 10, the phrase 'We are such stuff as dreams are made on' is a metaphor that suggests that human existence is fleeting and transient, lacking any true substance or permanence. **It implies that our lives are like fleeting dreams that disappear once we wake up and that there is no enduring reality or substance to human life.**

**Read the following extract and answer the questions that follow:**

*Is man no more than this? Consider him well. Thou ow'st the worm no silk, the beast no hide, the sheep no wool, the cat no perfume. —Ha! here's three on's are sophisticated. Thou art the thing itself; unaccommodated man is no more than such a poor, bare, forked animal as thou art.* — **Shakespeare, *King Lear***

## Question 71

**'Is man no more than this?' means:**

1.   Man is far more than what he seems to be.
2.   **Man is not as well endowed as some other animals.**
3.   Accommodated man is well endowed.
4.   As an animal, man is a superior animal.

**Correct Explanations:**

This quote from Shakespeare's "King Lear" comes from a scene where Lear, who has been driven to madness, confronts one of his daughters, who has betrayed him. In this quote, Lear is speaking to a group of animals, pointing out that they can offer specific attributes or materials, but that humans have none of these natural resources. The line "Is man no more than this?" **suggests that humans are not as well endowed as animals in terms of these specific things and that we must rely on our faculties and intelligence to survive.**

## Question 72

**Which one of the following best captures what Shakespeare means?**

1. Man just uses what animals possess.
2. Animals' attributes are external.
3. **Man can accommodate the same properties.**
4. Animals, unlike man, are more complex.

**Correct Explanations:**

In this quote, Shakespeare seems to be suggesting that while humans may not have the specific attributes or materials of certain **animals, we can adapt and accommodate these things to suit our needs.** For example, humans may not have furs like sheep or cats, but we have learned to make clothing and perfumes from these materials. The line "Thou art the thing itself; unaccommodated man is no more than such a poor, bare, forked animal as thou art" reinforces this idea, suggesting that humans would be no without the ability to adapt and innovate differently from any other animal.

## Question 73

**Who is the author of the essay "Lear, Tolstoy and the Fool"?**

1. Aldous Huxley
2. **George Orwell**
3. Virginia Woolf
4. Somerset Maugham

**Correct Explanations:**

**"Lear, Tolstoy and the Fool" is an essay by George Orwell. It was inspired by a critical essay on Shakespeare by Leo Tolstoy and was first published in Polemic No. 7 (March 1947).**

Orwell analyzes Tolstoy's criticism of Shakespeare's work in general and his attack on King Lear in particular. According to Orwell's detailed summary, Tolstoy denounced Shakespeare as a bad dramatist, not a true artist at all, and declared that Shakespeare's fame was due to propaganda by German professors towards the end of the eighteenth century. Tolstoy claimed that Shakespeare was still admired only because of a sort of mass hypnosis or "epidemic suggestion".

## Question 74

**What was poor Yorick in Hamlet?**

1. **Jester**
2. Actor
3. Soldier
4. Gravedigger

**Correct Explanation:**
**Yorick was a jester in William Shakespeare's play Hamlet. Although he never appears on stage, he is an important character in the play as his skull is famously held by Hamlet in the famous graveyard scene.** Yorick's presence in the play symbolizes the fleeting nature of life and reminds the characters of their own mortality.

## Question 75

**Arrange the following characters in their chronological sequence of appearance:**

A. Mirabell
B. Shylock
C. Jimmy Porter
D. Sir Epicure Mammon

**Choose the correct answer from the options given below**
1. D, B, A, C

   **2. B, D, A, C**
   3. D, B, C, A
   4. B, D, C, A

## Correct Explanations:

- ➢ Shylock is a fictional character in William Shakespeare's play The Merchant of Venice (c. **1600**).
- ➢ Sir Epicure Mammon is a theatrical character in the play The Alchemist (**1610**).
- ➢ Mirabell is a character in the The Way of the World (**1700**) by the English playwright William Congreve.
- ➢ Jimmy Porter, the lead character in John Osborne's **1956** play Look Back in Anger.

## Question 76

**What might the speaker mean when he addresses 'Time' in a Shakespearean sonnet and declares, "I will be true, despite thy scythe and thee "?**

   A. Time preserves human life.
   B. With time comes change.
   C. Time creates opportunities.
   D. Time removes human life.

**Choose the correct answer from the options given below:**

   1. A and B only
   2. C and D only
   3. B and D only
   4. A and C only

## Correct Explanations:

In the first lines of 'Sonnet 123,' the speaker asserts that he is not controlled by time. Time, a force he personifies, cannot "boast that" the speaker changes. He's not acting for Time's pleasure and enjoyment. Through this broader allusion to life and death, he's trying to allude more specifically to his relationship with the Fair Youth. His love is not something that can decay and change at one time. It is not subject to Time's degradations.

When the speaker addresses 'Time' in a Shakespearean sonnet and declares, "I will be true, despite thy scythe and thee," it means that the speaker intends to remain faithful and true despite the passage of time and the inevitability of aging and death. The speaker is acknowledging that time has a destructive power (symbolized by "thy scythe"), but asserts that they will remain committed to their beliefs or the object of their affection, despite the ravages of time. **So, the answer would be "Time removes human life."**

## Question 77

**Which character in Hamlet utters the line: "Something is rotten in the state of Denmark"?**

1. **Marcellus**
2. Bernardo
3. Ghost
4. Horatio

**Correct Explanations:**
**Yes, Marcellus does utter the line "Something is rotten in the state of Denmark" in Shakespeare's play "Hamlet". This line is spoken in Act I, Scene 4,** by Marcellus, one of the soldiers who is keeping watch outside the castle at Elsinore. The line is a foreboding one, suggesting that there is something deeply wrong with the state of affairs in Denmark. It has become a famous and widely quoted line, and is often used to refer to situations where there is something corrupt or amiss. The line has also been interpreted in a variety of ways, with some seeing it as a reference to the political corruption and intrigue of the time, while others view it as a metaphor for the moral decay of society as a whole.

## Question 78

**Which Shakespearean comedy is structured as a play within a play?**

1. A Midsummer Night's Dream
2. Love's Labour's Lost
3. The Comedy of Errors
4. The Taming of the Shrew

**Correct Explanations:**

**A Midsummer Night's Dream is a Shakespearean comedy that includes the performance of a play called "The Most Lamentable Comedy and Most Cruel Death of Pyramus and Thisbe"** by the Mechanicals, a group of amateur actors. The play within the play is a farcical and humorous rendition of the tragic love story of Pyramus and Thisbe, and it serves as a parody of the main plot's romantic complications. The structure of the play within the play is an example of a metatheatrical device, which is a theatrical technique that draws attention to the artifice of the drama and breaks the fourth wall between actors and audience.

Question 79

**Match List I with List II**

| LIST I | LIST II |
|---|---|
| A. Corne what come may, Time and the hour runs through the roughest day. | I. Othello |
| B. When sorrows come, they come not single spies. But in battalions! | II. King Lear |
| C. I am a man more sinned against than sinning. | III. Macbeth |
| D. But I will wear my heart upon my sleeve For Daws to peck at: I am not what I am. | IV. Hamlet |

**Choose the correct answer from the options given below:**

1. A-IV, B-III, C-II, D-I
2. A-II, B-III, C-I, D-IV
3. A-III, B- IV, C-II, D-I
4. A-I, B-II, C-IV, D-III

**Explanations:**
**Ans:** A-III, B- IV, C-II, D-I

A. ***"Corne what come may, Time and the hour runs through the roughest day." *This is a quote from Macbeth by William Shakespeare.** It is spoken by Macbeth's right-hand man, Angus, and means that time passes regardless of what is happening, even during the most difficult moments.

**B.** ***"When sorrows come, they come not single spies. But in battalions!"*** **This quote is from Hamlet by William Shakespeare.** It is spoken by King Claudius, who is reflecting on the troubles that have befallen him. He suggests that bad things often happen in groups, rather than one at a time.

**C.** ***"I am a man more sinned against than sinning."*** **This quote is from King Lear by William Shakespeare.** It is spoken by the main character, King Lear, who feels that he has been wronged more than he has wronged others.

**D.** ***"But I will wear my heart upon my sleeve For Daws to peck at: I am not what I am."*** **This quote is from Othello by William Shakespeare.** It is spoken by the character Iago, who is known for his manipulative and deceitful nature. He suggests that he will appear one way while actually being another.

Question 80

*"What needs my Shakespeare for his honoured bones*
*The labour of an age in piled stones?*
*Or that his hallowed reliques should be hid*
*Under a star-ypointing pyramid?"*

**These lines are written by**

1. Ben Jonson
2. **John Milton**
3. Robert Browning
4. William Wordsworth

**Explanations:**
**The lines are from Milton's poem "On Shakespeare", published in the second folio edition of Shakespeare's plays in 1632.** "On Shakespeare" is a poem by John Milton, published in the second folio edition of William Shakespeare's plays in 1632. In the poem, Milton praises Shakespeare as a great poet and dramatist and expresses his admiration for Shakespeare's works.

***On Shakespeare***
*John Milton - 1608-1674*

*"What needs my Shakespeare for his honour'd Bones,*

*The labour of an age in pilèd Stones,*
*Or that his hallow'd reliques should be hid*
*Under a stary pointing Pyramid?*
*Dear son of Memory, great heir of Fame,*
*What need'st thou such weak witnes of thy name?*
*Thou in our wonder and astonishment*
*Hast built thy self a live-long Monument.*
*For whilst to th' shame of slow-endeavouring art,*
*Thy easie numbers flow, and that each heart*
*Hath from the leaves of thy unvalu'd Book*
*Those Delphick lines with deep impression took,*
*Then thou our fancy of it self bereaving,*
*Dost make us Marble with too much conceaving;*
*And so Sepulcher'd in such pomp dost lie,*
*That Kings for such a Tomb would wish to die."*

## Question 81

**The book Political Shakespeare: Essays in Cultural Materialism was jointly edited by**

1. Gilles Deleuze and Felix Guattari
2. Alan Sinfield and Jonathan Dollimore
3. Bill Ashcroft and Helen Tiffin
4. Theodor Adorno and Max Horkheimer

**Explanations:**

**Ans**: Alan Sinfield and Jonathan Dollimore

**The book "Political Shakespeare: Essays in Cultural Materialism" was jointly edited by Jonathan Dollimore and Alan Sinfield.** It was first **published in 1985** and has since become a classic text in the field of cultural studies. **The book is a collection of essays** that apply the principles of cultural materialism to the study of Shakespearean texts and the cultural contexts in which they were produced. It argues that Shakespeare's plays are deeply embedded in the cultural, social, and political realities of their time and that they can be read as a form of cultural critique.

**Which of the following plays of William Shakespeare was translated into Bengali and directed by Girish Chandra Ghosh.**

1. The Tempest
2. Hamlet
3. Macbeth
4. King Lear

**Explanations:**
**Ans:** Macbeth

**Girish Chandra Ghosh (1844-1912) was a renowned Bengali playwright, actor, and director** who made significant contributions to Bengali theater in the late 19th and early 20th centuries. He is considered one of the pioneers of **Bengali theater and is often referred to as the "father of Bengali theater."**

Ghosh began his career as an actor in the mid-1860s and later became a playwright and director. He **wrote over 40 plays,** many of which were based on social and political issues of the time, and were known for their realistic portrayals of contemporary Bengali life. Ghosh's plays were performed by **his own theater company, the National Theater, which he founded in 1872.** The National Theater became one of the most popular theater companies in Bengal and played a significant role in the development of Bengali theater.

Girish wrote about 86 plays, most of which were based upon stories from Purana, Ramayana and Mahabharata. Among his famous works were Buddhadev Charit, Purna Chandra, Nasiram, Kalapahar, Ashoka, Shankaracharya, Chaitanyalila, Nimai Sannyas, Rup-Sanatan, Vilwamangal, Prahlad Charit. Most of his plays were performed in Star Theatre in Calcutta. **Girish also translated Shakespeare's Macbeth play into Bangla in 1893.**



**Which of the following works are written by John Dennis?**

A. The Advancement and Reformation of Modern Poetry
B. The Christian Hero
C. The Grounds of Criticism in Poetry
D. The Conscious Lovers

E. An Essay on the Genius and Writings of Shakespeare

**Choose the correct answer from the options given below:**

1. A, B and C
2. A, C and E
3. B, C and D
4. C, D and E

**Explanations**
**Answer:** 2. A, C and E

**John Dennis (1657-1734)** was an English critic and dramatist.

**Major essays:**
- *Remarks ...* (1696), on Blackmore's epic of Prince Arthur.
- *Letters upon Several Occasions written by and between Mr. Dryden, Mr. Wycherley, Mr. Moyle, Mr. Congreve and Mr Dennis, published by Mr Dennis (1696).*
- *two pamphlets in reply to Jeremy Collier's Short View of the Immorality and Profaneness of the English Stage.*
- ***The Advancement and Reformation of Modern Poetry (1701), perhaps his most important work.***
- ***The Grounds of Criticism in Poetry (1704)***, in which he argued that the ancients owed their superiority over the moderns in poetry to their religious attitude.
- *Essay on the Operas after the Italian Manner (1706).*
- *Essay upon Publick Spirit (1711)*, in which he inveighs against luxury, and servile imitation of foreign fashions and customs.
- *Essay on the Genius and Writings of Shakespeare in Three Letters (1712).*

**Dramatic works**
- *A Plot and No Plot (1697)*
- *Rinaldo and Armida (1698)*
- *Iphigenia (1700)*
- *The Comical Gallant (1702)* (adaptation of The Merry Wives of Windsor)
- *Liberty Asserted (1704)*

> ➤ *Gibraltar (1705)*
> ➤ *Orpheus and Eurydice (1707)*
> ➤ *Appius and Virginia (1709)*
> ➤ *The Invader of His Country (1719)*

## Question 84

**Mention the year in which Political Shakespeare, edited by Jonathan Dollimore and Alan Sintield, was published.**

1. 1980
2. 1984
3. 1987
4. 1985

**Explanations**
**Answer:** 4. 1985

**Jonathan Dollimore** is the author of four academic books, a memoir, and numerous academic articles. **With Alan Sinfield, he was the co-editor of and key contributor to *Political Shakespeare*** and the co-originator of the critical practice known as cultural materialism. Dollimore is credited with making major interventions in debates on sexuality and desire, Renaissance literary culture, art and censorship, and cultural theory.

## Question 85

**Which of the following plays may be considered as a parody of Shakespeare's Macbeth, and some parts of Hamlet and King Lear?**

1. G. B. Shaw's Pygmalion
2. Luigi Pirandello's Bellavita
3. August Strindberg's The Dance of Death
4. Alfred Jarry's Ubu Roi

**Explanations:**
**Answer: 4.** Alfred Jarry's Ubu Roi

**"Ubu Roi" is a play written by Alfred Jarry and first published and produced in 1896. Originally intended as a parody of one of Jerry's teachers, it quickly evolved into a satire of the French middle class.**

The central character, Père Ubu, is a gluttonous, greedy, and cruel individual who seizes the throne of Poland by slaughtering the royal family. With no qualms about sacrificing anyone to achieve his goals, Ubu's true cowardice is revealed when he confronts the surviving son of the slain king. The play's scatological references, pompous style, and distorted French language provoked a riot when it premiered. However, it later gained recognition and appreciation from Surrealists and Dadaists in the 1920s, who hailed it as the first Absurdist drama.

**"Ubu Roi" is a parody of Shakespeare's "Macbeth" and incorporates elements from "Hamlet" and "King Lear."** The story unfolds as Ubu's wife persuades him to lead a revolution, resulting in the murder of the King of Poland and most of the royal family. The King's son, Bougrelas, and the Queen manage to escape, but the Queen later dies. The ghost of the deceased king appears to his son, urging him to seek revenge.

As Ubu assumes the throne, he imposes heavy taxes on the people and ruthlessly eliminates the nobles for their wealth. Ubu's henchman is imprisoned but escapes to Russia, convincing the Tsar to declare war on Ubu. While Ubu heads off to confront the invading Russians, his wife attempts to steal the palace's riches. Bougrelas leads a revolt of the people against Ubu, and when Ubu's wife seeks refuge with him, she is driven away. Eventually, Ubu is defeated by the Russians, abandoned by his followers, and attacked by a bear. His wife disguises herself as the angel Gabriel to manipulate Ubu's forgiveness, leading to a confrontation. Bougrelas intervenes, seeking revenge on Ubu, but Ubu defends himself using the bear's corpse. Ubu and his wife flee to France, marking the end of the play.

## Question 86

**Which two plays of Anton Chekhov made creative use of Shakespeare's Hamlet?**

A. A Marriage Proposal
B. Three Sisters
C. The Cherry Orchard
D. Uncle Vanya
E. The Seagull

**Choose the correct answer from the options given below:**

1. A and D
2. C and E
3. B and D
4. B and E

**Explanations:**
**Answer: 4.** B and E

**Three Sisters is a Russian drama by Anton Chekhov, first performed in Moscow in 1901 and published as Tri sestry in the same year.** The play revolves around the Prozorov sisters who long for the excitement of Moscow, but are trapped in a dreary provincial life. Their hopes for a new life are shattered when their brother marries someone they consider unsuitable and jeopardises their home. Through the characters' boredom and longing, Chekhov portrays the aspirations and despair of the Russian middle class.

**The Seagull, another drama by Chekhov,** was performed in 1896 and published as Chayka in 1897. It explores themes of lost opportunities and generational conflicts, drawing intertextual references to **Shakespeare's Hamlet**. The play delves into the complexities of relationships and contains allusions to Shakespearean plot elements.

Question 87

**Match List I with List II**

| List I | List II |
|---|---|
| A. Charles Lamb | I. Imaginary Conversations |
| B. William Hazlitt | II. Specimens of the English Dramatic Poets who Lived about the Time of Shakespeare |
| C. Walter Savage Landor | III. Characters of Shakespeare's Plays |
| D. Thomas Love Peacock | IV. Gryll Grange |

**Choose the correct answer from the options given below:**

1. A-III. B-I, C-IV. D-II
2. A-I, B-II. C-III. D-IV
3. A-II, B-III, C-I. D-IV

4. A-IV, B-I. C-II. D-III

**Explanations:**
Answer: **3**. A-II, B-III, C-I. D-IV

**I. "Imaginary Conversations" is a collection of dialogues written by Walter Savage Landor, first published in 1824.** The book features fictional conversations between historical and literary figures, exploring various topics and ideas.

**II. "Specimens of the English Dramatic Poets who Lived about the Time of Shakespeare" is a work by Charles Lamb, published in 1808.** The book contains selected plays and excerpts from plays written by English dramatists who were contemporaries of William Shakespeare, providing insight into the theatrical landscape of that era.

**III. "Characters of Shakespeare's Plays" is a book written by William Hazlitt, published in 1817.** In this work, Hazlitt offers critical analysis and character sketches of the various characters found in William Shakespeare's plays, delving into their personalities, motivations, and significance within the plays.

**IV. "Gryll Grange" is a novel by Thomas Love Peacock, first published in 1861.** The book follows the story of Mr. Falconer, who retreats to the countryside estate of Gryll Grange. It satirises various social and intellectual movements of the time, including politics, philosophy, and education, through witty dialogues and humorous situations.

## Question 88

**Who, among the following, has written Lear (a play), an adaptation of Shakespeare's King Lear?**

1. Edward Bond
2. Arthur Miller
3. Steven Berkoff
4. Virginia Woolf

**Explanations:**
Answer: 1. Edward Bond

Edward Bond (born 18 July 1934) is an English playwright, theatre director, poet, theorist and screenwriter. He is the author of some fifty plays, among them Saved (1965), the production of which was instrumental in the abolition of theatre censorship in the UK. Other well-received works include **Narrow Road to the Deep North (1968), Lear (1971), The Sea (1973), The Fool (1975), Restoration (1981), and the War trilogy (1985).** Bond is broadly considered among the major living dramatists but he has always been and remains highly controversial because of the violence shown in his plays, the radicalism of his statements about modern theatre and society, and his theories on drama.

**Lear: Edward Bond's 1971 play reimagines Shakespeare's King Lear, presenting a paranoid autocrat who builds a wall to ward off imagined threats.** The rebellion of his daughters sparks a violent war, leading Lear on a journey of self-discovery, haunted by the ghost of a Gravedigger's Boy. His eventual act of dismantling the wall offers a glimmer of hope in this tale of practical activism.

**Narrow Road to the Deep North:** Edward Bond's satirical play from 1968 takes place in Japan's Edo period and follows poet Basho as he navigates the changing political landscape over several decades, offering a political parable on the British Empire.

**The Sea:** Set in a small seaside village during the Edwardian period, Edward Bond's 1973 comedy draws inspiration from Shakespeare's The Tempest, exploring the dynamics of rural life in a humorous and insightful manner, earning positive reviews from critics.

**Bingo: Scenes of Money and Death: Edward Bond's 1973 political drama delves into the life of an ageing William Shakespeare,** grappling with a guilty conscience for signing a contract that harms local farmers. Influenced by Bertolt Brecht, the play offers a fictionalised portrayal of Shakespeare and his moral struggles, sparking both praise and criticism for its depiction.



**"Did not Shakespeare hate and despise Iago and Edmund?" Identify the book in which this question has been mentioned.**

1. An Apology for Poetry
2. Kings of Norway
3. Fool of Quality
4. Aspects of Poetry

**Explanations:**
**Answer: 4.** Aspects of Poetry

**Criticism on Othello:**

**In John Campbell Shairp's "Aspects of Poetry,"** a provocative question is raised: **"Did not Shakespeare hate and despise Iago and Edmund?"** This inquiry delves into the complexities of Shakespeare's characterizations, particularly focusing on the nefarious figures of Iago from "Othello" and Edmund from "King Lear." Shairp's question invites readers to consider Shakespeare's personal sentiments towards his creations, suggesting a contemplation of the depth of villainy and moral depravity embodied by these characters. It prompts an exploration of the emotional and ethical engagement of the playwright with his own literary figures, opening a discourse on the nature of evil and the playwright's potential disdain for such embodiments of vice in his works.

**Thomas Rymer's Criticism:** Date: Late 17th century (specifically, his work "A Short View of Tragedy" was published in 1693).

- Criticized "Othello" for deviating from neoclassical principles, arguing it should focus on events occurring in a single day and location.
- Objected to the play's portrayal of a man of color, Othello, as a general in the Venetian military, which he saw as violating natural hierarchy and societal norms of the time.
- Found the marriage between Othello, a man of color, and Desdemona, a senator's daughter, implausible and objectionable.
- Despite his overt racism and hostility, Rymer acknowledged Shakespeare's effective use of language in Othello's courtship of Desdemona, recognizing it as a powerful tool for reconciling differences, though he viewed it negatively.
- Thomas Rymer criticized "Othello" for deviating from neoclassical dramatic form and found the play's plot and characters implausible

**August Wilhelm Schlegel's Criticism**: The criticism of Shakespeare's "Othello" highlighted in the provided text comes primarily from the 19th-century German poet and translator August Wilhelm Schlegel. Schlegel interpreted Othello's tragic downfall not as a complex character development but as a return to his innate, barbarous nature. Schlegel argued that Othello's violent jealousy and subsequent actions were indicative of his "wild nature," which he associated with his Moorish identity and the "glowing zone" of his origin, suggesting that such traits are characteristic of the most "ravenous beasts of prey" and "deadly poisons." He posited that Othello's jealousy was not one of emotional depth but of a "sensual kind" tied to his heritage, which Schlegel demeaningly linked to "the disgraceful confinement of women" and other "unnatural usages" prevalent in "burning climes." This interpretation reveals a deeply rooted racial bias, associating European identity with civility and morality, while portraying Moorish identity as inherently savage and immoral. Schlegel's critique reflects a broader 19th-century trend of reading "Othello" in a way that reinforced existing racial stereotypes and hierarchical views of European superiority over other races and cultures.

**Samuel Johnson (1709-1784)**, in contrast, defended "Othello" for its compelling depiction of human behavior. He admired the play's aesthetic value and argued that it offers profound insights into human nature, highlighting the distinct characteristics of its main characters: Othello's fiery openness and credulousness; Iago's cool malignity and subtlety; and Desdemona's soft simplicity and innocence. Johnson saw these as unmatched proofs of Shakespeare's mastery of human nature, suggesting it's a vain effort to find a comparable modern writer.

**Samuel Taylor Coleridge on Othello:** Samuel Taylor Coleridge viewed Othello not as inherently passionate or jealous but driven by moral indignation and wounded honor, generating sympathy for him as a "high and chivalrous Moorish chief." Coleridge also described Iago as a "passionless character, all will in intellect," famously coining the phrase "motive-hunting of motiveless malignity" to describe Iago's actions. Anna Jameson shifted focus towards Desdemona, arguing the tragedy's pathos lies in her character, characterized by gentleness and goodness, which Jameson sees as both her strength and her fatal flaw. Jameson contrasts Desdemona's purity with Iago's malevolence, suggesting the play's central conflict is between Desdemona's virtue and Iago's evil, rather than the marriage of Othello and Desdemona.

**A.C. Bradley's view on "Othello"** is characterized by his portrayal of the play as the most painfully exciting and terrible of Shakespeare's tragedies, invoking extreme feelings of pity, fear, sympathy, and repulsion in its audience. Bradley romanticizes Othello as a noble and mysterious everyman, whose downfall is orchestrated by Iago exploiting his virtues. He depicts Desdemona as the embodiment of the "eternal womanly," innocent and saintly, whose tragic fate underscores the theme of high aspirations being crushed. Bradley emphasizes the uniqueness of the play's construction, with a late conflict onset and a rapid acceleration to catastrophe, contributing to the audience's intense emotional experience. His approach treats the characters as real individuals, whose lives offer insights into human nature and tragedy.

**G. Wilson Knight criticized A.C. Bradley**'s romantic reading of the play, arguing that Othello focuses on the "vividly particular rather than the vague and universal" and emphasized the play's "formal beauty." L.C. Knights objected to Bradley's approach, accusing him of treating Shakespearean tragedies as novels and neglecting their status as poetry. Knights's criticism highlights an overemphasis on psychological dimensions at the expense of verbal constructions.

**F.R. Leavis** found Bradley's reading excessively sentimental, accusing him of over-identifying with Othello and missing the general's "self-approving self-dramatization." Leavis portrays Othello not as a naive noble victim but as an egoist, whose "self-pride becomes stupidity" and "an insane and self-deceiving passion."

**William Empson's view on "Othello"** is focused on the extensive use of the word "honest" within the play. He explores how this term is employed by different characters at critical points, highlighting shifts in its meaning over time. Empson suggests that Shakespeare uses the word "honest," especially in relation to Iago, to reflect a cultural transition toward individualism. This analysis is part of Empson's broader argument that Shakespeare was aware of the changing semantics of "honest" and manipulated it to convey deeper themes of deception and integrity within the play.

Question 90

**Who composed the poem "The Phoenix and the Turtle"?**

1. William Blake

2. William Shakespeare

3. William Cowper

4. Robert Burns

**Explanations:**

**Answer: 2.** William Shakespeare

**During the theatre closures of 1593 and 1594 due to the plague, William Shakespeare** turned to publishing two narrative poems centered on themes of sexuality, **"Venus and Adonis" and "The Rape of Lucrece,"** dedicating them to Henry Wriothesley, Earl of Southampton. "Venus and Adonis" depicts the goddess Venus unsuccessfully pursuing the young and chaste Adonis, whereas "The Rape of Lucrece" tells the tragic story of Lucrece, a faithful wife who is assaulted by the predatory Tarquin. Drawing inspiration from Ovid's "Metamorphoses," these works explore the aftermath of unchecked desire, highlighting the ensuing guilt and moral turmoil. Both poems enjoyed popularity and frequent reprints during Shakespeare's life.

## Question 91

**Match List I with List II**

| List I (Movie) | List Il (Inspiredby/Adaptation of) |
| --- | --- |
| A Kai Po Che! | I. Macbeth by William Shakespeare |
| B. Slumdog Millionaire | II. Romeo and Juliet by William Shakespeare |
| C. Maqbool | III. The 3 Mistakes of My Life by Chetan Bhagat |
| D.Ishaqzaade | IV.Q & A by Vikas Swarup |

**Match List I with List IlChoose the correct answer from the options given below:**

1.   A - I, B - II, C - III, D -IV
2.   A - II, B - 1, C - IV, D - III
3.   A - III, B - IV, C - 1, D - II
4.   A - IV, B - III, C - II, D - 1

**Explanations:**

**Answer: 3.** A - III, B - IV, C - 1, D - II

**"Three Mistakes of My Life," penned by Chetan Bhagat,** was unveiled in May 2008, marking Bhagat's third literary work with an opening print of 420,000 copies. Set in Ahmedabad, India, it unravels the camaraderie and trials of three friends. Its cinematic rendition, **"Kai Po Che!" directed by Abhishek Kapoor** and featuring actors Sushant Singh Rajput, Amit Sadh, and Rajkumar Rao, was released in February 2013.

**"Q & A," Vikas Swarup's** debut novel released in 2005, chronicles the ascent of Ram Mohammad Thomas from a waiter to the largest quiz show victor, followed by his subsequent arrest under suspicion of cheating. **Its film adaptation, "Slumdog Millionaire,"** diverged with new characters Jamal and Salim, securing multiple Oscars in 2008.

**"Maqbool," a 2004 film directed by Vishal Bhardwaj** and starring notable actors like Irrfan, Tabu, and Pankaj Kapur, is a crime drama that reimagines **Shakespeare's Macbeth** in the Hindi language, setting it against the backdrop of the Indian underworld.

**"Ishaqzaade,"** a 2012 action romance drama by Habib Faisal and produced by Aditya Chopra for Yash Raj Films, spins a contemporary Indian take on the classic ***Romeo and Juliet***, blending action with romance, earning a rating of 3 out of 5 stars from Filmfare for its fresh narrative twist on the timeless love story.

## Ben Jonson (1573–1637)

### Life:

- He was born **at Westminster, and educated at Westminster School**.
- **His father died** before Jonson's **birth**.
- He adopted the trade of his stepfather, who was a master **bricklayer**.
- He became a **soldier, serving in the Low Countries**.
- Engaged himself, both as actor and playwright, with the **Lord Admiral's company (1597)**.
- **Admiral's Men**, a theatrical company in **Elizabethan and Jacobean** England. It was later known successively as Nottingham's Men. It was closely **associated with Christopher Marlowe**. The first to produce **George Chapman's plays**.

- ➤ **In 1598 he killed a fellow-actor in a duel, narrowly escaping the gallows.**
- ➤ In 1603, with **James I's accession, masques** became popular, and Jonson successfully created many of them.
- ➤ **Mermaid Tavern**, near St. Paul's, hosted monthly meetings in 1612–13. **Ben Jonson** and **Francis Beaumont** attended, along with other scholars and intellectuals. No evidence suggests **Shakespeare** or **Raleigh** ever attended these meetings.
- ➤ **Buried in Westminster Abbey**, and over him was placed the epitaph "*O rare Ben Jonson!*"

**Works:**

- ➤ He Published *Timber, or Discoveries made upon men and matter, as they have flowed out of his daily readings, or had their reflux to his peculiar notion of the times, (London, 1641).*
- ➤ **It is in Jonson's *Timber, or Discoveries*...** that he famously quipped on the manner in which language became a measure of the speaker or writer: *"Language most shows a man: Speak, that I may see thee. It springs out of the most retired and inmost parts of us, and is the image of the parent of it, the mind. No glass renders a man's form or likeness so true as his speech. Nay, it is likened to a man; and as we consider feature and composition in a man, so words in language; in the greatness, aptness, sound structure, and harmony of it."* —**Ben Jonson, 1640 (posthumous)**
- ➤ He began with the comedy *Every Man in his Humour,* (1598); then followed *Every Man out of His Humour* (1599), *Cynthia's Revels (1600)*, and *The Poetaster* **(1601)**. (**Code:** In-Out Humour Reveals The Poetaster)

List of His Works:

**Play:**

- ➤ **A Tale of a Tub** (1596, revised 1633)
- ➤ **The Isle of Dogs** (1597, with Thomas Nashe; lost)
- ➤ **The Case is Altered** (1597–98)
  (**Code:** A tale of Dog's Case)
- ➤ **Every Man in His Humour** (1598)
- ➤ **Every Man out of His Humour** (1599)
- ➤ **Cynthia's Revels** (1600)
- ➤ **The Poetaster** (1601)
  (**Code:** In-Out Humour Reveals The Poetaster)
- ➤ **Sejanus His Fall** (1603)

- **Eastward Ho** (1605, with John Marston and George Chapman)
- **Volpone** (1605–06)
- **Epicoene, or the Silent Woman** (1609)
- **The Alchemist** (1610)
  (**Code**: VoELT Network)
- **Catiline His Conspiracy** (1611)
- **Bartholomew Fair** (1614)
- **The Devil is an Ass** (1616)
  (**Code**: Cats dont bark but mew on Devil)
- **The Staple of News** (1626)
- **The New Inn, or The Light Heart** (1629)
- **The Magnetic Lady, or Humours Reconciled** (1632)
- **The Sad Shepherd** (1637)
  (**Code**: Second Last Work)
- **Mortimer His Fall** (1637)
  (Code: Last Work)

**Masque**: Total 36 Masques:
- **The Masque of Blackness** (6 January 1605)
- **The Masque of Beauty** (10 January 1608)
- **The Masque of Queens** (2 February 1609)
- **Oberon, the Faery Prince** (1 January 1611)
  (**Code**: Black Beauty Queen and Prince)

**Other Works:**
- Epigrams (1612)
- The Forest (1616), including **To Penshurst**
- **On My First Sonne** (1616), **elegy**
- A Discourse of Love (1618)
- **Horace's Art of Poetry**, translated by Jonson (1640)
- **Underwood (1640)**
- English Grammar (1640)
- *Timber, or Discoveries made upon men and matter, as they have flowed out of his daily readings, or had their reflux to his peculiar notion of the times, (London, 1641) a commonplace book*
- **To Celia** (*Drink to Me Only With Thine Eyes*), poem

### Every Man in His Humour (1598)

- ➤ Was performed in London by **Lord Chamberlain's Men** in 1598.
- ➤ Play introduced a vigorous and direct anatomizing of **"the time's deformities"**—the language, habits, and humor to the English stage and the contemporary London scene.
- ➤ It has been suggested that **Shakespeare took the part of Kno'well,** the aged father.

### Plot:

- ➤ **Old Knowell** worries his son spends time on poetry.
- ➤ Knowell intercepts a letter and reads **disparaging remarks** about himself.
- ➤ Knowell, suspicious, orders **Brainworm** to deliver the letter secretly.
- ➤ **Brainworm reveals** to Edward that his father read the letter.
- ➤ Edward plans a **prank** with his cousin Stephen and **meets Wellbred.**
- ➤ Kitely fears his wife will **be tempted** by Wellbred's friends.
- ➤ **Brainworm disguises** as a soldier and stalls Knowell's journey.
- ➤ Brainworm sells Stephen a **fake sword**, which Bobadill exposes.
- ➤ **Brainworm admits** the sword deception, making Stephen calm.
- ➤ Brainworm tells Edward **Knowell follows him** and is nearby.
- ➤ Kitely, jealous, orders Cash to **watch his wife** for suspicious visitors.
- ➤ Wellbred and friends arrive at Kitely's house, **Cash alerts Cob.**
- ➤ **More disguises** and misunderstandings follow at Kitely's house.
- ➤ **Fights and lawsuits** escalate as jealousy and confusion grow.
- ➤ The play ends with **plagiarized poetry** and angry accusations.

### Every Man out of His Humour (1599)

- ➤ **Every Man Out of His Humour** premiered in 1599 by Jonson.
- ➤ **Sequel to Every Man in His Humour**, but more ambitious.
- ➤ Longest play ever written for **Elizabethan public theatre.**
- ➤ Aimed to be **equivalent to Aristophanes' Greek comedy.**
- ➤ Featured an "induction" and **between-act commentaries on drama.**
- ➤ The play was a **disaster, forcing Jonson to private theatres.**
- ➤ Young boys acted in **"private" theatres like children's company.**
- ➤ Contains allusion to **John Marston's Histriomastix in Act III.**
- ➤ Involved Jonson in the **War of the Theatres rivalry.**
- ➤ Scholars find references to **Sir Walter Raleigh and Gabriel Harvey.**

## The Poetaster (1601)

> - The play formed one element in the back-and-forth exchange between **Jonson and his rivals John Marston and Thomas Dekker** in the so-called **Poetomachia** or War of the Theatres of 1599–1601.
> - The principal character in the play is Ovid.
> - **The character of Horace in Poetaster represents Jonson** himself, while **Crispinus**, who vomits up a pretentious and bombastic vocabulary, is **Marston, and Demetrius Fannius is Dekker**.
> - Jonson attempted in Poetaster to express his views on **"the poet's moral duties in society."**
> - The play has been considered *"an attempt to combine undramatic, philosophical material on good poets with satire on bad poets."*

## Eastward Ho! (1605)

> - Play written by George Chapman, Ben Jonson, and John Marston.
> - Performed at the Blackfriars Theatre by a company of boy actors known as the Children of the Queen's Revels.
> - Eastward Ho! is a citizen or city comedy about Touchstone, a London goldsmith, and his two apprentices, Quicksilver and Golding.
> - The play's title **alludes to Westward Ho! by Thomas Dekker and John Webster who also wrote Northward Ho**! in response that year.

## Volpone (1605–06)

> - Drawing on elements of **city comedy and beast fable.**
> - It remains Jonson's most-performed play, ranked among the finest Jacobean-era comedies.

**Characters:** Thomas Hull in costume as Voltore, 1780

> - **Volpone (the Sly Fox)** – a greedy and rich childless Venetian magnifico
> - **Mosca (the Fly)** – his servant
> - **Voltore (the Vulture)** – a lawyer
> - **Corbaccio (the Raven)** – an avaricious old miser
> - **Bonario** – Corbaccio's son
> - **Corvino (the Carrion Crow)** – a merchant
> - Celia – Corvino's wife
> - Sir Politic Would-Be – ridiculous Englishman

- **Lady Would-Be (the parrot)** – English lady and wife of Sir Politic-Would-Be
- **Peregrine ("Pilgrim")** – another, more sophisticated, English traveller
- Nano – a dwarf, companion of Volpone
- Androgyno – a hermaphrodite, companion of Volpone
- Castrone – a eunuch, companion of Volpone
- The Avocatori – the judges of Venice

**Plot:**

- **Volpone** pretends to be a dying, wealthy old man.
- He tricks **three greedy men**, Corvino, Voltore, and Corbaccio.
- **Mosca**, Volpone's servant, helps manipulate these gold-diggers.
- **Corbaccio disinherits** his son Bonario for Volpone's fortune.
- Volpone seeks to **seduce Corvino's wife**, Celia, through trickery.
- Corvino offers Celia to Volpone for **promised inheritance.**
- Volpone tries to **rape Celia**, but Bonario interrupts.
- **Celia and Bonario** are falsely accused of adultery.
- **Mosca and Voltore** manipulate the court to protect Volpone.
- The **Would-Bes** are tricked by Volpone and Mosca.
- Volpone announces his "death," leaving **Mosca as his heir.**
- Mosca refuses to relinquish Volpone's **fortune and power.**
- Volpone realizes the scam spirals **out of control.**
- **Volpone reveals** the truth to the court, confessing everything.
- **Everyone is punished** for their greed and deceit.

### Epicoene, or the Silent Woman (1609)

- The play is about **Dauphine, who creates a scheme to get his inheritance from his uncle Morose.**
- The plan involves setting **Morose up to marry Epicoene, a boy disguised as a woman.**
- It was initially performed by the **Blackfriars Children, or Children of the Queen's Revels, a group of boys players, in 1609.**
- Excluding its two prologues, the play is written **entirely in prose.**

**Characters:**

- **Morose:** A gentleman that loves silence
- Sir Dauphine Eugenie: A Knight, Morose's nephew
- Ned Clerimont: A Gentleman, Dauphine's friend
- **Truewit:** Dauphine's other friend

- ➢ **Epicoene**: A young Gentlewoman, supposedly the silent woman
- ➢ Sir John Daw: A Knight, Epicoene's servant
- ➢ Sir Amorous la Foole: A Knight
- ➢ Thomas Otter: A land and sea Captain
- ➢ **Cutbeard:** A barber, also aids in tricking Morose
- ➢ **Mute**: One of Morose's servants
- ➢ Madame Haughty: Ladies Collegiates
- ➢ Madame Centaure, Ladies Collegiates
- ➢ Mistress Mavis, Ladies Collegiates
- ➢ Mistress Trusty, The Lady Haughty's woman
- ➢ Mistress Otter, The Captain's wife
- ➢ Parson
- ➢ Pages
- ➢ Servants

## Plot:

- ➢ **Morose**, a wealthy man, hates noise and disturbances.
- ➢ He plans to disinherit **Dauphine** by marrying soon.
- ➢ **Dauphine schemes** with barber Cutbeard to stop Morose.
- ➢ Cutbeard presents **Epicœne**, a supposedly silent woman, to Morose.
- ➢ Morose tests Epicœne's silence and **obedience** before marrying her.
- ➢ **Dauphine arranges** the match to sabotage Morose's plans.
- ➢ Meanwhile, the **Ladies Collegiates** discuss using sex to control men.
- ➢ **Truewit**, Dauphine's friend, tries to stop the marriage.
- ➢ Despite warnings, Morose marries **Epicœne** in excitement.
- ➢ Epicœne quickly turns into a **loud, nagging wife** after marriage.
- ➢ **Morose's house** is overrun by noisy guests and chaos.
- ➢ **Mistress Otter** dominates her husband, adding to the confusion.
- ➢ Morose seeks a **divorce** but can't find legal grounds.
- ➢ **Dauphine reveals** that Epicœne is a disguised boy.
- ➢ The **marriage is annulled**, and Morose loses his inheritance.

## The Alchemist (1610)

### Plot:

- ➢ **November 1610**, London is plagued, Lovewit leaves his townhouse.
- ➢ **Lovewit's servant, Jeremy**, becomes "Face" and schemes.
- ➢ Face teams up with **Subtle**, a con man, and **Doll Common**, a prostitute.
- ➢ They turn Lovewit's house into a **scamming headquarters**.

- **Subtle pretends to be a master** of alchemy, astrology, and magic.
- **Dapper**, a clerk, seeks a spirit to aid his gambling.
- **Abel Drugger**, a tobacconist, asks for help setting up his shop.
- **Sir Epicure Mammon** believes Subtle can create the **philosopher's stone**.
- Sir Epicure dreams of **wealth, power, and numerous concubines**.
- **Puritan elders**, Tribulation Wholesome and Ananias, also pay for the stone.
- They want the stone to **gain wealth** for their Protestant sect.
- **Pertinax Surly**, Sir Epicure's friend, doubts the whole scheme.
- The play is a **satire of greed and folly**, like *Volpone*.
- Each customer is **punished according to their vices and hypocrisy**.
- Subtle and Face **quarrel over Dame Pliant**, a wealthy widow.
- **Surly suspects their schemes** but is outwitted by Subtle and Face.
- Subtle and Face send **all their customers packing**, avoiding exposure.
- **Lovewit returns unexpectedly**, and Subtle and Doll flee.
- **Face, now Jeremy again**, conspires with Lovewit to cover everything up.
- **Lovewit marries Dame Pliant** and keeps the swindled goods.

Ben Jonson's poem "To the Immortal Memory and Friendship of that Noble Pair, Sir Lucius Cary and Sir H. Morison" is not categorized as an Ode in the Horatian manner, and Alfred Tennyson's "Ode on the Death of the Duke of Wellington" is not included in the list as an option.

The title of poet laureate was first granted in England in the 17th century for poetic excellence. The tradition of a poet acting in service to a British sovereign is a long one, but the origins of the modern post can be traced to Ben Jonson, who was granted a pension by James I in 1616.

**A Tale of a Tub was the first major work written by Jonathan Swift,** composed between 1694 and 1697 and published in 1704. It is arguably his most difficult satire, yet considered by some to be his best[by whom?. The Tale is a prose parody divided into sections of "digression" and a "tale" of three brothers, each representing one of the main branches of western Christianity.

**A Tale of a Tub is a Caroline era stage play, a comedy written by Ben Jonson.** The last of his plays to be staged during his lifetime, A Tale of a Tub was performed in 1633 and published in 1640 in the second folio of Jonson's works.

**Questions:**

Question 92

**Match List I and List II List I**

| List I **Critics** | List II **Text** |
| --- | --- |
| A. Horace | I. A Defence of Rhyme |
| B. John Dryden | II. Timber: or, Discoveries |
| C. Samuel Daniel | III. Ars Poetica |
| D. Ben Jonson | IV. Of Dramatic Poesy |

**Choose the correct answer from the options given below:**

1. A – II, B – I, C – IV, D – III
2. A – III, B – IV, C – II, D – I
3. A – III, B – IV, C – I, D – II
4. A – II, B – IV, C – I, D – III

**Explanations:**
**Answer 3:** A – III, B – IV, C – I, D – II

**A. Horace's "Ars Poetica" is a treatise on the art of poetry.** It was written in ancient Rome around 18 BCE and provides guidelines for writing poetry, including the importance of unity, clarity, and avoiding clichés.

**B. John Dryden's "Of Dramatic Poesy" is a critical essay written in 1668.** It is a conversation between four characters discussing the relative merits of ancient versus modern drama. The essay also explores the idea of the "rules" of drama and whether they should be followed or broken.

**C. Samuel Daniel's "A Defence of Rhyme" is a 16th-century treatise defending the use of rhyme in poetry.** At the time, there was a debate about whether rhyme was an appropriate technique for serious poetry. Daniel argues that rhyme can be used effectively to enhance the beauty and musicality of poetry.

**D. Ben Jonson's "Timber: or, Discoveries" is a collection of notes and observations on literature and language.** It was written in the early 17th century and covers a wide range of topics, including poetry, drama, and the use of language. The work is notable for its insights into Jonson's own creative process and his thoughts on other writers of his time.

## Question 93

**Who among the following called the  Poetasters,  "The rhyming friends"?**

1. Lucan
2. Horace
3. Pindar
4. Plato

**Explanations:**
**Answer:** Dropped

"Poetaster" is a play written by Ben Jonson, a prominent English playwright and poet of the Renaissance period. The play was first performed in 1601 and satirizes the literary and social circles of the time. In Ben Jonson's play "Poetaster," the principal character is indeed Ovid. It is widely recognized by scholars and critics that Jonson used the characters in the play to satirize and parody his contemporaries in the literary world. The character of Horace is commonly understood to represent Jonson himself, while Crispinus is believed to be a caricature of John Marston, and Demetrius Fannius represents Thomas Dekker. These characterizations reflect the rivalries and tensions among playwrights and poets of the time.

Some commentators have speculated on identifying other characters in the play, suggesting connections to historical and literary figures such as George Chapman and even William Shakespeare. However, these arguments have not gained widespread acceptance among scholars.

## Question 94

**Arrange the following plays in their chronological order:**

(A) The Tempest
(B) All For Love
(C) Volpone
(D) The School for Scandal

**Choose the correct answer from the options given below :**

1. (A), (C), (B), (D)

2. (C), (B), (A), (D)
3. (C), (A), (B), (D)
4. (A), (D), (B), (C)

**Explanations:**
**Answer: 3.** (C), (A), (B), (D

**(C) Volpone** - Written by Ben Jonson, it was first performed in **1605** and is a satirical comedy that explores themes of greed, deception, and corruption in Venetian society.

**(A) The Tempest** - Written by William Shakespeare, it is believed to be one of his last plays and was likely composed around **1610-1611.** It is a complex play that combines elements of romance, comedy, and tragedy, centring around themes of power, magic, and forgiveness.

**(B) All For Love - Written by John Dryden, it was first performed in 1677** and is a tragedy based on the story of Antony and Cleopatra. It explores themes of love, loyalty, and the conflict between personal desires and duty.

**(D) The School for Scandal - Written by Richard Brinsley Sheridan, it premiered in 1777** and is a witty comedy of manners that satirizes gossip, hypocrisy, and social conventions of the time. It remains one of the most popular and enduring plays of the 18th century.

## Question 95

**Which of the following are true of the dramatic legacy of Ben Jonson?**

A. Jonson's physiological interpretation of character and personality did not have any precedent.
B. Taking after the practice of the Moralities and Interludes, Jonson named his dramatis personae aptronymically.
C. Chapman's All Fools and Middleton's A Trick to Catch the Old One belong to the genre of Comedy of Humours that Jonson is said to have pioneered.
D. John Marston and Thomas Dekker collaborated with Jonson in writing for a children's company of players.

**Choose the correct answer from the options given below:**

1. A and B only
2. B and C only

3. **C and D only**
4. D and A only

**Correct Explanations:**
**The following statements are true of the dramatic legacy of Ben Jonson:**

**C. Chapman's All Fools and Middleton's A Trick to Catch the Old One belong to the genre of Comedy of Humours that Jonson is said to have pioneered.**

**D. John Marston and Thomas Dekker collaborated with Jonson in writing for a children's company of players.**

**The following statements are false or misleading:**

A, Jonson's physiological interpretation of character and personality did not have any precedent. This is not entirely true, as Jonson's approach to character was influenced by earlier writers like Robert Burton and his work on melancholy, as well as classical theories of humours and physiognomy.

B. Taking after the practice of the Moralities and Interludes, Jonson named his dramatis personae aptronymically. This is not entirely true, as Jonson did use some aptronyms in his plays, but he also used a variety of other naming conventions and techniques. Additionally, the use of aptronyms was not unique to Jonson, but was a common feature of Renaissance drama more broadly.

Question 96

**Name the playwright who wrote the play *Epicene or The Silent Woman***

1. William Congreve
2. Thomas Kyd
3. Ben Jonson
4. Thomas Farquhar

**Explanations:**
**Ans**: Ben Jonson

**The play "Epicene, or The Silent Woman"** was written by **Ben Jonson**, a prominent English playwright and poet who lived from 1572 to 1637. Jonson was a contemporary of William Shakespeare and is best known for his satirical plays, which often poked fun at the social and political issues of his time. **"Epicene, or The Silent Woman" was first performed in 1609** and is one of Jonson's most popular and enduring works, known for its witty dialogue, complex characters, and satirical commentary on the role of women in society.

The plot revolves around a wealthy old man named **Morose who is obsessed with silence and wants to disinherit his nephew if he ever speaks loudly in his presence. Morose is also convinced by his friend Dauphine that he should marry a woman named Epicene who is said to be the epitome of silence. However, Epicene turns out to be a fraud and is actually a man in disguise, hired by Dauphine and Morose's other friends to teach him a lesson about his obsession with silence.**

The play features a range of colourful characters, including **Morose, Dauphine, and Epicene**, as well as other friends and acquaintances of Morose who all have their own agendas and motivations. Other major characters include the lawyer **Truewit, who helps Dauphine to pull off the prank, and Clerimont, a friend of Dauphine who is in love with Morose's niece.**

Question 97

**Which of the playwrights have been correctly matched with their works?**

A.   William Wycherly - The Rivals
B.   Ben Jonson - Volpone, or the Fox
C.   William Congreve - The Country Wife
D.   Aphra Behn - The Dutch Lover
E.   Richard Sheridan - A School for Scandal

**Choose the correct answer from the options given below:**

1.   C, D and E
2.   B, C and D
3.   A, C and E
4.   B, D and E

**Explanations:**
**Ans:** B, D and E

**Volpone, or the Fox is a comedy written by Ben Jonson** and first performed in 1605. The play is set in Venice and revolves around the wealthy and cunning Volpone, who pretends to be dying in order to receive gifts from his wealthy acquaintances. The play is a biting satire of greed and materialism, and explores themes of deception, corruption, and the corrupting influence of wealth.

**The Dutch Lover is a Restoration comedy written by Aphra Behn and first performed in 1673**. The play is set in Holland and revolves around the romantic entanglements of the wealthy merchant Jeronimo and his love interest, the beautiful and headstrong Lucinda.

**A School for Scandal is a comedy of manners written by Richard Brinsley Sheridan** and first performed in 1777. The play is set in London and revolves around the scandalous behavior of a group of wealthy aristocrats, who engage in gossip, deceit, and manipulation.

**Extra Perk:**

**The Rivals is a comedy of manners written by Richard Brinsley Sheridan and first performed in 1775.** The play is set in Bath, England, and revolves around the romantic pursuits of the wealthy Captain Jack Absolute, who is in love with the beautiful Lydia Languish. The play is known for its witty dialogue, intricate plot, and memorable characters, including the eccentric Mrs. Malaprop.

**The Country Wife is a Restoration comedy written by William Wycherley and first performed in 1675.** The play is set in London and follows the exploits of the philandering Horner, who feigns impotence in order to gain access to the wives of wealthy men. The play is known for its frank sexual content and bawdy humor, and is considered a classic of English Restoration theatre.

## Question 98

Which of the following two poems are linked with each other in terms of form?

A. "The Last Ride Together"
B. "Ulysses"
C. "Upon Appleton House: To My Lord Fairfax"
D. "To Penshurst"
E. "The Waste Land"

**Choose the correct answer from the options given below:**

1. A and E only.
2. A and B only.
3. A and D only.
4. **C and D only.**

**Explanations:**
**"Upon Appleton House: To My Lord Fairfax" and "To Penshurst" are linked with each other in terms of form.** Both poems are examples of **country-house poems, which were popular in the seventeenth century.** These poems describe the beauty and tranquility of country estates and the noble families who lived there. They often use a descriptive and contemplative style, praising the virtues of country life and rural landscapes. Additionally, both poems were written by poets associated with the metaphysical school of poetry: Andrew Marvell wrote "Upon Appleton House," and Ben Jonson wrote "To Penshurst."

**Other Explanations:**
**"The Last Ride Together" is a poem by Robert Browning** that explores the theme of unrequited love. The speaker is addressing his beloved, who is about to marry someone else. He asks for one last ride together before he lets her go. The poem is structured as a dramatic monologue, with the speaker trying to persuade his beloved to spend one last moment with him. The poem is notable for its use of dramatic irony, as the reader knows that the beloved will not accept the speaker's offer.

**"Ulysses" is a poem by Alfred, Lord Tennyson** that explores the theme of the search for meaning and purpose in life. The poem is written in the voice of the legendary hero Ulysses, who is now an old man, looking back on his life. He expresses his desire to set out on one final adventure, to seek new experiences and regain his former glory. The poem is notable for its use of blank verse and its complex syntax, which reflects Ulysses' restless, searching spirit.

**"Upon Appleton House: To My Lord Fairfax"** is a poem by Andrew Marvell that celebrates the beauty and harmony of nature. The poem is written in the voice of the speaker, who is visiting his friend's country estate. The poem is structured as a series of descriptions of the landscape, the animals, and the people who inhabit the estate. The poem is notable for its use of vivid imagery and its celebration of the natural world.

**"To Penshurst" is a poem by Ben Jonson** that celebrates the beauty and harmony of country life. The poem is written in the voice of the speaker, who is visiting the country estate of his patron. The poem is structured as a series of descriptions of the landscape, the animals, and the people who inhabit the estate. The poem is notable for its use of vivid imagery and its celebration of the natural world.

**"The Waste Land" is a poem by T.S. Eliot** that is widely regarded as one of the most important works of modernist poetry. The poem is structured as a series of fragmented scenes and voices, which reflect the dislocation and fragmentation of modern life. The poem is notable for its use of allusions and quotations from a wide range of literary and cultural sources, including Shakespeare, Dante, and Hindu mythology.



**Which two of the following plays were written by Ben Jonson?**

A. Flowers for Latin Speaking
B. The Devil is an Ass
C. Sappho and Phao
D. The Woman in the Moon
E. The Staple of News

**Choose the correct answer from the options given below:**

1. A and D
2. A and C
3. B and E
4. D and E

**Explanations**
**Answer:** 3. B and E

**Complete List of Plays by Ben Jonson**

**Comedies:**
- *A Tale of a Tub (c. 1596, 1633)*
- *The Isle of Dogs (1597) - lost*
- *The Case is Altered (c. 1597–98)*
- *Every Man in His Humour (1598)*
- *Every Man out of His Humour (1599)Cynthia's Revels (1600)*
- *The Poetaster (1601)*
- ***Eastward Ho (1605) - collaboration with John Marston and George Chapman***
- *Volpone (c. 1605–06)*
- *Epicoene, or the Silent Woman (1609)*
- *The Alchemist (1610)*
- *Bartholomew Fair (1614)*
- ***The Devil is an Ass (1616)***
- ***The Staple of News (1626)***
- *The New Inn, or The Light Heart (1629)*
- *The Magnetic Lady, or Humours Reconciled (1632)*

**Tragedies:**

- *Sejanus His Fall (1603)*
- *Catiline His Conspiracy (1611)*
- *The Sad Shepherd (1637)* - unfinished
- *Mortimer His Fall (1641)* - fragment

**Other Explanations**
**Nicholas Udall (1504-1556)** was an **English playwright,** cleric, and schoolmaster, credited **with writing *Ralph Roister Doister,*** considered the first comedy in the English language. He also translated parts of Erasmus's Apophthegms and oversaw the English version of the Paraphrases of Erasmus, published in 1548 as The first tome or volume of the Paraphrase of Erasmus vpon the newe testamente. **Udall's translations included Pietro Martire's *Discourse on the Eucharist* and Thomas Gemini's *Anatomia.*** His renowned

play, Ralph Roister Doister, was likely performed as entertainment for Queen Mary around 1553 but remained unpublished until 1566. Additionally, he authored a Latin textbook, *Flowers for Latin Speaking (1533)*, incorporating material from his comedy and works by the Roman poet Terence.

**Eight of John Lyly's plays survive in quarto**, published during his lifetime in fourteen separate editions, all but the last written in prose:

> ➢ *Campaspe* performed 1583/84
> ➢ ***Sapho and Phao*** performed 1584
> ➢ *Gallathea* performed 1587/88
> ➢ *Endymion, the Man in the Moon* performed 1588
> ➢ *Midas* performed 1589/90
> ➢ *Mother Bombie* performed c.1590
> ➢ *Love's Metamorphosis* performed c.1589/90
> ➢ ***The Woman in the Moon*** probably performed 1590-95

# CHAPTER 2

## Jacobean Period (1603-1625)

### Introduction:

- The **Jacobean Era** coincided with **James VI of Scotland's reign.**
- **James inherited the English crown in 1603** as James I.
- The Jacobean Era succeeded the **Elizabethan Era** and preceded the **Caroline Era.**
- Notable styles include **Jacobean architecture, arts, and literature.**
- The **Gunpowder Plot** occurred on **5 November 1605**, led by **Guy Fawkes.**
- Plotters aimed to assassinate the king and destroy **Parliament.**
- **Plot was exposed and plotters were hanged**, drawn, and quartered.
- **Jacobean literature** questioned the **stability of the social order.**
- **Shakespeare's greatest tragedies** were written during this period.
- **John Webster's** dramas explored the **problem of evil.**
- Comedy included **Ben Jonson's acid satire** and works of **Beaumont and Fletcher.**
- **Metaphysical poets like John Donne** used intellectual complexity.
- **Francis Bacon** and **Robert Burton** brought **tough prose styles.**
- The **King James Bible** (1611) was the era's monumental prose achievement.
- In 1617, **George Chapman** completed **English translations of Homer's Iliad and Odyssey.**
- **The Jacobean era ended with a severe economic depression in 1620–1626**, complicated by a serious outbreak of bubonic plague in London in 1625.

### Gunpowder Plot (1605)

- The **Gunpowder Plot** was an **attempted regicide** in **1605** against **King James I.**
- The plan was to **blow up the House of Lords** during **Parliament's State Opening.**
- **Led by Robert Catesby**, the group aimed for **regime change** due to **religious persecution.**

- ➤ **Guy Fawkes** was in charge of the **explosives**, using his **military expertise**.
- ➤ The conspirators intended to install **Princess Elizabeth** as the new monarch after the revolt.

## Bible

**"Mr. White is CooKing"**

- ➤ **Whi** = **W**yclif's Bible (1384-1388)
- ➤ **Te** = **T**yndale's Bible (1526)
- ➤ **Coo** = **Co**verdale's Bible (1535)
- ➤ **Kings** = **King** James Bible (1611)

**"Matthew is the great and genuine Bishop"**
- ➤ Matthew's Bible (1537)
- ➤ The Great Bible (1539)
- ➤ Geneva Bible (1560)
- ➤ Bishops' Bible (1568)

## Jacobean Drama & Theatre

- ➤ **Jacobean drama** refers to plays from **James I's reign**.
- ➤ It focuses on **moral corruption** and **revenge tragedies**.
- ➤ **Ben Jonson** led the shift to **harsh satire** in comedies.
- ➤ **Jacobean tragedies** emphasized **violence** and **pessimism** about life.
- ➤ **John Webster's The White Devil** shows **brilliant yet violent characters**.
- ➤ **The Duchess of Malfi** features characters **pursuing ambition through crimes**.
- ➤ **Middleton and Rowley's The Changeling** is a **Jacobean drama model**.
- ➤ Violent acts, like **cutting off fingers** or **gouging eyes**, were common.
- ➤ **Shakespeare** embraced **Jacobean themes**, intensifying his plays' **violent undertones**.
- ➤ **Iago** from **Othello** exemplifies the **Jacobean villain**, manipulative and ambitious.
- ➤ **Iago** manipulates others to commit **extreme violence** like **Othello killing Desdemona**.

- ➢ **Regan's act** in **King Lear** epitomizes the era's **violent dramatizations**.
- ➢ **Jacobean villains** were **intelligent, clever, manipulative**, and **relentlessly ambitious**.
- ➢ **Musical dramas**, or **masques**, were a key part of **Jacobean theatre**.
- ➢ **Shakespeare's The Tempest** is the finest example of a **Jacobean masque**.

## Revenge tragedy

- ➢ **Revenge tragedy** focuses on **revenge** and its **fatal consequences**.
- ➢ **Ashley H. Thorndike** formalized the genre in **1902**.
- ➢ **The Spanish Tragedy** (Thomas Kyd) started the genre in **16th century**.
- ➢ **Gorbuduc** by **Norton and Sackville** is an early **revenge tragedy**.
- ➢ **Shakespeare's Hamlet** is the most famous **revenge tragedy**.
- ➢ **Antonio's Revenge** (John Marston) features **ghost urging for revenge**.
- ➢ **Revenge of Bussy d'Ambois** by **Chapman** explores **hesitation in revenge**.
- ➢ **Titus Andronicus** by **Shakespeare** is another key **revenge play**.
- ➢ **The Revenger's Tragedy** (Middleton) showcases **ultimate scenes of carnage**.
- ➢ **The Tragedy of Hoffman** by **Henry Chettle** is a lesser-known **revenge drama**.

## City Comedy

- ➢ **City comedy** focuses on **urban life** and **middle-class manners**.
- ➢ The genre satirizes **contemporary London life**, often with **biting humor**.
- ➢ **John Marston's The Dutch Courtesan** (1605) is a **key example**.
- ➢ **Ben Jonson's Bartholomew Fair** (1614) satirizes **London's social dynamics**.
- ➢ **Thomas Middleton's A Chaste Maid in Cheapside** (1613) explores **citizen comedy** themes.
- ➢ **Ben Jonson's comedies of humor** laid the foundation for **city comedy**.
- ➢ **Thomas Middleton, John Marston**, and others developed the **genre's conventions**.
- ➢ **Shakespeare's Merry Wives of Windsor** touches on **city comedy** elements.

- ➤ **City comedy** avoids **romantic plots** in favor of **socio-economic themes**.
- ➤ **London's rapid population growth** and urbanization influenced **city comedy settings**.
- ➤ **City comedies** often depict **London as a place of vice and folly**.
- ➤ **Jonson's Epicoene** and **Middleton's A Trick to Catch the Old One** are **notable examples**.
- ➤ **Reformation and mercantilism** shaped **London's socio-economic landscape** in these plays.
- ➤ **John Ford's 'Tis Pity She's a Whore** re-works **city comedy features** into a **tragic drama**.
- ➤ **City comedy** emerged as a response to the **changing urban environment**.
- ➤ **List of city comedies:**
    - ○ ***Every Man in his Humour (1598)***, by Ben Jonson
    - ○ *The Family of Love (c. 1602)*, by Thomas Middleton
    - ○ *The Wise Woman of Hoxton* (c. 1604), by Thomas Heywood
    - ○ *A Trick to Catch the Old One* (c. 1604), by Thomas Middleton
    - ○ *The Dutch Courtesan* (c. 1604), by John Marston
    - ○ ***Westward Ho*** (1604), by Thomas Dekker and John Webster
    - ○ ***Eastward Ho*** (1605), by George Chapman, Ben Jonson, and John Marston
    - ○ ***Northward Ho*** (1605), by Thomas Dekker and John Webster
    - ○ *Michaelmas Term* (c. 1605), by Thomas Middleton
    - ○ *A Mad World, My Masters* (c. 1605), by Thomas Middleton
    - ○ *Cupid's Whirligig* (1607), by Edward Sharpham
    - ○ *Your Five Gallants* (c. 1607), by Thomas Middleton
    - ○ *Ram Alley, or Merry Tricks* (1608), by Lording Barry
    - ○ ***Epicœne, or The Silent Woman (1609)***, by Ben Jonson
    - ○ ***The Alchemist (1610)***, by Ben Jonson
    - ○ ***The Roaring Girl (c. 1611)***, by Thomas Middleton and Thomas Dekker
    - ○ ***A Chaste Maid in Cheapside (c. 1611)***, by Thomas Middleton
    - ○ ***Bartholomew Fair (1614)***, by Ben Jonson
    - ○ *Anything for a Quiet Life* (c. 1621), by Thomas Middleton (and, possibly, John Webster)
    - ○ ***A New Way to Pay Old Debts*** (c. 1621), by Philip Massinger
    - ○ *The City Madam* (c. 1632), by Philip Massinger.

## Tragicomedy

- **Tragicomedy** blends **tragic** and **comic** elements in dramatic literature.
- It can be a **serious play** with a **happy ending**.
- **Battista Guarini** defined **tragicomedy** in the **Renaissance**.
- **Tragicomedy** includes **compassion**, but avoids **tragic conclusions**.
- It features **low-born characters, laughter**, and **jests**.
- **John Fletcher's The Faithful Shepherdess** is a notable tragicomedy.
- **Shakespeare's The Merchant of Venice** (1596-97) is a key example.
- **The Winter's Tale** (1610–11) is another of **Shakespeare's tragicomedies**.
- **The Tempest** (1611–12) also showcases **tragicomic elements**.
- **Tragicomedy** thrived in **England**, ignoring **Neoclassical genre rules**.

## Masque & Antimasque

- **Masques** were **festive courtly entertainments** in **16th-17th century Europe**.
- Masques featured **music, dancing, singing**, and **elaborate stage design**.
- **Courtiers, like Anne of Denmark**, often performed in **masques**.
- **Antimasque**, a **comic or grotesque dance**, preceded the **masque**.
- **Ben Jonson** conceived the **antimasque** as a **spectacle of disorder**.
- **Antimasques** featured **lower-class characters**, contrasting with the **masque's order**.
- **Masque**: Total 36 Masques:
    - **The Masque of Blackness** (6 January 1605)
    - **The Masque of Beauty** (10 January 1608)
    - **The Masque of Queens** (2 February 1609)
    - **Oberon, the Faery Prince** (1 January 1611)
    - (**Code**: Black Beauty Queen and Prince)

## Thomas Heywood (1575–1650)

- He was born in Lincolnshire about 1575, was educated at Cambridge.
- Became an author and dramatist in London.
- He himself asserts that he had a hand (*"or at least a main finger"*) **in two hundred and twenty plays**, of which **twenty-three survive**.
- He also wrote masques, mythological cycles, and chronicle plays.

> ➢ *A Woman Killed with Kindness*, a domestic tragedy first performed in **1603** at the **Rose Theatre by Worcester's Men company. Code:** *(Hey, Kind Woman Anne why would you cheat Frank with a guest Wen)*
> ➢ Frankford's happiness is ruined by the treachery of a guest, Wendoll, to whom he has been hospitable. Frankford discovers that his wife, Anne, has been adulterous with Wendoll, but instead of taking revenge, he decides to "kill her even with kindness".
> ➢ *The Captives and A Pleasant Comedy, Called a Maidenhead Well Lost (both in 1634);*
> ➢ *The Fair Maid of the West (1631);*
> ➢ *If You Know Not Me, You Know Nobody (1605–06)*: It is about Elizabeth I.

## Question 100

**Name the playwright who composed the play A Woman Killed with Kindness.**

1. Francis Beaumont
2. Beaumont and Fletcher
3. Thomas Kyd
4. **Thomas Heywood**

**Explanations:**
**"A Woman Killed with Kindness" is a play by the English playwright Thomas Heywood.** It was first performed in 1603 and is considered one of Heywood's most famous works. The play tells the story of Anne, a virtuous and loyal wife, who is betrayed by her husband John's infidelity with her cousin. The play explores love, betrayal, forgiveness, and morality and is known for its sympathetic portrayal of women in a patriarchal society. The play's title is often ironic, as Anne is not killed with kindness but rather through the consequences of her husband's actions.

## Question 101

**Arrange the works in the chronological order of the staging/ publication of the following plays:**

A. A Woman Killed with Kindness
B. John Bull's Other Island
C. The Double Dealer

D. The Shoemaker's Holiday
E. The Conscious Lovers

**Choose the correct answers from the options given below:**
1. B, D, C, A and E
2. D, A, C, E and B
3. C ,D, A,B and E
4. E, B, D, C and A

**Explanations:**
**Ans:** D, A, C, E and B

The chronological order of the staging of the plays is:

> *The Shoemaker's Holiday (1600)*
> *The Double Dealer (1693)*
> *A Woman Killed with Kindness (1603)*
> *The Conscious Lovers (1722)*
> *John Bull's Other Island (1904)*

**Extra Perk:**

**The Shoemaker's Holiday: Written by Thomas Dekker,** it was first performed in 1600. The play is a romantic comedy that explores themes of social mobility and class conflict in the context of the shoemaking trade in London.

**A Woman Killed with Kindness: Written by Thomas Heywood, it was first performed in 1603.** The play is a tragedy that tells the story of a woman who is betrayed by her husband and ultimately dies from the kindness of a man who tries to help her.

**The Double Dealer: Written by William Congreve, it was first performed in 1693.** The play is a comedy of manners that satirizes the hypocrisy and corruption of the aristocracy.

**The Conscious Lovers: Written by Richard Steele, it was first performed in 1722.** The play is a sentimental comedy that emphasizes the importance of virtue and sincerity in romantic relationships.

**John Bull's Other Island: Written by George Bernard Shaw, it was first performed in 1904.** The play is a satirical comedy that explores Irish identity and culture through the experiences of an Englishman who travels to Ireland to open a business.

## Thomas Dekker (1570–1641)

- ➢ Wrote to support himself, and he had a hand in at least 42 plays written in the next 30 years.
- ➢ **John Marston and Thomas Dekker collaborated with Jonson** in writing for a children's company of players.
- ➢ Thirteen more plays survive in which Dekker collaborated with such figures as **Thomas Middleton, John Webster, Philip Massinger, John Ford, and William Rowley.**

**List of Major Works: Code: (*Deck your Shoes in Attire Honey*)**

- ➢ *The Shoemakers Holiday (1600)*
  - o **Lacy disguises as a shoemaker** to pursue his love, Rose.
  - o **Eyre becomes prosperous and Lord Mayor** of London.
  - o **Ralph reunites with Jane**, stopping her wedding to Hammon.
- ➢ *Satiro-mastix (produced 1601)*
  - o In the dispute known as **"the poets' war"** or **"the war of the theatres,"** he was satirized in **Ben Jonson's Poetaster (produced 1601) as Demetrius Fannius**, *"a very simple honest fellow. . . a dresser of plays."*
  - o Dekker's attack on Jonson in the play **Satiro-mastix**
- ➢ *The Honest Whore, Part 2 (1630).*
  - o **Part 1 is a collaboration between Thomas Dekker and Thomas Middleton,**
  - o **Part 2 is the work of Dekker alone. The Admiral's Men acted in the plays.**
  - o **Hippolito converts Bellafront** to honesty, though she falls for him.
  - o **Bellafront resists temptation** as her husband, Matheo, exploits her.
  - o **Orlando Friscobaldo rescues Bellafront** while the comic subplot lightens the drama.

## John Marston (1576-1634)

- **Satirists** of the Shakespearean era, whose best-known work is *The Malcontent* (1604). (**CODE**: MARSHMAL)
  - **Altofronto, deposed Duke, seeks revenge in Genoa.**
  - Disguised as **Malevole**, he criticizes the corrupt court.
  - **Duke Pietro values Malevole's honest observations.**
  - **Malevole exposes Pietro's wife** and Mendoza's scheming.
  - **Altofronto manipulates Mendoza's attempts to seize power.**
- Marston was educated at the University of Oxford and resided from 1595 at the Middle Temple, London.
- **Marston wrote Histrio-mastix in 1599**, mocking Jonson.
- Character **Chrisoganus**, a **"Master Pedant"** and "translating scholler," the audience was able to recognize the **learned Ben Jonson.**
- Feud with **Ben Jonson** sparked the **"war of theatres."**
- Jonson depicted Marston as **Crispinus in *Poetaster*.**
- Crispinus was mocked for his **pretentious vocabulary.**
- *Poetaster* was performed in **1601, escalating their feud.**
- For the **Children of Paul's, a theatre company, Marston** wrote *Antonio and Mellida (1600); its sequel, Antonio's Revenge (1601*); and *What You Will (1601).*
- In 1605 Marston collaborated with Jonson and George Chapman on **Eastward Ho,** a comedy of the contrasts within the city's life. (**CODE**: BENJEMEN).

## John Webster (1580-1632)

- Best known for his tragedies The White Devil and The Duchess of Malfi.
  - (**CODE**: White Web Malfi's Devil Case)
- *The Devil's Law-Case* (c. 1620; published 1623).
- Collaborations (not all extant). With Thomas Dekker, his main collaborator, he wrote Westward Ho (1604) and Northward Ho (1605), published in 1607.
  - (**Code**: Web in the NeW Deck)
- **His later plays were collaborative city comedies:**
  - **Anything for a Quiet Life** (c. 1621) co-written with Thomas Middleton.
  - **A Cure for a Cuckold** (c. 1624) was co-written with William Rowley. In 1624, he co-wrote a topical play about a recent scandal.

- o *Keep the Widow Waking* (with John Ford, Rowley, and Dekker). The play is lost, but its plot is known from a court case.
- o He is believed to have contributed to the tragicomedy *The Fair Maid of the Inn* with John Fletcher, Ford, and Phillip Massinger.
- o His Appius and Virginia, probably written with Thomas Heywood, is of uncertain date.

## The White Devil (1612)

**Full original title:** *The White Divel; or, The Tragedy of Paulo Giordano Ursini, Duke of Brachiano. With The Life and Death of Vittoria Corombona the famous Venetian Curtizan.*

- ➤ **Count Lodovico** is banished for murder and debauchery.
- ➤ **Brachiano** desires Vittoria despite being married.
- ➤ Flamineo plots to unite **Brachiano** and Vittoria.
- ➤ **Isabella** and Camillo are murdered by Brachiano's order.
- ➤ Vittoria is falsely condemned and imprisoned for murder.
- ➤ **Lodovico** and **Francisco** plot to avenge Isabella's death.
- ➤ **Brachiano** is poisoned by disguised conspirators.
- ➤ Flamineo fakes madness and survives assassination attempts.
- ➤ Vittoria is killed by **Lodovico** and **Gasparo** in revenge.
- ➤ **Giovanni** discovers the plot and arrests the conspirators.

## The Duchess of Malfi (1612-1613)

- ➤ It was first performed privately at the **Blackfriars Theatre**, later to a larger audience at **The Globe,** in 1613–1614.
- ➤ **The Duchess** secretly marries her steward, **Antonio.**
- ➤ Her **brothers, Ferdinand and the Cardinal**, disapprove.
- ➤ **Bosola** is hired to **spy** on her.
- ➤ **Bosola** suspects the Duchess is **pregnant**.
- ➤ **Apricots** expose her pregnancy to **Bosola**.
- ➤ The Duchess gives birth to a **son**.
- ➤ **Bosola** informs the **furious brothers** of the birth.
- ➤ **Ferdinand** confronts her, urging her **suicide**.
- ➤ The **Duchess, Antonio, and children** flee to **Ancona**.
- ➤ The **Cardinal** banishes them and **takes their rings**.
- ➤ **Bosola** imprisons the Duchess and her **children**.
- ➤ The Duchess and her **children** are **strangled**.
- ➤ **Ferdinand** goes **mad** and blames **Bosola**.

> ➢ **Bosola** mistakenly kills **Antonio** while ambushing.
> ➢ In a final **battle**, all **three die.**

## Question 102

**The Duchess of Malfi is based on:**

1. a French romance
2. an Italian novella
3. a Geman fable
4. a Scottish chronicle

**Explanations:**

**Answer: 2.** an Italian novella

"The Duchess of Malfi" is a play written by John Webster and first performed in 1613 or 1614. The play is a tragedy and is widely considered one of the greatest examples of Jacobean drama. It is believed to be based on a true story, although the exact details of the historical events are unclear.

**"The Duchess of Malfi" is indeed based on an Italian novella, "Giovanni and Lussuriosa," which was published in 1565 by Italian writer Matteo Bandello.** The novella tells the story of a duchess who marries beneath her station, and the tragic consequences that follow. John Webster adapted this story into his play "The Duchess of Malfi," which was first performed in the early 17th century.

## Francis Beaumont (1584–1616) and John Fletcher (1575–1625)

> ➢ The first Beaumont and Fletcher folio of 1647 contained 35 plays; 53 plays were included in the second folio in 1679.
> ➢ The plays generally recognised as Beaumont/Fletcher collaborations:
>   - *The Woman Hater, comedy (1606; printed 1607)*
>   - ***The Knight of the Burning Pestle (1611)***
>   - *Cupid's Revenge, tragedy (c. 1607–12; printed 1615)*
>   - *Philaster, or Love Lies a-Bleeding, tragicomedy (c. 1609; printed 1629)*
>   - ***The Maid's Tragedy, tragedy*** *(c. 1609; printed 1619)*
>   - *A King and No King, tragicomedy (1611; printed 1619)*
>   - *The Captain, comedy (c. 1609–12; printed 1647)*
>   - *The Scornful Lady, comedy (c. 1613; printed 1616)*
>   - *Love's Pilgrimage, tragicomedy (c. 1615–16; 1647)*

- o *The Noble Gentleman, comedy (licensed 3 February 1626; printed 1647).*
  - o ***The Faithful Shepherdess*** *(by Fletcher alone)*
  - o ***Code***: *Miad Mount Burning Fletcher*
- ➢ Beaumont/Fletcher plays, later revised by Massinger:
  - o *Thierry and Theodoret, tragedy (c. 1607?; printed 1621)*
  - o *The Coxcomb, comedy (1608–10; printed 1647)*
  - o *Beggars' Bush, comedy (c. 1612–13?; revised 1622?; printed 1647)*
  - o *Love's Cure, comedy (c. 1612–13?; revised 1625?; printed 1647).*

## Thomas Middleton (1580-1627)

- ➢ English Jacobean playwright and poet.
- ➢ Born in London, wrote much for the stage, and in **1620 was made City Chronologer**.
- ➢ ***The Changeling (1624)*** praised by **Lamb** and others;
- ➢ *Women beware Women (1622),*
- ➢ ***The Witch*, which bears a strong resemblance to Macbeth.**
- ➢ ***The Spanish Gipsy (1623)***, a romantic comedy suggesting As You Like It.
- ➢ Along with ***Dekker he wrote The Roaring Girle, or Moll Cutpurse (1611)***, which is a close dramatic parallel to the earliest novels.
- ➢ Middleton wrote Tragedy, history, and city comedy.
- ➢ His best-known plays are tragedies.
  - o ***A Trick to Catch the Old One (1605)***
  - o ***The Roaring Girl (1611)***
  - o ***A Chaste Maid in Cheapside (1613)***
  - o ***The Witch (1616)***
  - o ***Women Beware Women (1622)***
  - o ***The Spanish Gypsy (1623)***
  - o ***The Changeling (with William Rowley) (1624)***
  - o ***Revenger's Tragedy:*** It attributed the play to Cyril Tourneur or refused to *arbitrate between Middleton and Tourneur. "A Faire Quarrell"*
  - o ***"A Game at Chess"***
  - o ***"A Trick to Catch the Old One"***
- ➢ **Code: A trick of Three women Roaring Girl, Chaste Maid and The Witch if you change and then reverse the woman who is in the middle.**

> **Chapman's All Fools and Middleton's A Trick to Catch the Old One belong to the genre of Comedy of Humours that Jonson is said to have pioneered.**

## Women Beware Women (1622)

> **Bianca elopes** with the poor Leantio.
> **Leantio locks Bianca** up while away.
> **Duke of Florence** sees and woos Bianca.
> Bianca becomes **Duke's mistress**, leaving Leantio.
> **Hippolito loves his niece**, Isabella, in secret.
> **Livia lies**, saying Isabella isn't Hippolito's relative.
> **Leantio is killed** by Hippolito after affair discovery.
> Livia confesses Isabella **is related** to Hippolito.
> **Bloodshed ensues** during Duke and Bianca's masque.
> **Bianca accidentally poisons** the Duke and herself.

## The Changeling (1624)

> Jacobean tragedy written by Thomas Middleton and William Rowley.
> Widely regarded as being among the best tragedies of the English Renaissance.
> Beatrice falls for Alsemero, orchestrates Alonzo's murder with De Flores, leading to deception, betrayal, and their tragic deaths.
> **Beatrice falls in love** with Alsemero after meeting him.
> **Alsemero and Beatrice plan** to marry in secret.
> **De Flores, obsessed with Beatrice**, agrees to kill Alonzo.
> **Beatrice convinces De Flores** to murder Alonzo.
> **De Flores kills Alonzo** and demands Beatrice's virginity.
> **Beatrice reluctantly agrees** to De Flores' demand.
> **Alibius locks his wife**, fearing she'll be unfaithful.
> **Antonio and Franciscus try** to woo Isabella in disguise.
> **Beatrice plans a bed trick** to hide her secret.
> **Diaphanta sleeps with Alsemero** in Beatrice's place.
> **De Flores sets a fire** and kills Diaphanta.
> **Beatrice becomes trapped** in secrets and murders.
> **Alsemero overhears Beatrice** and De Flores' confession.
> **Beatrice admits** to the murder of Alonzo.
> **Alsemero accuses Beatrice** of adultery and murder.
> **De Flores and Beatrice** are locked in Alsemero's closet.

- **De Flores fatally stabs** Beatrice and himself.
- **Beatrice asks for forgiveness**, welcoming her death.
- **De Flores dies, satisfied** with his actions.
- **Justice is restored**, and grief replaces tragedy.

## Question 103

**The book Women Beware Women was published in the year?**

1. 1612
2. 1620
3. 1621
4. 1622
5. 1657
6. Drop

**Correct Option Explanation:**
**Women Beware Women is a Jacobean tragedy written by Thomas Middleton and first published in 1657.**

## Philip Massinger

- His finely plotted plays, including *A New Way to Pay Old Debts, The City Madam, and The Roman Actor,* are noted for their satire, realism, and political and social themes.
- *A New Way to Pay Old Debts (1625)*
- Its central character, **Sir Giles Over-reach**
- became one of the more popular **villains** on English and American stages through the 19th century.

## John Ford (1586–1639)

- English playwright and poet of the Jacobean and Caroline eras, born in Ilsington in Devon, England.
- *'Tis Pity She's a Whore (1626)*
  - **A brother and sister and their forbidden love.**
  - **Young Parman nobleman Giovanni is desperately in love with his sister Annabella, and is overjoyed when she reciprocates his feelings.**

## James Shirley (1596-1666)

- ➤ **An English poet and dramatist.**
- ➤ **Famous for** *The Schoole of Complement (1625)*

## Cyril Tourneur (1575–1626)

In the work of Tourneur we have horrors piled on horrors. His two plays *The Revenger's Tragedy (1600) and The Atheist's Tragedy (1611*).

## Question 104

**Who among the following has authored The Revenger's Tragedy?**

1. **Cyril Tourneur**
2. John Webster
3. John Fletcher
4. Thomas Heywood

**Correct Explanations:**
**The Revenger's Tragedy** is an English-language Jacobean revenge tragedy which was performed in 1606, and published in 1607 by George Eld. **It was long attributed to Cyril Tourneur, but** "The consensus candidate for authorship of The Revenger's Tragedy at present is Thomas Middleton, although this is a knotty issue that is far from settled."

## PROSE

## FRANCIS BACON, BARON VERULAM, VISCOUNT ST. ALBANS (1561–1626)

- ➤ Bacon was born in London, the son of Sir Nicholas Bacon, the Lord Keeper of the Great Seal.
- ➤ Studied at Cambridge, and then entered Gray's Inn (1576).
- ➤ Bacon introduced this **new form of literature** in English with the publication of his ten **essays** in 1597.
- ➤ He became a **member of Parliament in 1584**.
- ➤ Bacon's career **flourished under James I's accession**.
- ➤ **Knighted in 1603**, Attorney-General in 1613.
- ➤ Bacon **enforced King James's divine right theories**.

- ➤ Became **unpopular with the House of Commons**.
- ➤ **Appointed Lord Chancellor** and Baron Verulam in 1618.
- ➤ Viscount **St. Albans title granted in 1621**.
- ➤ **Parliament accused Bacon of bribery** in 1620.
- ➤ Bacon **confessed**, fined £40,000, briefly imprisoned.
- ➤ Exiled from **Court and office** after charges.
- ➤ Bacon focused on **literary and scientific pursuits**.
- ➤ **Bacon has been called the father of empiricism.**

## His Works:

- ➤ Bacon wrote both in **Latin and English**, and of the two he considered the Latin works to be the more important.
- ➤ **His Essays, which first appeared in 1597.** Then they numbered ten;
- ➤ This number grew to **thirty-eight in the 1612 edition**.
- ➤ The number reached **fifty-eight in the 1625 edition**.
- ➤ The essays are the result of his direct observations of people and matters.
- ➤ His other English works were *The Advancement of Learning (1605),* containing the substance of his philosophy;
- ➤ *Apophthegms (1625),* a kind of jest-book; and *The New Atlantis,* left unfinished at his death, a philosophical romance modeled upon More's Utopia.
- ➤ His Latin works were to be fashioned into a vast scheme, which he called *Instauratio Magna*, expounding his philosophical theories.

## Major Works

## Philosophical works

- ➤ *The Twoo Bookes of Francis Bacon. Of the Proficience and Advancement of Learning Divine and Humane* (1605);
    - o It inspired the **taxonomic structure** of the highly influential Encyclopédie by Jean le Rond d'Alembert and Denis Diderot,
    - o *"So that as Tennis is a game of no use in itself, but of great use in respect it maketh a quick eye, and a body ready to put itself in all positions, so, in the Mathematics the use which is collateral, an intervenient, is no less worthy, than that which is principle and intended."*
- ➤ *Instauratio Magna (1620), also known as Novum Organum*;
    - o ("Part II of The Great Instauration"),
    - o The title is a reference to **Aristotle's work Organon,** which was his treatise on logic and syllogism.

- o   This is now known as the **Baconian method.**
- o   For Bacon, finding the essence of a thing was a simple process of reduction, and the use of **inductive reasoning.**

➢ ***Historia Naturalis et Experimentalis ad Condendam Philosophiam: Sive Phaenomena Universi (1622),*** also known as ***Historia Ventorum; Historia Vitae & Mortis (1623);***

➢ *De Dignitate et Augmentis Scientiarum (1623).*

➢ ***New Atlantis (1626)***
- o   An **incomplete utopian novel** published posthumously in 1626.
- o   A utopian land where *"generosity and enlightenment, dignity and splendour, piety and public spirit"* are the commonly held qualities of the inhabitants of the mythical **Bensalem.**
- o   The plan and organisation of his ideal college, **Salomon's House (or Solomon's House),** prefigured the modern research university in both applied and pure sciences.

## Literary and historical works

➢ ***Essayes (1597),***

➢ ***10 essays enlarged to 38 as The Essaies of Sr Francis Bacon Knight (1612),***

➢ ***58 as The Essayes or Counsels, Civill and Morall (1625);***

➢ ***Francisci Baconi De Sapientia Veterum Liber (1609);***

➢ ***The Historie of the Raigne of King Henry the Seventh (1622).***


*"Crafty men contemn studies, simple men admire them, and wise men use them; for they teach not their own use; but that is a wisdom without them, and above them, won by observation. Read not to contradict and confute; nor to believe and take for granted; nor to find talk and discourse; but to weigh and consider. Some books are to be tasted, others to be swallowed, and some few to be chewed and digested; that is, some books are to be read only in parts; others to be read, but not curiously; and some few to be read wholly, and with diligence and attention. Some books also may be read by deputy, and extracts made of them by others; but that would be only in the less important arguments, and the meaner sort of books; else distilled books are like common distilled waters, flashy things. Reading maketh a full man; conference a ready man; and writing an exact man. And therefore, if a man write little, he had need have a great memory; if he confer little, he had need have a present wit; and if he read little, he had need have much cunning, to seem to know that he doth not. Histories make men wise; poets witty; the mathematics subtile; natural philosophy deep; moral grave; logic and rhetoric able to contend."* **Of Studies**

"Studies serve for delight, for ornament and for ability. ------------------------------------------------------- except they be bounded in by experience."

"To spend too much time in studies is sloth; to use them too much for ornament, is affectation; to make judgment wholly by their rules, is the humor of a scholar."

"Crafty men contemn studies, simple men admire them, and wise men use them; for they teach not their use; but that is a wisdom without them, and above them, won by observation."

"Read not to contradict and confute, nor to believe and take for granted, nor to find talk and discourse, but to weigh and consider."

"Some books are to be tasted, others to be swallowed, and some few to be chewed and digested; that is, some books are to be read only in parts; others to be read, but not curiously; and some few to be read wholly, and with diligence and attention. Some books also may be read by deputy, and extracts made of them by others; but that would be only in the less important arguments, and the meaner sort of books; else distilled books are, like common distilled waters, flashy things."

"Reading maketh a full man; conference a ready man; and writing an exact man; and, therefore, if a man write little, he had need have a great memory; if he confer little, he had need have a present wit: and if he read little, he had need have much cunning, to seem to know that he doth not."

"Histories make men wise; poets witty; the mathematics subtile; natural philosophy deep; moral grave; logic and rhetoric able to contend."

"Bowling is good for the stone and reins; shooting for the lungs and breast; gentle walking for the stomach; riding for the head; and the like."

"So, if a man's wit be wandering, let him study the mathematics; for in demonstrations, if his wit be called away never so little, he must begin again; if his wit be no apt to distinguish or find differences, let him study the schoolmen, for they are 'Cymini sectores;' if he be not apt to beat over matters, and to call upon one thing to prove and illustrate another, let him study the lawyer's cases: so every defect of the mind may have a special receipt."

**Famous Essays:**
- Of Truth (1625)
- Of Revenge (1625)
- Of Adversity (1625)
- Of Marriage and Single Life (1612, slightly enlarged 1625)
- Of Envy (1625)
- Of Love (1612, rewritten 1625)
- Of Seditions and Troubles (1625)
- Of Atheism (1612, slightly enlarged 1625)
- Of Friendship (1612, rewritten 1625)
- Of Expense (1597, enlarged 1612, again 1625)
- Of Discourse (1597, slightly enlarged 1612, again 1625)
- Of Plantations (1625)
- Of Ambition (1612, enlarged 1625)
- Of Beauty (1612, slightly enlarged 1625)
- **Of Studies (1597, enlarged 1625)**
- Of Anger (1625)

## Nicholas Breton (1553?-1625?)

- ➢ English writer of religious and pastoral poems, satires, dialogues, and essays.
- ➢ His ***Passionate Shepheard (1604)*** is full of sunshine, fresh air, and unaffected gaiety. The third pastoral in this book—"Who can live in heart so glad / As the merrie country lad"—is well known;

## Question 105

**List I with List II**

| List I (Text) | List II (Author) |
| --- | --- |
| A. Advancement of Learning | I. Susan Sontag |
| B. Past and Present | II. Francis Bacon |
| C. English Traits | III. Thomas Carlyle |
| D. Illness as Metaphor | IV. R. W. Emerson |

**Choose the correct answer from the options given below:**

1. A -I , B -III , C -IV , D -II

2. A -III , B -IV , C -II , D -I
3. **A -II , B -III , C -IV , D -I**
4. A -IV , B -I , C -II , D -III

**Correct Explanations:**

**The Advancement of Learning is a book written by Francis Bacon in 1605.** The work is divided into two parts, the first of which focuses on the shortcomings of current educational practices and the need for a new approach to learning. Bacon argues that knowledge should be based on empirical observation and experimentation rather than on received wisdom and tradition. He believed that science could help to improve human understanding and benefit society as a whole.

**Past and Present is a book written by Scottish essayist, historian, and philosopher Thomas Carlyle.** It was published in April 1843 and explores the relationship between the past and the present, with a particular focus on the Industrial Revolution and its effects on British society. Carlyle was critical of the capitalist system and the ways in which it prioritized profit over people. He believed that the Industrial Revolution had led to a loss of community and a decline in traditional values and social structures.

**English Traits is a book written by Ralph Waldo Emerson and published in 1856.** The work is based on Emerson's travels in England, where he spent several months studying the culture and customs of the country. Emerson was particularly interested in the ways in which the English language and literature had influenced American culture. The book is a reflection on the unique characteristics of English society, including its love of tradition, its attachment to the land, and its sense of individualism.

**Illness as Metaphor is a book by Susan Sontag published in 1978.** In the work, Sontag challenges the language used to describe diseases and the people affected by them. She argues that certain illnesses, such as tuberculosis and cancer, have been stigmatized in ways that are unjust and harmful to those who suffer from them. Sontag also critiques the idea that people are responsible for their own illnesses, and that illness is a punishment for moral failings. The book has been influential in shaping the way we think about illness and its social and cultural contexts.

## Question 106

**Which two of the following inspired the rise of the periodical essay?**

    A. Robert Burton
    B. Francois Rabelais
    C. Francis Bacon
    D. Michel de Montaigne

**Choose the most appropriate answer from the options given below:**

    1. C and A only
    2. A and B only
    3. C and D only
    4. B and D only

**Explanations:**
Answer: 3. C and D only

**Francis Bacon and Michel de Montaigne both inspired the rise of the periodical essay through their works, which emphasized the importance of individual experience and observation.**

## Question 107

**Arrange the following in the chronological order of publication:**

    A. Advancement of Learning
    B. The Origin of Species
    C. On Heroes and Hero Worship
    D. The Lives of the Poets

**Choose the correct answer from the options given below:**

    1. D, A, C, B
    2. D, A, B, C
    3. A D, C, B
    4. A D, B, C

**Explanations:**
**Answer: 3.** A D, C, B

**"Advancement of Learning" is a work by Francis Bacon, published in 1605.** It is considered to be one of Bacon's most important works, and it outlines his ideas about the nature of knowledge and how it should be acquired.

**"The Lives of the Poets" is a collection of biographical essays by Samuel Johnson, published in 1779.** The essays provide detailed accounts of the lives and works of several important English poets, including John Milton, Alexander Pope, and John Dryden.

**"On Heroes and Hero Worship" is a series of lectures by Thomas Carlyle, published in 1841.** In the lectures, Carlyle discusses the concept of heroism and examines the lives of several notable figures from history, including Muhammad, Shakespeare, and Napoleon.

**"The Origin of Species" is a book by Charles Darwin, published in 1859.** It is considered to be one of the most important scientific works ever written, and it outlines Darwin's theory of evolution by natural selection.

## Question 108

**In  Advancement of learning  Francis Bacon divides poetry into three divisions:**

1. Philosophical religious, imaginative
2. Epic, dramatic, lyrical
3. Narrative, representative, allusive
4. Odes, sonnets, eclogues

**Explanations:**
**Answer: 3.** Narrative, representative, allusive

Bacon classifies 'Poesie' into three broad groups roughly based on qualities:

- Narrative poetry
- Representative poetry
- Allusive/ parabolic or allegorical.

In *The Advancement of Learning,* **Francis Bacon** classifies poetry into three main divisions: **Narrative, Representative, and Allusive.** He explains that poetry creates a better world than the one we live in, granting it **access to all times and places.** This imaginative world transcends limitations and includes experiences from different eras, from barbaric times to modern civilization. For Bacon, poetry operates on a higher level than history and philosophy because it provides moral lessons through its allegorical nature.

- **Narrative Poetry**: Bacon describes narrative poetry as the **imitation of history,** often dealing with themes like war, love, and mirth. These poems capture historical events in verse, making them memorable and easier to retain. For instance, Bacon refers to **narrative poetry as a mirror of history**, depicting past events with vividness.

➢ **Representative Poetry**: This division of poetry presents a **visible history**, where actions and events are dramatized and **enacted as if they were happening in the present**. While still rooted in historical facts, representative poetry emphasizes **action and dramatic reenactment** rather than a linear recount of past events.

➢ **Allusive/Allegorical Poetry**: The **allusive or allegorical mode** of poetry involves expressing deeper meanings through symbolism and metaphors. Bacon emphasizes that **allegorical poetry contains moral lessons** and has the power to deliver complex messages through simple narratives. These **parables and allusions** allow readers to derive multiple meanings from a single story, making poetry a superior form of expression.

In conclusion, **Bacon places poetry above history and philosophy**. He aligns with **Sir Philip Sidney** in viewing poetry as an imaginative force that not only **revives history but also teaches moral lessons**, enriching our understanding of the world through its allegorical nature.

## Question 109

**Match List I with List II**

| List I (Essay) | List II (Essayist) |
|---|---|
| A. "The Tory Fox-Hunter" | I. Francis Bacon |
| B. "What I Believe" | II. Joseph Addison |
| C. "The Death of the Moth" | III. E.M.Forster |
| D. "Of Ambition" | IV. Virginia Woolf |

**Choose the correct answer from the options given below:**
1. A -I , B -III , C -IV , D -II
2. A -III , B -IV , C -II , D -I
3. **A -II , B -III , C -IV , D -I**
4. A -IV , B -I , C -II , D -III

**Correct Explanations:**
**"The Death of the Moth and Other Essays" is a collection of essays by Virginia Woolf,** first published in 1942, which includes a variety of her essays on topics such as literary criticism, personal reflections, and nature. The title

essay is a meditation on the inevitability of death, observed through the struggles of a moth in its final moments.

**"What I Believe" is a humanist essay by E. M. Forster,** first published in 1938, in which the author discusses his personal philosophy and beliefs, including his rejection of religious dogma and his embrace of the humanistic principles of tolerance, individuality, and empathy.

**"Of Ambition" is an essay by Francis Bacon,** a prominent English philosopher and statesman of the Elizabethan era, in which he explores the nature of ambition and its impact on individuals and society.

**"The Tory Fox Hunter" is an essay by Joseph Addison,** an 18th-century English essayist and poet, in which he satirizes the cultural and social practices of the aristocracy, particularly their enthusiasm for fox hunting.

## Question 110

Francis Bacon's The Advancement of Learning attempted to draw a distinction between two kinds of 'truth'. Which are these?

1. **Theological Truth and Scientific Truth**
2. Theological Truth and Aesthetic Truth
3. Aesthetic Truth and Objective Truth
4. Metaphysical Truth and Aesthetic Truth

**Explanations:**

In The Advancement of Learning, Francis Bacon distinguished between two kinds of truth - the truth of theology and the truth of philosophy or natural science. According to Bacon, theological truth was concerned with the spiritual realm and was based on faith and revelation. In contrast, scientific truth was concerned with the natural world and was based on empirical observation and experimentation.

Bacon believed that **scientific truth was superior to theological truth** because it was based on observable and measurable phenomena, while theological truth was based on faith and revelation, which were often subjective and open to interpretation.

## Question 111

**Find the chronological order of the writers in terms of the period they belonged to:**

- A. Richard Steele
- B. Charles Lamb
- C. John Dryden
- D. Francis Bacon
- E. Matthew Arnold

**Choose the correct answer from the options given below:**

1. ABCDE
2. BDECA
3. CBDAE
4. **DCABE**

**Explanations:**
1. Francis Bacon (1561-1626)
2. John Dryden (1631-1700)
3. Richard Steele (1672-1729)
4. Charles Lamb (1775-1834)
5. Matthew Arnold (1822-1888)

## Question 112

**Francis Bacon's The Advancement of Learning was dedicated to**

1. King James I
2. King Henry IV
3. King Richard II
4. Queen Elizabeth I

**Explanations**
**Answer:** 1. King James I

**Francis Bacon (1561-1626),** also known as Lord Verulam, was a renowned English philosopher and statesman who held prominent positions such as Attorney General and Lord **Chancellor of England during the reign of King James I.** His contributions spanned the realms of natural philosophy and the scientific method, making him a leading figure in the advancement of knowledge during the Scientific Revolution. One of his influential works is **"The Advancement of Learning" (1605), which provided a framework for the taxonomic** structure later adopted by the highly influential Encyclopédie by Jean le Rond d'Alembert and Denis Diderot. Notably, Bacon's book, according to his biographer-essayist Catherine Drinker Bowen, stands as a pioneering essay in support of empirical philosophy, leaving a lasting impact on the development of knowledge and understanding.

## Question 113

**What is the correct chronological sequence of the following English non-fictional prose writers according to their years of birth?**

    A. Joseph Addison
    B. Francis Bacon
    C. Charles Lamb
    D. Virginia Woolf
    E. Matthew Amold

**Choose the correct answer from the options given below:**

    1. A. D. C. B. E
    2. B. A. C. E. D
    3. C. A. D. E. B
    4. D. C. B, A, E

**Explanations**
**Answer:** 2. B. A. C. E. D

**Sir Francis Bacon (1561-1626)** was an influential English philosopher and statesman who held the positions of Attorney General and Lord Chancellor of England during the reign of King James I.

**Joseph Addison (1672-1719)** was an English essayist, poet, and dramatist. Alongside Richard Steele, he played a leading role in the creation and direction of the periodicals The Tatler and The Spectator. Addison's remarkable writing abilities earned him significant government positions during the Whig party's tenure.

**Charles Lamb (1775-1834**) was an English essayist and critic, renowned for his collection of essays titled Essays of Elia (1823–33). Lamb attended Christ's Hospital, where he studied until 1789. He was a contemporary of Samuel Taylor Coleridge and Leigh Hunt during his time there.

**Matthew Arnold (1822-1888)** was an English Victorian poet and a prominent literary and social critic. Notably, he launched scathing attacks on the contemporary tastes and manners of different social classes such as the "Barbarians" (the aristocracy), the "Philistines" (the commercial middle class), and the "Populace." Arnold championed the concept of "culture" in works like Culture and Anarchy (1869).

**Virginia Woolf (1882-1941)** is best known as a novelist, particularly for her works Mrs. Dalloway (1925) and To the Lighthouse (1927). However, Woolf also made significant contributions to the field of literary criticism, writing groundbreaking essays on artistic theory, literary history, women's writing, and power dynamics.

## Question 114

**Who was the author of Novum Organum?**

1. Robert Burton
2. Francis Bacon
3. Thomas Browne
4. Montaigne

**Explanations:**
**Answer**: 2. Francis Bacon

The Novum Organum, also known as Novum Organum, sive Indicia Vera de Interpretatione Naturae (Latin for "New Organon, or True Directions Concerning the Interpretation of Nature") or Instaurationis Magnae, Pars II ("Part II of The Great Instauration"), is a **philosophical work written by Francis Bacon. Published in 1620**, it draws inspiration from Aristotle's Organon but presents a new and improved system of logic called the Baconian method. In the Novum Organum, Bacon introduces his ideas for interpreting nature and argues for the superiority of his logical approach over traditional syllogism.

## Question 115

**Which work of Francis Bacon explains the new logic or inductive method of reasoning?**

1. Apophthegms
2. The History of Henry VII
3. Novum Organum
4. De Augmentis Scientiarum

**Explanations:**
**Answer: 3.** Novum Organum

**The "Novum Organum," or "New Organon,"** published by Francis Bacon in 1620, serves as a philosophical manifesto proposing a novel system of logic to surpass the Aristotelian syllogism found in Aristotle's Organon. **Bacon champions inductive reasoning over simple reduction to uncover the essence of phenomena, a method now known as the Baconian method.** Bacon's framework for this monumental reform included:

➢ "Partitions of the Sciences" to classify knowledge
➢ the "New Method" (Novum Organum) introducing a new system of logic;
➢ a "Natural History" to compile observational data;
➢ the "Ladder of the Intellect" for ascending through levels of understanding;
➢ "Anticipations of the Second Philosophy" as precursors to new insights; and finally,
➢ the "Second Philosophy or Active Science," aimed at applying knowledge for practical benefits.

## Question 116

**Given below are two statements: one is labelled as Assertion A and the other is labelled as Reason R**

**Assertion A:** Michel de Montaigne established the term 'essay' as a new literary form in his text Essays.
**Reason R:** Francis Bacon is generally considered as the father of English essay.

**In the light of the above statements, choose the correct answer from the options given below**

    1. Both A and R are true and R is the correct explanation of A.
    2. Both A and R are true but R is NOT the correct explanation of A.
    3. A is true but R is false
    4. A is false but R is true.

**Explanations:**
**Answer: 2.** Both A and R are true but R is NOT the correct explanation of A.

Michel de Montaigne, a French writer, truly pioneered the essay as a literary form with his work "Essays" published in 1580. His personal reflections and insights established a new way for writers to express their thoughts on various topics, marking the beginning of the essay as a distinct genre in literature. Montaigne's essays covered a wide range of subjects and were characterized by their exploratory nature, blending personal anecdotes with intellectual musings. This innovation provided a model for the essay as a flexible and intimate form of writing.

On the other hand, Francis Bacon, an English philosopher and statesman, is often referred to as the father of the English essay. His collection of essays, first published in 1597, was seminal in developing the essay form in the English language. Bacon's essays differed from Montaigne's by being more compact and focused, often dealing with philosophical, moral, and practical subjects. While both Montaigne and Bacon were pivotal in the development of the essay, their contributions represent parallel developments rather than a direct line of influence from one to the other.

Therefore, while both statements are true—**Montaigne established the essay as a literary form and Bacon is considered the father of the English essay—they do not directly explain one another.** Montaigne's contribution was foundational in a broad, genre-defining sense, and Bacon's work further established the form within the English literary tradition.

## Robert Burton (1577-1640)

> An English writer and fellow of Oxford University, best known for his comprehensive book *The Anatomy of Melancholy*.

## The Anatomy of Melancholy (1621)

- The final edition came to more than 500,000 words total.
- (**Full title:** *The Anatomy of Melancholy, What it is: With all the **Kinds, Causes, Symptomes, Prognostickes, and Several Cures** of it. In **Three** Maine Partitions with their several **Sections, Members, and Subsections**. Philosophically, Medicinally, Historically, Opened and Cut Up)*
- **"Melancholy...is either in disposition or inhabit"** Burton defined the subject.
- **"Melancholy...comes upon every small occasion of sorrow."**
- It arises from **"need, sickness, trouble, fear, grief."**
- Causes **"heaviness and vexation of spirit."**
- **"No man living is free"** from melancholy's effects.
- **"Melancholy...is the character of Mortality."**
- Burton describes melancholy as a **"serious ailment"** and fixed.
- It develops into a habit, **"pleasant or painful."**
- **Burton drew from psychology, physiology, and astronomy.**
- **"Beginning with Hippocrates, Aristotle, and Galen."**
- Burton includes **Latin poetry and ancient references**.
- The book is lengthy, **"nearly 900 pages"**.
- The text is **divided into three sections**.
- First section: **"causes and symptoms"** of melancholy.
- Second section: **"cures for melancholy"** are discussed.
- Third section explores **"melancholy of lovers"**.
- **Characteristically, the introduction includes an author's note** titled **"Democritus Junior to the Reader"**.
- It also contains a **Latin poem and a warning**.
- The introduction has **an abstract and another poem** for explanation.
- The book concludes with an **"extensive index"** called **"a readerly pleasure in itself."**

## Joseph Hall (1574-1656)

- Hall's Virgidemiarum: ***Six Books (1597–1602; "A Harvest of Blows")*** was the first English satire successfully modeled on Latin satire.
- The first writer **in English to emulate Theophrastus,** an ancient Greek philosopher who wrote a book of characters with Characters of Vertues and Vices (1608).

### Sir Thomas Overbury (1581–1613)

- Known for being the victim of a murder which led to a scandalous trial.
- His poem *A Wife* (also referred to as *The Wife),* which depicted the virtues that a young man should demand of a woman, played a significant role in the events that precipitated his murder.

### John Earle, (1601-1665)

- Anglican clergyman, best known as the author of Micro-cosmographie.
- Or, A Peece of the World Discovered; in Essayes and Characters (1628; enlarged 1629 and 1630).

### Charles I, the Civil War and The Eikon Basilik

- **Eikon Basilike is an autobiography by Charles I.**
- **The penultimate chapter is a farewell to his eldest son.**
- Charles I wrote, **'Farewell, till We meet in Heaven.'**
- The book portrays Charles I as a **just and pious King.**
- **Thirty-five editions were printed in the first year.**
- The **small format allowed readers to conceal** the book.

### Roger Ascham (1515–68)

- He was appointed **tutor to Elizabeth (1548)** and secretary to Queen Mary.
- His two chief works were *Toxophilus (1544)*, a treatise, in the form of a dialogue, on archery.
- *The Scholemaster (1570)*, an educational work containing some ideas that were then fairly fresh and enlightening.
- In *Toxophilus* he declares his intention of *"writing this English matter in the English speech for Englishmen."*
- In style he is plain and strong, using only the more obvious graces of alliteration and antithesis.

### John Lyly (1553–1606) (Already Discussed)

- Endymion (1591)
- Campaspe (1584)
- Sapho and Phao (1584)

- Gallathea (1592)
- Midas (1592)
- Mother Bombie (1594)
- The Woman in the Moon (1595-1597)

---

**Code**: Lill Anneffer Indian Saga of Moon

---

**Richard Hooker (1553–1600)Born near Exeter, and educated at Corpus Christi College, Oxford, where he was elected a Fellow (1577).**

- In 1582 he took orders, and later was appointed to a living in Kent, where he died.
- His great work, at which he labored during the greater part of his life, was *The Laws of Ecclesiastical Polity*.

## Question 117

**The theological treatise Ecclesiastical Polity was written by**

1. Richard Hakluyt
2. Francis Bacon
3. Raphael Holinshed
4. Richard Hooker

**Explanations:**
**Ans:** Richard Hooker

*Ecclesiastical Polity* **is a work of political philosophy and theology by Richard Hooker,** a 16th-century English theologian. The book was written **to defend the Church of England against the Puritans** who wanted to strip it of its traditional structure and practices. Hooker argued that the Church of England was not only justified in its practices but that these practices were essential for the health and well-being of both the Church and the state.

## Michael Drayton (1563–1631)

- **He** epresents the later epoch of **Elizabethan literature.**
- Born in **Warwickshire, studied at Oxford**, and became a tutor.
- Drayton moved to **London around 1590** and produced many poems.
- His first book was **The Harmony of the Church (1591).**

- ➢ He wrote several **long historical poems**, including **England's Heroical Epistles**.
- ➢ **The Barons' Wars (1603)** is another of his long historical poems.
- ➢ His most important longer poem is **Polyolbion**, a tedious geographical description of England.
- ➢ **Polyolbion** is written in **alexandrines** and includes interspersed tales.
- ➢ Drayton's **shorter poems** include his well-known poem on **Agincourt**.
- ➢ He also wrote verse tales and pastorals like **The Man in the Moon**.
- ➢ **Nymphidia** is one of his most skillful and attractive shorter poems.
- ➢ Drayton is rarely an inspired poet, but **"Since there's no help"** is an exception.
- ➢ The sonnet **"Since there's no help"** is considered his most inspired work.
- ➢ Drayton was **painstaking, versatile,** and sometimes **delightful** in his poetry.
- ➢ **Nymphidia** showcases his skill in creating **charming and whimsical** verse.

## Thomas Campion (1567–1620)

- ➢ He was born in **London** and educated at **Cambridge**.
- ➢ He studied law at **Gray's Inn** but became a **physician** in 1606.
- ➢ Campion wrote popular **masques** during his career.
- ➢ His main fame comes from his **attractive lyrics** set to music.
- ➢ **Campion** composed some of the music for his own lyrics.
- ➢ His best-known collections include **A Booke of Ayres (1601)**.
- ➢ **Songs of Mourning (1613)** and **Two Bookes of Ayres (1613)** are also well-known collections.
- ➢ Campion was known for his **skillful adaptation** of words to tunes.
- ➢ He mastered **complicated meters** and had a knack for **sweet phrasing**.
- ➢ Campion excelled in the **technical aspects** of poetry, despite lacking the highest lyrical genius.
- ➢ **Thomas Campion wrote *Observations in the Art of English Poesie* (1602)**.

## Phineas Fletcher (1582–1650) and Giles Fletcher (1588–1623)

- ➤ They were **brothers and poets**.
- ➤ Both were **educated at Cambridge** and later took **holy orders**.
- ➤ **Phineas Fletcher's** chief poem is **"The Purple Island"** (1633).
- ➤ **The Purple Island** allegorically describes the **human body** in **twelve cantos**.
- ➤ The poem contains **much digression**, allowing for **real poetical passages**.
- ➤ The poem's structure is **cumbrous and artificial** but shows **Spenserian influence**.
- ➤ **Phineas's stanza** resembles the **Spenserian** but omits the **fifth and seventh lines**.
- ➤ **Giles Fletcher's** best-known work is **"Christ's Victorie and Triumph"** (1610).
- ➤ The poem is **epical**, with **four cantos** describing **Christ's triumph**.
- ➤ **Giles's style** is **descriptive, imaginative**, and **ornate in diction**.
- ➤ The poem's **melodious diction** partly inspired **Milton's Paradise Regained**.
- ➤ **Giles's stanza** is similar to **Spenserian**, lacking the **seventh line**.
- ➤ The **Fletchers** were known for their **Spenserian imitation**.
- ➤ They lacked **Spenser's genius** but excelled in **intensity, color, and melody**.
- ➤ Their works show **great metrical artistry** and **high-quality imitation**.

## Samuel Daniel (1562–1619)

- ➤ He was born near **Taunton in Somerset**.
- ➤ He was **educated at Oxford** and became a **tutor** to the son of the **Countess of Pembroke**.
- ➤ In **1599**, he was briefly **Poet Laureate**.
- ➤ In **1603**, he was made **Master of the Queen's Revels** by **James I**.
- ➤ His works include the **sonnet-series "Delia"** (1592).
- ➤ He wrote the romance **"The Complaint of Rosamund"** (1592).
- ➤ His historical poem **"The Civil Wars"** was published in **1595**.
- ➤ He also wrote **masques**, including **"The Queenes Wake"** (1610) and **"Hymen's Triumph"** (1615).
- ➤ His **sonnets** continue the tradition of **Sidney, Spenser, and Shakespeare**.

- ➢ His **longer poems** are considered **prosy and dull**, though the **masques** show **imaginative touches**.
- ➢ **A Defense of Rhyme:** Prose treatise defending the English verse's lack of adherence to classical standards, a response to **Thomas Campion's Observations in the Art of English Poesie (1602)**.

## Question 118

**Match List I and List II List I**

| List I **Critics** | List II **Text** |
| --- | --- |
| A. Horace | I. A Defence of Rhyme |
| B. John Dryden | II. Timber: or, Discoveries |
| C. Samuel Daniel | III. Ars Poetica |
| D. Ben Jonson | IV. Of Dramatic Poesy |

**Choose the correct answer from the options given below:**

1. A – II, B – I, C – IV, D – III
2. A – III, B – IV, C – II, D – I
3. A – III, B – IV, C – I, D – II
4. A – II, B – IV, C – I, D – III

**Explanations:**

**Answer 3:** A – III, B – IV, C – I, D – II

**A. Horace's "Ars Poetica" is a treatise on the art of poetry.** It was written in ancient Rome around 18 BCE and provides guidelines for writing poetry, including the importance of unity, clarity, and avoiding clichés.

**B. John Dryden's "Of Dramatic Poesy" is a critical essay written in 1668.** It is a conversation between four characters discussing the relative merits of ancient versus modern drama. The essay also explores the idea of the "rules" of drama and whether they should be followed or broken.

**C. Samuel Daniel's "A Defence of Rhyme" is a 16th-century treatise defending the use of rhyme in poetry.** At the time, there was a debate about whether rhyme was an appropriate technique for serious poetry. Daniel argues that rhyme can be used effectively to enhance the beauty and musicality of poetry.

**D. Ben Jonson's "Timber: or, Discoveries" is a collection of notes and observations on literature and language.** It was written in the early 17th century and covers a wide range of topics, including poetry, drama, and the use of language. The work is notable for its insights into Jonson's own creative process and his thoughts on other writers of his time.

Chronological order of the works with their respective dates:

- **Plato's Republic** – c. **375 BCE**
- **Aristotle's Poetics** – c. **335 BCE**
- **Horace's Ars Poetica** – c. **19 BCE**
- **Longinus's On the Sublime** – c. **1st century CE**
- **Stephen Gosson's School of Abuses** – **1579**
- **Philip Sidney's An Apology for Poetry** – **1595** (published posthumously)
- **Thomas Campion's Observations in the Art of English Poesie** – **1602**
- **Samuel Daniel's A Defense of Rhyme** – **1603**
- **John Dryden's "Of Dramatic Poesy"** – **1668**

## Sir John Davies (1569-1626)

English poet and lawyer whose **_Orchestra, or a Poem of Dancing,_** reveals a typically Elizabethan pleasure in the contemplation of the correspondence between the natural order and human activity.

**In 1599 he published Nosce Teipsum (Know thyself) and Hymnes of Astraea. Queen Elizabeth became an admirer of Davies's work,** and these poems contain acrostics that spell out the phrase Elisabetha Regina.

## Emilia Lanier (1569–1645)

- English poet and the **first woman to assert herself as a professional poet**
- Her volume **_Salve Deus Rex Judaeorum (Hail, God, King of the Jews, 1611_**).
- Attempts have equated her with Shakespeare's "Dark Lady."
- **"Salve Deus Rex Judaeorum,"** about the crucifixion of Christ, is written from a woman's point of view.

## Elizabeth Cary, Viscountess Falkland (1585–1639)

- English poet, dramatist, translator, and historian.

> ➤ She is the **first woman known to have written and published an original play** in English: ***The Tragedy of Mariam***. She was recognized as an accomplished scholar by writers of her time from an early age.

## Lady Mary Wroth (née Sidney; 1587 – 1651/3)

- ➤ English noblewoman and a poet of the English Renaissance.
- ➤ Lady Wroth was among **the first female English writers** to have achieved an enduring reputation.
- ➤ **Mary Wroth was niece to Mary Herbert née Sidney** (Countess of Pembroke and one of the most distinguished women writers and patrons of the 16th century) and **Sir Philip Sidney,** a famous Elizabethan poet-courtier.
- ➤ **Poetic Career:**
  - ○ ***Love's Victory (c.1620)*** – pastoral closet drama.
  - ○ *The Countess of Montgomery's Urania (1621)* – The first extant prose romance by an English woman.
  - ○ *Pamphilia to Amphilanthus (1621)* – The second-known sonnet sequence by an English woman.

## Usage Policy for NerdSchool Notes

**Created by:** Instructors from NerdSchool
**Owned by:** NERDSTABLE PVT LTD

The following notes are the intellectual property of **NERDSTABLE PVT LTD** and are made available exclusively to students who have paid for access. By using these notes, you agree to the terms and conditions outlined below:

### Policy of Usage:

**Personal Use Only:** These notes are intended for your **personal study and exam preparation**. You are permitted to **read** and **print** them for your own reference.

**No Unauthorized Distribution or Sale:** You **may not sell**, **distribute**, or **replicate** these notes in any form, whether digitally or physically. This includes sharing copies with others, regardless of the medium (online platforms, printed materials, etc.).

**No Plagiarism:** You **may not claim** the contents of these notes as your own. Any form of direct publication or submission under your name, without proper citation, is strictly prohibited.

**Non-Transferable Access:** Access to these notes is restricted to the individual purchaser. **Sharing your login credentials** or any other means of access to these materials with others is a violation of this policy.

### Additional Guidelines:

**For Educational Use Only:** These notes are designed to help students succeed in their academic exams and should be used responsibly. They are meant to supplement your learning, not to replace the guidance of instructors or textbooks.

**No Commercial Use:** The content in these notes cannot be used for **commercial purposes**. This includes using the material in any form of paid tutoring or educational courses that you offer without the explicit permission of NERDSTABLE PVT LTD.

**Proper Attribution:** If you wish to reference any part of these notes in your own academic work, proper **citation** must be made to **NerdSchool and NERDSTABLE PVT LTD**.

**Legal Action:** Any violation of these terms, including unauthorized distribution or commercial use, may result in **legal action**.